Gail Marshall argues that the professional and personal history of the Victorian actress was largely defined by her negotiation with the sculptural metaphor, and that this was authorised and determined by the Ovidian myth of Pygmalion and Galatea. Drawing on evidence of theatrical fictions, visual representations, and popular culture's assimilation of the sculptural image, as well as theatrical productions, she examines some of the manifestations of the sculptural metaphor on the legitimate English stage, and its implications for the actress in the later nineteenth century. Within the legitimate theatre, the 'Galatea-aesthetic' positioned actresses as predominantly visual and sexual commodities whose opportunities for interpretative engagement with their plays were minimal. This dominant aesthetic was effectively challenged only at the end of the century, with the advent of the 'New Drama' and the emergence of a body of autobiographical writings by actresses.

ACTRESSES ON THE VICTORIAN STAGE

Feminine Performance and the Galatea Myth

GAIL MARSHALL

University of Leeds

CAMBRIDGE
UNIVERSITY PRESS

CAMBRIDGE UNIVERSITY PRESS
Cambridge, New York, Melbourne, Madrid, Cape Town, Singapore, São Paulo

Cambridge University Press
The Edinburgh Building, Cambridge CB2 2RU, UK

Published in the United States of America by Cambridge University Press, New York

www.cambridge.org
Information on this title: www.cambridge.org/9780521620161

First published 1998
This digitally printed first paperback version 2006

A catalogue record for this publication is available from the British Library

Library of Congress Cataloguing in Publication data
Marshall, Gail, 1965–
Actresses on the Victorian stage: feminine performance and the Galatea
myth / Gail Marshall.
p.   cm. – (Cambridge studies in nineteenth-century literature and
culture; 16)
Includes bibliographical references and index.
ISBN 0 521 62016 3 (hardback)
1. Women in the theatre – Great Britain – History – 19th century.
2. Actresses – Great Britain – Biography.   3. Mentoring.   4. Creation
(Literary, artistic, etc.)   I. Title.   II. Series.
PN2582.W65M37   1998
792'.028' 082094109034 – dc21   97-26258   CIP
[B]

ISBN-13 978-0-521-62016-1 hardback
ISBN-10 0-521-62016-3 hardback

ISBN-13 978-0-521-02746-5 paperback
ISBN-10 0-521-02746-2 paperback

For Shirley, Brian, and
Robin Marshall

Contents

Illustrations

Acknowledgements

I am grateful for the editors' permission to reprint, as part of chapter 3 of this book, material which first appeared in an article, 'Actresses, Statues, and Speculation in *Daniel Deronda*', *Essays in Criticism* 44 (1994); for the permission of the National Trust to quote from manuscript material held in the Ellen Terry Memorial Museum, Smallhythe, Kent; and for the permission of the Special Collections librarian, Brotherton Collection, University of Leeds, to quote from material held in the Bram Stoker archive. Permission details for illustrations are given on pp. x–xi.

This book first took shape as part of doctoral work undertaken at Cambridge University between 1988 and 1992. During that period I was supervised by Adrian Poole, who was, and has continued to be, generous and supportive. I would also like to acknowledge as formative influences on this work, Inga-Stina Ewbank, out of whose MA module at Leeds the idea for my thesis came; and Roy Gibson, whose scholarship on Ovid was extremely helpful to me, and whose friendship has been crucial. I would also like to thank Adrian and Roy for their comments on drafts of the book, and to thank Sara Jan for reading part of the typescript, and for her generosity in sharing her own work on Ibsen with me.

I have been a student or lecturer at three institutions, Newnham College, Cambridge, Bedford College of Higher Education, and the School of English, University of Leeds, during my work on this project, and I would like to acknowledge the way in which all of these places have contributed to the finished work. I would like to thank the following people in particular for help in a variety of ways: John Barnard, Mark Batty, Stephen Bending, Julia Borossa, Richard Brown, Melissa Calaresu, Shirley Chew, Jean Chothia, Frank Felsenstein, Denis Flannery, Jean Gooder, Fiona Green, Emma Liggins, David Lindley, Nancy Proctor, Roger Rees, Mark Robson, Gaye Rowley, Alistair Stead, Jane Steed, John Stokes, Julia Swindells, and Ian and Liz Wallis.

During archive work at the Ellen Terry Museum in 1996, I was very lucky to work with the museum's curator, Margaret Wear, for whose help I am grateful. I would also like to thank Josie Dixon at Cambridge University Press for her guidance, Gillian Beer for her support as series editor, and the Press's readers for their comments.

My final acknowledgements are to my family, to whom this book is dedicated, for making it possible.

Introduction

In 1832, Mrs Jameson published a study of Shakespeare's female characters under the title *Characteristics of Women, Moral, Poetical, and Historical.*
The work went through seven editions in the nineteenth century,
changing its title in 1896 to the more accurate *Shakespeare's Heroines.* Her
original title, however, helpfully signals the universalising tendencies of
a study which derives exemplary, and implicitly prescriptive, readings
from Shakespeare's heroines. One of Jameson's most fascinating para-
digmatic moments occurs in her chapter on Hermione, whom Jameson
classifies as one of Shakespeare's 'Characters of the Affections'. She
writes thus of the moment when Hermione, who has been introduced as
a statue in this scene, descends from her pedestal to the sound of soft
music, and speechlessly throws herself into her husband's arms:

It appears to me that her silence during the whole of this scene (except where
she invokes a blessing on her daughter's head) is in the finest taste as a poetical
beauty, besides being an admirable trait of character. The misfortune of
Hermione, her long religious seclusion, the wonderful and almost supernatural
part she has just enacted, have invested her with such an awful and sacred
charm that any words put into her mouth must, I think, have injured the
solemn and profound pathos of the situation.[1]

This event, she writes, is one of 'inexpressible interest'. It was a moment
which was compellingly re-enacted throughout the nineteenth century,
in new editions of Jameson, in performances of *The Winter's Tale* (where
it functioned not only as a moment of psychological, but also of spectacular, interest), in domestic *tableaux vivants*, and in George Eliot's
fictional adaptation in *Daniel Deronda* (1876).

The interest lies principally perhaps in Jameson's account of Hermione's return to human being as a complex and contradictory dramatic moment, not least because 'the feelings of the spectators become
entangled between the conviction of death and the impression of life, the

idea of a deception and the feeling of a reality' (vol. II, p. 20). Jameson goes on to suggest, however, that the audience's difficulty lies, not in the incredible nature of the realised event, the 'wonderful and almost supernatural' action of Hermione's coming to life, but rather in the inherent difficulty of reconciling the implications of Hermione's living state, most notably her potential for speech, with her essential character, which has been most amply fulfilled by her statue-state: the attribute which is singled out as 'an admirable trait of character', Hermione's silence, is one which seems necessarily to qualify the achievement of her return to life.

Jameson's narrative signals the contradictions inherent in the ubiquitous metaphors of sculpture and statuary which were applied to nineteenth-century women. Specifically, she implies that the statue-state, Hermione's manifestation as a 'sacred and awful' icon, is in fact the character's most appropriate conclusion, and one which is irretrievably compromised by a return to life. Jameson wonders whether we could

fancy this high-souled woman – left childless through the injury which has been inflicted on her, widowed in heart by the unworthiness of him she loved, a spectacle of grief to all, to her husband a continual reproach and humiliation – walking through the parade of royalty in the court which had witnessed her anguish, her shame, her degradation, and her despair? Me thinks that the want of feeling, nature, delicacy, and consistency would lie in such an exhibition as this. (vol. II, pp. 17–18)

Hermione acts best then, and is granted most authorial approval, when she elects to adopt the dignity and silence of death, so closely allied to and commemorated by statuary, as her resource following Leontes' rejection. It is notable that Jameson describes as 'that most beautiful scene', not Hermione's 'coming to life', but her being 'discovered to her husband as the statue or image of herself' (vol. II, p. 18). Hermione is thus most exemplary as a Shakespearean woman, her moral characteristics most evident and best fulfilled, when she is not living, but assuming the guise of a marble icon. It is in this state that Hermione comes closest to, through literally embodying, the 'abstract notions of power, beauty, love, joy' which '[haunt] our minds and [illuminate] the realities of life', and which Jameson held were made peculiarly manifest in sculpture.[2] For Hermione then, her physical descent from the pedestal, her return to life, is a compromising act.

It is essential to note that this disruption is necessitated and confirmed through the imperatives of maternity. With her son dead, and her daughter believed to be so, Hermione had in some measure been free to be taken for dead herself. However, when Perdita returns to Leontes' court, Hermione can no longer remain hidden, but is 'brought to life'. She breaks her silence only to bless her daughter. The physical and temporal dimensions implicit in the narrative of maternity conspire to disrupt Hermione's adoption of, and others' consigning her to, the idealised state of marble and/or death. Motherhood, itself later to be idealised within Victorian culture, acts here as a troubling element which actively disrupts Hermione's status as an icon of 'immutable truth and beauty' (vol. II, p. 23). The appropriateness of the statue-metaphor for the figure of the woman deprived of maternity was recognised earlier by Henry Siddons, who in his *Practical Illustrations of Rhetorical Gesture and Action* (1822) observes of depictions of Niobe that:

It appears to me that fixity, or want of motion, is a quality which the aspect of a *rock* impresses more easily on thought than the idea of *silence* – and that a grief, deep and full, such as a mother so cruelly robbed of her children ought to be represented, should in fact be motionless: she is totally plunged in the representation of her afflicting fate; and as the soul fixes (as we may say) with a haggard eye on this solitary idea, the whole body [...] preserves also a fixed and single attitude.[3]

Motherhood, by comparison, necessitates speech, relationship, a recognition of the temporal, finite implications of the female body which are glossed into a semantics of atemporal virtues by the conventions of Classical statuary which the maligned Hermione adopts.[4]

Hermione's descent from her pedestal then represents an uneasy conjunction of forces: it idealises the persistence of her reification whilst purporting to witness her return to 'life'. In this moment, we can, I think, begin to understand something of the dimensions and implications both of the use of Victorian statuary's celebration of the female form, and of writers' application of the sculptural metaphor. For Hermione and for the Victorians, sculpture is a way of achieving, rather than simply commemorating, the association of timeless ideals with women. The timelessness, the material persistence of sculpture, particularly in its apparently time-defying Classical mode, absorbs the contradictions between eternal ideals and temporal female forms, whilst absorbing also the life and autonomy of the female model or celebrated woman. Jameson reveals the attractiveness of the statue-state for women, the exaltation generated by that form, and the benefits of reverence and respect that may accrue to it. She is also, however, aware of the uneasiness of the art–life relationship actually 'embodied' in the statue, and of the hampering implications for women of a too-ready identification with the marble-form. In particular, Jameson highlights the way in which speech, the access to, and necessity for, language, is denied in the identification between woman and the idealised marble, thus denying also the possibility of articulating independent subjectivity.

Implicit in her study of dramatic characters, inspired as Jameson's introduction tells us by conversations with the actress Fanny Kemble, is the extent to which the public appearances of actresses are almost ineluctably vulnerable to definition by means of sculptural reference. Valerie Traub has argued that *The Winter's Tale*, along with *Hamlet* and *Othello*, are plays which 'give women speech only to silence them [...] make women move only to still them', that, indeed, 'the plays enact the process of female objectification as the dramatic process'.[5] Traub argues persuasively that fear for their own subject-status also leads the plays' heroes variously to 'monumentalize'[6] their partners. In Hermione's case, she is turned into a statue. However, questions of agency are of course elided in this formulation, as are the complications of desire in Traub's assertion that 'monumentalizing [...] is the strategy by which female erotic energy is disciplined and denied' (p. 28). In the work which follows, I will rather be concerned to argue that, on the Victorian stage at least, it was precisely the 'statuesque' actress who was a highly charged icon of sexual desirability, whose own 'erotic energy' was variously camouflaged, denied, even facilitated by her access to the theatrical rhetoric of statuary. However, if the actress was to achieve recognition for other forms of energy, for instance, creative, interpretative, transformative, or professional, then that rhetoric had to be abandoned.

In *Actresses on the Victorian Stage*, I examine some of the various manifestations of the sculptural metaphor on the English stage, and in writings about it, concentrating on the second half of the nineteenth century. I will argue that much of the professional and personal history of the Victorian actress is defined by her negotiation with the imposition upon her of the contractual dimensions inherent in the sculpture metaphor; and that this metaphor is essentially authorised, and its dimensions determined, by the popular Ovidian myth of Pygmalion and Galatea. However, as my first chapter shows, actresses were not alone in being subject to Pygmalion-like attentions; they were simply the most public Galateas in a century which, as we will see, readily adopted the authority of the sculptor-king for its own ends.

The history of the association of statuary and the stage is a substantial one, based for a late-Western culture on its conceptualisation of its Classical inheritance. As Richard Jenkyns notes, quoting Schlegel, the legacies of sculpture and drama were closely linked. Schlegel suggested that, 'It is only before the groups of Niobe or Laocoön that we first enter in the spirit [...] of Sophocles.'[7] Much valuable work has been done in recent years on the relationship between the Victorian stage and painting, a conjunction which has been described by Michael Booth as both 'intimate and meaningful'.[8] In my own work I would like more fully to reinstate the sculptural as a similarly vital part of the spectacular Victorian stage, one which has its own distinctive cultural connotations and history, and its own specifically gendered ramifications which are not wholly absorbed by the pictorial aesthetic. As such, this work supplements that of Booth and Martin Meisel,[9] drawing implicitly on both, and on their underlying premise that the theatre is profoundly determined by its broader cultural setting: 'it is unlikely that [the Victorians'] standards of theatrical taste were formed only in the theatre' (Booth, *Victorian Spectacular Theatre*, p. 3). I will, however, be arguing for a discrete genesis for the theatrical realisation of statuary. It has a different history from the on-stage tableau, though it may act as part of that tableau. It is a vital part of the contemporary spectacular stage, but its roots lie in a specifically Classical inheritance, in the practice of defining women by means of statuary, and in the later entertainments of wax-works and other popular shows which deliberately imitated sculpture.

As well as offering a new way of writing the history of Victorian actresses then, the work which follows also suggests that the Victorian interest in statuary, both contemporary and Classical, should be re-garded as a significant determining factor within a predominantly visual theatrical aesthetic. The links between stage and sculpture are cemented in the late-eighteenth and early-nineteenth centuries in acting manuals and in a range of Classical motifs on the popular English stage, a brief account of which is given before I turn to examine the peculiarly Victorian appropriation of the statuesque actress. As will become clear, the specific type of statuary which is consistently invoked is that from the Greek Classical Era and the Hellenistic period, and their Roman copies. I am not, however, specifically concerned with the history of Classical drama on the Victorian stage, but rather with how the connotations of a Victorian–Classical aesthetic are manifested in what I shall come to term the 'Galatea-aesthetic'; how this informs the work of the actress; and further how the concomitant assumptions of Pygmalion infiltrate the legitimate English theatre and its conventions.[10] As will become apparent, it is in part through these conventions that the legitimate stage achieves its definition in opposition to both the French and the popular English theatres. It is no coincidence that it was in the 1880s that the neo-Classical influence was at its most prominent on the legitimate stage, and that it was also during this decade that the theatre was perceived as being most 'respectable'.

As well as looking at specific productions, I will be considering how the Galatea-aesthetic infiltrates reviewing practices and determines audience reactions, and how fictional depictions of the actress, in particular those of George Eliot in *Daniel Deronda* (1876), narrativise the recourse to sculpture, and accommodate the reference to a further, plastic art-form. In my account of *Daniel Deronda*, I will also be concerned to set out the extent to which, as Jameson implies, the manipulation of language necessarily acts to disrupt the fixity, the time-bound restrictions, of the statue. In her assessment of how entrapment within the physical and sculptural is necessarily shattered by the imperatives of language and narrative, Eliot envisages a crucial qualification of sculpture's lapidary powers. The way in which the intervention of language necessarily reshapes the sculptural metaphor emerges again in my final chapter and conclusion, which consider how the Galatea-aesthetic stands up to the challenges of the 'new' drama of the 1890s: specifically how it deals with that drama's enabling actresses to achieve a more intellectual, interpretative engagement with the textuality of plays; and how it comes to be challenged by actresses' employment of a variety of forms of autobiography. Autobiographical activity became a primary form of resistance to the popular and readily available narrative of Pygmalion and Galatea for such late-Victorian actresses as Eleanora Duse, Elizabeth Robins, and particularly for Ellen Terry. The latter's personal and professional encounters with the dimensions of sculpture and the sculptor pervaded her life, stretching from her first professional appearance in *A Winter's Tale* in 1856, to the complicated publication history of her autobiography in 1908, and its revised version in 1933. Ellen Terry's story forms a narrative thread throughout this book, and makes clear the ways in which the Pygmalion and Galatea myth operated both practically and metaphorically to shape and define women's theatrical lives.

In his *Italian Journey*, Goethe uses the Pygmalion and Galatea narrative to describe his first experience of Rome:

Wherever I walk, I come upon familiar objects in an unfamiliar world; everything is just as I imagined it, yet everything is new. It is the same with my
observations and ideas. I have not had a single idea which was entirely new or
surprising, but my old ideas have become so much more firm, vital and
coherent that they could be called new.

  When Pygmalion's Galatea, whom he had fashioned exactly after his
dreams, endowing her with as much reality and existence as an artist can,
finally came up to him and said: 'Here I am', how different was the living
woman from the sculptured stone.[11]

Goethe's use of the Pygmalion narrative engagingly captures the wonder of the Ovidian story, and, uniquely, places the male figure as one
transformed beyond all possibility, in this case by the marvel of Rome.
As we will see in the work which follows, however, for the later Victorians there was not such a tangible difference between the sculptured
stone and the living woman as Goethe suggests.

CHAPTER I

Victorian Pygmalions

From its start, the nineteenth century in Britain was imbued with new possibilities for the proliferation of sculpturally informed aesthetic judgements and criteria, for it was then that Britain, France and America imported into their museums what were to become the best-known examples of Classical sculpture, statues which '[entered] deeply into the visual consciousness of educated Europe', which 'were used as touchstone[s] by artists, art lovers, collectors and theorists alike for the gauging of taste and quality'.[1] However, as we will see, the statues also came to form and inform ideological notions of femininity, and specifically the extent to which femininity might be contained by an extension of the viewing practices applied to newly available Classical statues. Amongst these statues were the Elgin Marbles (first exhibited in London in 1817); the Apollo Belvedere and the Spinario (exhibited in Paris in 1798 and 1800 respectively, and then both returned to Rome and re-exhibited there in 1816); and the Praxitelean Hermes (discovered at Olympia in 1877, and exhibited in cast-form in the British Museum shortly afterwards). But two of the most popular sculptures were the Venus de' Medici and the Venus de Milo. The former was well known to travellers in Europe from the eighteenth century onwards, but was not seen outside Italy, except in the form of casts until, like the Apollo Belvedere and the Spinario, it was forcibly removed from Rome by French troops and exhibited in Paris. It too was subsequently repatriated. The Venus de Milo was a genuine nineteenth-century find. Excavated by a peasant on the Aegean island of Melos in 1820, it was shown in Paris in 1821, and was a timely replacement for the Venus de' Medici.

Both statues achieved tremendous exposure and popularity. Nathaniel Hawthorne, though personally undecided in his evaluation of the Venus de' Medici, nonetheless acknowledged that for his time she was 'one of those lights that shine along a man's pathway'.[2] Her French

provenance notwithstanding, the Venus de Milo was prominently exhibited in the Greek Court of the Crystal Palace exhibition of 1862,
where she was idealised by an admiring Samuel Phillips, author of the
exhibition guide, as affording 'perhaps the most perfect combination of
grandeur and beauty in the female form'.[3] A cast of the Venus de Milo
was installed in the British Museum for the express purpose of helping to
train artists. The young American sculptor Harriet Hosmer copied the
Museum's Venus as she passed through London *en route* to work in the
Rome studio of the English sculptor John Gibson.[4] In March 1886, the
permission of the Museum's trustees was sought to add a cast of the
Venus de' Medici, to help overcrowding around the Venus de Milo and
Praxitelean Hermes. The figure of the Venus de' Medici was, after all,
according to the Museum's Officers' reports, 'one of those which the
[Royal] Academy accepts as a test of the drawing of the candidate for
admission'.[5] The legacy of such a Classical training is most evident in
the popular art of G. F. Watts, Edward Poynter, Lawrence Alma-
Tadema, Albert Moore, Frederic Leighton, and Edward Burne-Jones,
the 'Olympian Dreamers'[6] whose works dominated the Royal Academy
in the second half of the nineteenth century.

The cultural prominence of the two figures of Venus is indisputable.
Less clear, however, is the nature of the response and popularity
accorded them and other versions of the Roman goddess of love. They
infiltrated the realm of popular culture in the form of anatomically
specific waxworks, the female versions of which were known as Venuses
(the rare male model was called Adonis). First shown in London in 1825,
an early advertisement claimed that, 'The exterior of the Model represents a Female Figure formed from the Venus de Medicis, the interior
exemplifies on dissection the various functions of the Human Body, and
displays to perfection the order and beauty that prevails throughout the
works of the CREATOR.'[7] Such exemplary motives are called into
question, however, by the evidence of separate male and female viewing
periods, and the descent of later exhibitions into what Richard Altick
terms more explicitly 'necro-erotic' spectacle (p. 339). The practice of
establishing separate viewing days for women was also observed at an
exhibition in New York of casts from the Louvre, where fig leaves were
tied on to the statues. In 1818 railings were erected around two casts of
Venus which had been 'disfigured'.[8] Similar instances of gender segre-
gation and the indecent treatment of casts were noted by Frances
Trollope when visiting the Pennsylvania Academy of Fine Arts in
Philadelphia (Haskell and Penny, *Taste and the Antique*, pp. 90–1). For

east-coast Americans the minimally-draped statues smacked all too publicly and uncomfortably of unbridled sexuality, and prompted carefully controlled viewing, which of course ensured mutual ignorance of the opposite sex's reactions. By contrast, in 1840, John Ruskin wrote from Italy that the Venus de' Medici, 'usually in her casts a foolish little schoolgirl, is one of the purest and most elevated incarnations of woman conceivable',[9] terms scarcely consistent either with Venus' status in Classical literature, or apparently with the American reaction.

Particularly striking in both the American visitors' and Ruskin's responses is the way in which they curtail Venus' narrative possibilities, her status as a character of multiple legends; and how both her Classical status and her antiquity are telescoped in a moment of gazing made relevant to, and determined by, the viewer. In an admonitory, even perhaps punitive, process the mischievous powers of Venus are countered and her objectification achieved in the present gaze of her viewer. Devoid of the full implications of her Classical status, the Venus becomes more easily assimilable to a nineteenth-century context. The purity, even blankness, of the marble state (quite unlike Classical statues' often highly coloured forms) seems peculiarly to authorise the play of the viewer's imaginative or ideological predilections. Her timelessness, confirmed by a passing apprehension of her antiquity, and modern ignorance about the person of the sculptor, paradoxically facilitate a historically determined response. The viewer, not the sculptor, is encouraged to believe that he or she controls signification and meaning, the viewer in some measure becoming responsible for, even generating, the statue's meaning. This responsibility is taken to extremes in 'Taken On Trust' (plate 1) where not only the connotations, but also the actual form of the Classical statue are reworked for an ignorant late-Victorian's convenience in a *Punch* cartoon which seems to demand both amusement and the complicity of its viewer.

The polarities expressed in the American museum visitors' and Ruskin's responses to sculptures of Venus came to be absorbed by those figures themselves. Venus is rendered simultaneously sexually available (although not, as in her literary guise, sexually active) and angelically idealised.[10] Of Frederic Leighton's imposing nude, *Venus Disrobing*, exhibited at the Royal Academy in 1867, the *Athenaeum* protested that 'Nakedness is not the leading characteristic of the figure', and the *Art Journal* described her as 'eminently chaste' in spite of her lack of drapery, her actions, and her history (quoted in Wood, *Olympian Dreamers*, p. 48). The naked, or only partially draped, Classical body becomes a signifier

TAKEN ON TRUST.

Viscount Conamorey (whose recollections of the antique are somewhat hazy). "AW—A—WHAT
BEAUTIFUL ARMS AND HANDS YOU 'VE GOT, MRS. BOUNDER! THEY REMIND ME OF THE VENUS
OF MILO'S!" *Mrs. B. (who has never even seen the Venus of Milo).* "OH! YOU FLATTERER!"

Plate 1 'Taken On Trust', *Punch*, 99 (1890)

both of the Fall and of a state of innocence, any sign of modesty (as
shown by the Medici Venus, who shields her genitals from view) both an
admission and a forestalling of knowledge. The simultaneity of these
significations was famously exploited in the 'Attitudes' of Emma Hamilton (an account of which will be given below), and also infiltrated
popular perceptions of Lillie Langtry, society beauty, one-time mistress
of the Prince of Wales, and from the early 1880s, an actress. The painter
Graham Robertson describes his first sighting of Langtry thus:

she might have been a milliner's assistant waiting upon a customer for all her gown said to the contrary, or a poorly paid governess hurrying to her pupils. As I drew near the pavement the girl looked up and I all but sat flat down in the road.

For the first time in my life I beheld perfect beauty. The face was that of the lost Venus of Praxiteles, and of all the copies handed down to us must have been incomparably the best, yet Nature had not been satisfied and had thrown in two or three improvements [...] the figure in its poise and motion conveyed an impression of something wild, eternally young, nymph-like.[11]

A few days later Robertson realised that

My dowdy divinity of Hyde Park Corner, my pathetic nursery governess, had been the world-famous Jersey Lily, the Venus Annodomini, the Modern Helen. Never since the days of the Gunnings had such universal worship been paid to beauty. The Langtry bonnet, the Langtry shoe, even the Langtry dress-improver, were widely stocked and as widely bought [...] this was a beauty beyond the reach of the brush: Praxiteles, who had first conceived it, should have returned to earth to carve it afresh [...] It was strange to me that the beauty of Mrs Langtry attracted the public so much: those who thronged to stare at her could have obtained precisely the same thrill from the Metope of the Parthenon, yet the Elgin Room at the British Museum was never inconveniently crowded. (pp. 70–1)

The potency of the recourse to Classical references is impressive, authorising as it does a range of commercial as well as aesthetic possibilities.[12]

Langtry was also invoked by Oscar Wilde in his poem 'The New Helen', as 'the Lily of love, pure and inviolate! / Tower of ivory!', resplendent in the 'white glory' of her loveliness.[13] Langtry's simultaneously scandalous reputation is safely absorbed into the writers' Classical references, a process perhaps most publicly acted out in Leighton's 1880–1 painting, *Idyll*, which includes a languorous, barely draped portrait of Langtry. She had then recently lost the protection of the Prince of Wales, and, as Stephen Jones suggests, the Classicism of Leighton's painting may have been viewed as the most appropriate way of re-introducing Langtry to society.[14] The fundamental doubleness of the Classical reference was not, however, usually acknowledged by nineteenth-century spectators, unless it was the energy of contradiction and irreconcilability which suggested to Walter Pater that 'some spirit' in the Venus de Milo was 'on the point of breaking out', that she was, like Hermione, about to exemplify, through living out, those contradictions.[15]

Classical statuary was a highly charged site of ideological and commercial practices in the nineteenth century. However, as the practice of employing statue-imagery to describe women demonstrates, it was one simultaneously most dangerous and tempting for, when seeming most celebratory of, Victorian women. In *Liber Amoris, or The New Pygmalion* (1823) Hazlitt describes the lower-class girl with whom he is infatuated thus:

> Her words are few and simple; but you can have no idea of the [...] graces with which she accompanies them, unless you can suppose a Greek statue to smile, move, and speak [...] I have her face constantly before me, looking so like some faultless marble statue, as cold, as fixed and graceful as ever statue did.[16]

Hazlitt's lover, like Hermione, is almost mute, and like Venus, is cut off from her origins and narrative by the overwhelming dimensions of the statue-image. The strength of the metaphor both enables and confirms Hazlitt's act of sculpting the image of his ideal from living flesh. The same process is successfully acted out, albeit in a more critical framework, in Vernon Lee's novel, *Miss Brown* (1884), a parody in large part of the Pre-Raphaelite circle, and of their practice of taking their models (including Annie Miller, Jane Burden, Fanny Cornforth, and Lizzie Siddal) from positions of social obscurity, if not degradation, and turning them into Pre-Raphaelite 'stunners' who even now enthral their audiences. Lee's heroine, 'Miss Brown', is one such woman. Discovered as a reluctant children's maid by the poet and painter Walter Hamlin, she is educated with a view to his possibly marrying her, thus saving her beauty from being lost forever in a nursery. From the start Hamlin is motivated by selfish, artistic concerns, by his desire for the inspiration Miss Brown brings him. He sees her as 'some sort of strange statue' rather than a living being, and she is said to have a likeness to 'certain mournful and sullen heads of Michelangelo, the type was so monumental, and at the same time so picturesque'.[17] In this moment the personality of Anne Brown is obliterated. The desired woman is intensely vulnerable to the sculptor-like attentions of her lover.

This vulnerability is illustrated by the propensity of novelists to employ metaphors of 'moulding' and 'sculpting' to describe male appropriations of a female partner. It quickly becomes apparent that the resulting artefact is conceived of as being entirely in thrall to, her significance exhausted by, her place as the creation and as the art-object of her lover. In Henry James's revision of *The Portrait of a Lady* (1881) for the New York edition of 1908, for instance, the art-connoisseur Gilbert

Osmond is attracted to Isabel Archer because, barring a too precipitate readiness, she was 'as smooth to his general need of her as handled ivory to the palm', 'she might have been moulded to his own special use'.[18] George Meredith's 'egoist', Sir Willoughby Patterne, wanted his fiancée 'simply to be material in his hands for him to mould her; he had no other thought'.[19] He wants her to be 'coldly, statue-like, Dian-like' (p. 95), but as Clara Middleton says of herself, in a spirit of self-knowledge not often available to statue-women, she is 'not a piece of drawing-room sculpture' (p. 159).

The image of the desirably sculpted woman is given an ironic turn in Thomas Hardy's *The Well-Beloved* (1897), the story of a sculptor who pursues his elusive vision of the 'well-beloved' for his whole life without ever being able simultaneously to recognise and capture her. The 'well-beloved' flits from one sculptural form to another, from 'a very Juno', to 'a Minerva'.[20] During a life-time of pursuit, Jocelyn Pierston,

threw into plastic creations that ever-bubbling spring of emotion which, without some conduit into space, will surge upwards and ruin all but the greatest man. It was probably owing to this [...] that he was successful in his art, successful by a seemingly sudden spurt, which carried him at one bound over the hindrance of years.

He prospered without effort. He was A. R. A. (p. 33)

His inspiration, like that of the late-Victorian neo-Classical painters, had captured the public taste, and he goes on to be described as a Victorian 'Praxiteles, or rather our Lysippus' (p. 54). He eventually finds, in the descendant of his earliest love, one whom he desires, and plans to mould her appropriately, 'to pack her off to school for two or three years, marry her, enlarge her mind by a little travel, and take his chance of the rest' (p. 75). Pierston fails in his pursuit, however, for the woman he chooses is one who is also in search of her own elusive well-beloved. The only consummation of Pierston's passion is that achieved through his sculpture, a most appropriate end, Hardy seems to suggest, for one who worships an abstraction, regardless of the beings in whom that abstraction may seem briefly to reside. Pierston thus suffers for restricting female life to the dimensions of an objectified statue.

The cooperation between statuary and desire, and its dangers for women, are powerfully demonstrated in *The Mill on the Floss* (1860), where Maggie Tulliver's arm is described in terms of Greek sculpture at precisely the moment when Stephen Guest is moved to shower kisses on it:

Who has not felt the beauty of a woman's arm? – the unspeakable suggestions of tenderness that lie in the dimpled elbow, and all the varied gently-lessening curves, down to the delicate wrist, with its tiniest, almost imperceptible nicks in the firm softness. A woman's arm touched the soul of a great sculptor two thousand years ago, so that he wrought an image of it for the Parthenon which moves us still as it clasps lovingly the time-worn marble of a headless trunk. Maggie's was such an arm as that – and it had the warm tints of life.

A mad impulse seized on Stephen; he darted towards the arm, and showered kisses on it.[21]

Maggie experiences the moment as one of affront and appropriation, the imposition of her 'viewer's' desires upon a form which the statue-metaphor has encouraged him to believe he can control. In this moment, Maggie loses her own specificity for Stephen: the impossibility of their situation is absorbed by the dimensions of the prevailing metaphor, and Stephen presumes to kiss Maggie. Her immediate reaction, and indeed the rest of Eliot's novel, demonstrate that Maggie is not a compliant 'sculpture', but this moment attests nonetheless to the vulnerability of the desired woman to the sculptor-like attentions of her lover.

The depiction of this incident invoked the wrath of the *Saturday Review*. Although, the reviewer suggests, 'There is nothing wrong in writing about such an act, and it is the sort of thing that does sometimes happen in real life', there is something profoundly wrong in the female novelist's handling of this incident, for her treatment of it '[leaves] behind a feeling of hesitation, if not repulsion, in the reader'.[22] The reviewer goes on,

There are very few men who would not shrink from putting into words what they might imagine to be the physical effects of love in a woman. Perhaps we may go further, and say that the whole delineation of passionate love, as painted by modern female novelists, is open to very serious criticism. There are emotions over which we ought to throw a veil; and no one can say that, in order to portray an ardent and tender love, it is necessary to describe the conquest of a beautiful arm over honour and principle. (p. 119)

The prevailing sense here is that Eliot has told too much, but the grounds of her excess shift uneasily from the veiled suggestion of her impropriety in trying to assume the sensual experiences of a man, to the cruder, but more readily condemnatory, and perhaps less disturbing, threat that in revealing so much Eliot is being indecorous and unfeminine. In fact, what Eliot is demonstrating here is an awareness of a Pygmalion-like assumption of authority on the male lover's part. It is her display of that knowledge that so affronts the *Saturday Review*, for such an articulation, and Eliot's writing in this instance as a woman, explicitly contravene the workings of the Pygmalion-mechanism, and threaten to break the mould of Galatea, which relies for its persistence on the statue's silent objectification.

VICTORIAN PYGMALIONS

Attempts to 'mould' young women through romantic attachment are authorised by aesthetic responses to Classical statuary, the implications of which are demonstrated in stories and case-studies of men who reputedly fell in love with statues. In 'Florentine Nights' (1835), for instance, Heinrich Heine had written of a statue which was actually responsible for setting the terms of a young boy's sexual awakening. His feelings are prompted by a statue which had 'been thrown from off its pedestal into the high grass; but there it lay, free from mutilation, the marble goddess with pure lovely features and the noble deep-cleft bosom, which seemed, as it glowed out of the grass, like a Greek revelation'.[23] The narrator later returns to '[kiss] the lovely goddess with such passion and tenderness and despair as I have never in this life kissed with again' (p. 184). Thus is prompted a lifetime of obsession with statues, and dead women.

In his introduction to Heine's prose writings, Havelock Ellis offers this vignette of a complementary moment late in Heine's life:

He went out for the last time in May 1848. Half blind and half lame, he slowly made his way out of the streets, filled with the noise of revolution, into the silent Louvre, to the shrine dedicated to 'the goddess of beauty, our dear Lady of Milo'. There he sat long at her feet; he was bidding farewell to his old gods; he had become reconciled to the religion of sorrow; tears streamed from his eyes, and she looked down at him, compassionate but helpless: 'Dost thou not see, then, that I have no arms, and cannot help thee?' (p. xvi)

In volume two of Ellis's *Studies in the Psychology of Sex*, Heine's example is just one of a series of male obsessions with statuary, which ranges from the Ancient Greeks to the cases of a Parisian gardener who fell in love with a statue of Venus in a park in 1877, and the young man who was arrested because of his 'moonlight visits to the statue of a nymph on the terrace of a country house'.[24] The two latter cases are also cited in Benjamin Tarnowsky's *The Sexual Instinct and its Morbid Manifestations* (first published in Russia in 1885) where he writes of the possibility that pictures and statues might become the objects of erotomaniacs' adoration.[25] The phenomenon is also cited, according to Ellis, in works by Eulenberg and Bloch, and in Richard von Krafft-Ebing's *Psychopathia Sexualis*, where those who violate statues are treated as a type of *frotteur*.[26] The practice was thus well established within the new science of sexology. It was, however, left to Havelock Ellis to coin a term for this 'falling in love with statues, [this] rare form of erotomania, founded on the sense of vision and closely related to the allurement of beauty' (*Psychology of Sex*, vol. II, p. 188), and which was thus defined as an aesthetically conditioned perversion. The term Ellis used was 'Pygmalionism', for the choice of which he was indebted to his Victorian heritage, to a culture which abounded in examples of the influence of the archetypal Pygmalion, the Cypriot sculptor-king of Ovid's *Metamorphoses*.[27]

There may initially seem to be a contradiction in Ellis's adopting for the title of this obsession the name of one who, through the media of his adoration and the intervention of Venus, brought his statue to life. In the *Metamorphoses* Ovid tells how, disgusted by the unchaste women of Cyprus, the celibate king Pygmalion sculpts a statue 'more beautiful / Than ever woman born' to succour his loneliness.[28] However, so moved is he by his work, that Pygmalion falls in love with the statue and woos it ardently. His love comes to express itself in the hope that the statue will live, and at Venus' festival he prays:

> 'Vouchsafe,
> O Gods, if all things you can grant, my bride
> Shall be' – he dared not say my ivory girl
> – 'The living likeness of my ivory girl.'   (p. 233)

Impressed by his fervour Venus, goddess of love and patron of Cyprus, miraculously brings the statue to life, using as her agent the desiring lips and hands of Pygmalion:

> Again he kissed her and with marvelling touch
> Caressed her breast; beneath his touch the flesh
> Grew soft, its very hardness vanishing.   (p. 233)

This relationship is consummated with Venus' blessing:

> The goddess graced the union she had made,
> And when nine times the crescent moon had filled
> Her silver orb, an infant girl was born,
> Paphos, from whom the island takes its name.   (p. 234)

Galatea's giving birth seems to confirm her miraculous incarnation, but the terms of that incarnation's achievement make it clear that her metamorphosis into a human being is only partially achieved: she will only ever be 'living marble', the living likeness of an ivory girl. Crucially, in the Ovidian legend, the statue (who has only subsequently come to be known as Galatea[29]) lacks both a name and a voice, because she is not born into conscious subjectivity. As J. Hillis Miller notes, 'For Galatea to see at all is to see Pygmalion and to be subject to him. It is as if Narcissus' reflection in the pool had come alive and could return his love.'[30] Her experiencing self is constrained by the circumstances of her creation, and she remains only and always the image of Pygmalion's desire. Galatea literally bodies forth that desire, and the ultimate derivation of her being from Venus restricts her to a range of purely physical representations.

In the *Metamorphoses*, we come to see how Pygmalion's love for the woman retains the same parameters as his love for the statue. In his eyes, as in the eyes of Walter Hamlin, Willoughby Patterne, Gilbert Osmond, and Jocelyn Pierston, the woman he loves is adored insofar as she embodies his desires and demonstrates herself malleable to her lover–creator. The sculptor John Gibson acted out the part of a modern Pygmalion when he created, and then temporarily refused to part with, his statue *The Tinted Venus* (first exhibited in 1862). Gibson records that it was commissioned by a Mr Preston from Liverpool, and that he took unprecedented care over its manufacture: 'This representation I kept in hand for five years, working on the marble whenever I felt disposed, and referring often to nature. Thus it became, I may say, the most carefully laboured work I ever executed, for I wrought the forms up to the highest standard of the ideal.'[31] The statue was later to become notorious for the way in which Gibson chose to tint its flesh and clothing, thus making it even more lifelike and, to his contemporaries, more explicitly sexual than the white marble statues of Ancient Greece and Rome:

I took the liberty to decorate it in a fashion unprecedented in modern times. I tinted the flesh like warm ivory – scarcely red – the eyes blue, the hair blond, and the net which contains the hair golden [...] The drapery is left the colour of the marble – the border ornament is pink and blue. At her feet is a tortoise, on the back of which is inscribed in Greek 'Gibson made me at Rome'. (p. 211)

Like Pygmalion, when his work was complete, Gibson, 'often sat down quietly and alone before my work, meditating upon it and consulting my own simple feelings [...] At moments I forgot that I was gazing at my own production; there I sat before her, long and often. How was I ever to part with her!' (pp. 211–12). The parting was indeed difficult, and only came after Mrs Preston's prolonged protests, during the course of answering which Gibson makes a revealing analogy between the statue and Mrs Preston herself: 'There is no doubt that I am using you abominably ill – yes – but the truth is I cannot screw up my courage to send away my Goddess. It is almost as difficult for me to part with her as it would be for Mr Preston to part with you' (p. 213).

Gibson's playful elision of Mrs Preston and his Venus supports a reading of Havelock Ellis which would suggest that Pygmalionism's dimensions replicate a conservative division of sexual characteristics. Ellis's analysis of vision as part of the process of sexual selection in man reinforces the legend's connotations of female passivity and spectacle in the assertion that beauty is the most powerful and subtle source of sexual allurement, 'appealing at once to the sexual and to the aesthetic impulses' (*Psychology of Sex*, vol. II, p. 186), but also that that beauty 'in the human species is, above all, a feminine attribute, making its appeal to men' (vol. II, p. 189). We are told that women experience no 'corresponding cult for the beauty of man' (vol. II, p. 189) but rather that their sexual enthusiasm is excited by visual stimuli which are the translation of tactile qualities signifying male energy and activity.[32] From the popular myth of Pygmalion, Ellis extracts a series of paradigms which enmesh any subsequent metaphorical resort to statuary, and the women so described, within a narrative of male creativity and determination, and female stasis and mimesis. It seems then that Pygmalionism may, in fact, be read in some measure as an exemplification, rather than a perversion, of the instinct of sexual selection.[33]

This is best demonstrated in some of the numerous nineteenth-century adaptations of Ovid's legend into poetry. These range from the innocence of Arthur Hallam's 'Lines Spoken in the Character of Pygmalion' (1832) to the necrophiliac fantasy of Robert Buchanan's juvenile poem 'Pygmalion. An Allegory of Art', a poem which in its sensuous extremes far exceeds the licence to which Buchanan was later to take exception in Dante Gabriel Rossetti's work.[34] At the start of his poem, Buchanan's Pygmalion is in mourning for the death of his fiancée, which took place on the morning of their wedding. He has an idealised statue made of her, and when the statue comes to life Pygmalion swoons at its loveliness, and statue and sculptor embark on a riot of sensual gratification, which was deliberately denied the living woman:

Three days and nights the vision dwelt with me,
Three days and nights we dozed in dreadful state,
Look'd piteously upon by sun and star.[35]

The dumb statue is merely the site of the gratification of its creator's desires, and the poem's gaudy vision ends appropriately: pestilence grips Pygmalion's city, and in a lurid image of Pre-Raphaelite distinctness, the statue dies:

the light,
With gleams of crimson on the ruinous hair,
[Spangled] a blue-vein'd bosom whence the robe
Fell back in rifled folds; but dreadful change
Grew pale and hideous on the waxen face,
And in her sleep she did not stir, nor dream.   (vol. II, p. 257)

With its death, all evidence of the statue's wonderful metamorphosis disappears, and attention is focused finally, as it was initially, on the plight of the forlorn sculptor. Hallam's poem contains none of the salacious details and prolonged courtship of Ovid's and Buchanan's accounts, but relates Pygmalion's adoration of the finished statue, his desire that she might live, and the almost instantaneous recognition that she is moving:

Let her live and love!
I dare not look again – my brain swims round –
I dream – I dream – even now methought she moved –
If 'tis a dream, how will I curse the dawn
That wakes me from it! There – that bend again –
It is no dream – Oh, speak to me and bless me.[36]

Fundamentally distinct both in tone and in their exploration of Ovid's legend, both nineteenth-century poems nonetheless presuppose the aptness of this narrative as an archetype through which to explore aspects of sexual desire and relationship. Hallam's letter to Emily Tennyson about this poem, and the private charade which prompted it, elides Pygmalion's desire for his own inanimate creation, whose being and vitality are dependent on him, with Hallam's desire literally to 'act out' this scene of desire with Emily. He writes to her thus:

My most decided success was in the character of Pygmalion. Charlotte Sotheby was my Statue: she looked it to perfection: when the curtain drew up, & shewed her standing motionless on the pedestal, draped in white, & a white veil concealing all her head except the beautiful features not unlike in truth the work of Grecian art – when I, dressed as a sculptor, chisel in hand, poured forth a speech (in verse) of my own composition in praise of my supposed statue, ending with a prayer to Venus that she might live, & at the word slowly & gracefully the form began to move, to bend forward, to descend, to meet my embrace – the room rang with acclamations, & I – I thought of several things, but of none so much, as of the pleasure I should have in describing this to you, & perhaps on some occasion acting it with you. (quoted in *Writings of Arthur Hallam*, p. 111)

Hallam employs this scenario as a means of courting Emily, of elaborately narrating a simple desire to embrace her as he had embraced Charlotte Sotheby, but embedded within this articulation of desire are the aspects of control and determination which are equally a part of Pygmalion and his statue's story.

The articulation of male desire in these poems takes its dimensions from a legend which confers absolute powers of determining the parameters of sexual desire on the figure of the sculptor and king. There is here no danger of an emasculating *femme fatale* or an otherwise disruptive female sexual presence. The function of the sculptural reference in defining women is demonstrated in Elizabeth Blackwell's *The Human Element in Sex* (1884), where she writes of the 'power of sex in women' that it is, 'strikingly shown in the enormous influence which they exert upon men for evil. It is not the cold beauty of a statue which enthrals and holds so many men in terrible fascination. It is the living active power of sexual life embodied in its separate overpowering female phase'.[37] Blackwell's opposition between the statue-woman and the active power of female sexuality is revealing, for it is that power which, in the 'erotic novelette' of the Pygmalion story,[38] is explicitly denied to Pygmalion's statue, that power of activity and fascination which the figure of Pygmalion is particularly well placed to deny in his complementary functions as sculptor, king, and parthenogeneticist. Burne-Jones's Pygmalion, in his *Pygmalion and the Image* series (1878) may kneel in homage to his living 'Image' without any fear of subjugation, because he is worshipping his own inspiration and desire (plate 2), in whom, as Thomas Lovell Beddoes confirms in 'Pygmalion. The Cyprian Statuary', romantic satisfaction is guaranteed:

> The living form with which the stone be blest
> Was the loved image stepping from his breast.
> And therefore loves he it and therefore stays
> About the statue-rock's feet, from hour to hour,
> Anchored to her by his own heart.[39]

Plate 2   Edward Burne-Jones, *Pygmalion and the Image – IV, The Soul Attains* (1878)

There is little distinction in any of the nineteenth-century Pygmalion poems between the 'statue' as animate and as inanimate female object, and crucially, coming to life offers no access to a language with which to express a dissenting subjectivity. Most of the statues are born with a blush into silence, although Buchanan's does murmur 'sounds like prattled infants' speech' (vol. II, p. 255); and W. C. Bennett offers his statue the compensation of being

> Silent, and yet how tuneful with sweet speech,
> Utterance divine, that from the listening soul
> Drew echoes, though the dull ear heard it not![40]

The essence of the woman's desirability lies in the connotations of her marble state, her approximation to a statuesque ideal, rather than her living vitality. Buchanan opens his poem with an extended treatment of the likeness between the narrator's dead bride and the commemorative statue, 'White-limb'd, immortal' (vol. II, p. 250), which takes her place. Charlotte Sotheby's 'Grecian' features are shown to great effect in the charade, and Beddoes writes that the statue's 'marble symmetry was white / As brow and bosom should be' (p. 80).

It is important to note the way in which most of the nineteenth-century poets, however, deviate from their Ovidian source in one particular which serves to confirm their sense of the greater desirability of the statue: with few exceptions, modern Galateas are returned to stone at the end of their narrative. This makes of the statue's 'life' rather a fleeting episode than the miraculous metamorphosis which is the climax of Ovid's story, and renders the marble state both the ultimate as well as the initial site of desire. The statue continues to exercise a fetishistic attraction, and its marble state may appear, as it does in Dowson's 'Epigram' (1896), the most appropriate culmination of the narrator's desire:

> Because I am idolatrous and have besought,
> With grievous supplication and consuming prayer,
> The admirable image that my dreams have wrought
> Out of her swan's neck and her dark, abundant hair:
> The jealous gods, who brook no worship save their own,
> Turned my live idol marble and her heart to stone.[41]

The poem's sado-masochistic fantasy exemplifies the Victorian Pygmalions' practice of turning a living woman into a statue, rather than taking a marble form and miraculously metamorphosing it into a living form. Victorian Pygmalions are more likely to be enthralled by the static than by the live form.

The privileging of closure over living form is mirrored in the connotations of the creativity embraced by the Pygmalions of nineteenth-century, as opposed to Ovid's, poetry. In their accounts of Ovid's legend, J. Hillis Miller, Marina Warner, and Erich Gombrich all cite it as partaking of the essence of creativity. For Hillis Miller, Pygmalion's desire for the statue is a prototype of prosopopoeia, 'the fundamental generative linguistic act making a given story possible' (p. 13). Warner and Gombrich go further in attesting to the story as evidence of the lambent numinosity which perpetually fires the artist's creation. Gombrich's contention that without the secret hopes and fears of the legend there might be no art (p. 80) is supported by Warner's suggestion that, 'when [the statue] steps out of illusion into reality through her creator's desire, she fulfils the delusory promise of art itself, the nearest equivalent to generation in the single, uncoupled manner of the gods that a man can reach', that she fulfils 'the great seduction of illusionistic art [...] that through art man can become a lord of creation'.[42]

Ovid's narrative ends with Venus blessing the union of Pygmalion and Galatea, and enabling the erstwhile statue to bear a child, 'Paphos, from whom the island takes it name' (p. 234). The ending generates new wonders, sending our thoughts 'spinning and growing on into the silence which succeeds the conclusion'.[43] Victorian Pygmalions, however, sacrifice this sense of wonder for endings of control and closure, choosing to privilege the elements of completion over those of transformation, what Gillian Beer describes as 'completed ceremony' over 'indefatigable process' (p. 65). Suggestions of generation and growth are replaced by narratives capitalising on the completeness of the woman created, and her sufficiency for the uses imposed on her. Further, when the statue dies or is returned to stone, all evidence of the wonderful metamorphosis, of such life as the statue had, disappears.

It is possible to see Victorian Pygmalion legends as responding to contemporary anxieties about women and their ability to 'metamorphose' into unprecedented professional and intellectual forms in the nineteenth century. Women seemed ever more likely to descend from the pedestalled position in which they were placed metaphorically as the embodiment of virtues in the Victorian home.[44] That descent is forestalled by the practice of Victorian Pygmalions who reinstate the statue-form at the conclusion of their narratives. Statuary thus becomes a prohibiting form, as Ovid had envisaged in the story which precedes that of Pygmalion in the *Metamorphoses*. The story of the Propoetides is told nowhere else in Classical literature, and seems to have been deliberately invented by Ovid as a foil to, or elaboration of, the Pygmalion-narrative. It is the sight of the Propoetides and their wickedness which prompts Pygmalion's celibacy, and make him resort to moulding his own woman:

Pygmalion had seen these women spend
Their days in wickedness, and horrified
At all the countless vices nature gives
To womankind lived celibate and long
Lacked the companionship of married love.   (p. 232)

These women had offended Venus, on what grounds is unclear, but
most scholars suppose some form of sexual impropriety. For their
punishment, the Propoetides' 'cheeks grew hard, [and] / They turned
with little change to stones of flint' (p. 232). In this story then, the
immobilisation of the woman within an inanimate form is a punishment
rather than a celebration, a stilling of her powers to disturb. She is
immured within a static form which has the additional benefit of acting
as a public warning through its status as spectacle. Victorian Pygmalion-
narratives, with their greater concentration on, and frequent return to,
the statue-state, may seem then to combine the two aspects of celebration and immurement in the creation of their statue-women, conjoining
both admiration and admonition in their motivation to 'mould' the
statue.[45]

GALATEA AND 'THE GIRL OF THE PERIOD'

That this dual significance of both statuary and sculptor is implicit in
Victorian adaptations of Pygmalion's narrative becomes clear when we
consider the extent to which conservative rhetoric in the debate over the
'woman question' is informed by assumptions about male–female relations, and masculine rights of determination, which are at the heart of
the Pygmalion legend. If we look at a seminal moment in Victorian
women's history, at the furore surrounding 'The Girl of the Period'
article of 1868, we see not only how Pygmalion-like assumptions con-
strain women's social and marital positions; but also how the metaphor
of woman as statuary carries much of the rhetorical burden of conservative arguments; and how woman's position is constructed as one mediating between the dichotomies of sculptor and statue, and of Galatea
and the Propoetides.

'The Girl of the Period' article was published anonymously in the
Saturday Review on 14 March 1868, and became 'perhaps the most
sensational middle article that the *Saturday Review* ever published'.[46] The
article was written by Eliza Lynn Linton, a successful novelist and
journalist who was fast becoming the most notorious female scourge of
those she would come to christen the 'Wild Women', or 'Shrieking

Sisterhood'. Lynn Linton's particular charge in this instance was that in place of 'the simple and genuine girl of the past, with her tender little ways and pretty bashful modesties', the 'Girl of the Period' was evolving into a 'loud and rampant modernization with her false red hair and painted skin, talking slang as glibly as a man, and by preference leading the conversation to doubtful subjects'.[47] The grounds for this charge, Lynn Linton suggested, lay in the extent to which young women were drawn to imitation of the *demi-mondaine* in cosmetics, costume, 'slang, bold talk and general fastness' (p. 340). The 'queens of the *demi-monde*', Lynn Linton interestingly suggests, appear to the young girl in the form of debased icons reminiscent of the Propoetides: she sees 'only the coarse gilding on the base token, and shuts her eyes to the hideous figure in the midst and the foul legend written round the edge' (p. 340).

The Pygmalion story surfaces more substantially in a number of specific charges against her accused. Lynn Linton's first accusation is that the 'Girl of the Period is a creature who dyes her hair and paints her face, as the first article of her personal religion' (p. 340). The girl is thus seen to be graphically claiming the right to be her own Pygmalion, literally to shape and colour herself as Pygmalion (and more recently Gibson) would have done his statue. At the root of Lynn Linton's accusation, and indeed of her whole argument, is the charge that the young woman is seeking to be self-made, to remake herself according to her own desires and observations, that is, to override the Pygmalion-rights of men. Her primary fault is to be guilty of disregarding men, for 'if she could be made to see herself as she appears to the eyes of men, she would mend her ways before too late' (p. 340). Lynn Linton's solution to this 'national madness' is to wait patiently until 'our women have come back again to the old English ideal, once the most beautiful, the most modest, the most essentially womanly in the world' (p. 340), that is, until women have returned to an idealised state, a figure of superlatives possible only in a marble rather than a living form.

The 'Girl of the Period' or 'GOP' as she became known, was soon a notorious commercial figure, giving her name to an Almanac, a Song-ster, a burlesque, and a parasol.[48] Most considered responses to Lynn Linton's article were negative, ridiculing it as an excessive, vulgar and odious piece of writing.[49] In *He Knew He Was Right* (1869), Trollope implicitly ridicules Lynn Linton's position by having his American feminist, Wallachia Petrie, who is a figure of fun throughout the novel, regard as 'pretty true' what the *Saturday Review* 'has said about English women'.[50] Opinion was undecided as to whether the anonymous author

Plate 3   '"The Girl of the Period!" or, Painted by a Prurient Prude', *The Tomahawk*, 4 April 1868

was male or female, with perhaps slightly more commentators detecting a masculine voice. However, *The Tomahawk*, a popular comic periodical, was adamant in its detection of a female hand behind the 'Girl of the Period', and exploited this insight in a crude cartoon entitled ' "The Girl of the Period!" or, Painted by a Prurient Prude' (plate 3). The cartoon takes up the main theme of Lynn Linton's argument against the 'Girl of the Period', her desire to usurp male creativity and determination, but turns it against Lynn Linton by showing her as one who likewise appropriates to herself the right of creating, in this case painting rather than moulding, others. What the cartoon seems primarily concerned to challenge is not Lynn Linton's observations (indeed an article in the same number of *The Tomahawk* substantially agreed with Lynn Linton[51]), but rather her self-appointed right to determine creation and representation, just as she had challenged young women's rights to do the same.[52]

The most interesting aspect of the 'Girl of the Period' debate, however, lies in the extent to which both sides are concerned to attest to, and to defend, social structures and relations based on the gender demarcation of Pygmalion's story. In the arguments of both Lynn Linton and her opponents the Pygmalion-trope figures as a readily accessible paradigm with universally acknowledged characteristics and functions, one of the most pervasive of which was the consigning of women to a realm of derivation and lack of originality. As a commentator in *Tinsleys' Magazine* puts it, 'Men assume that women ought to think precisely as they do.'[53] While Lynn Linton argued that the 'Girl of the Period' challenged this assumption, some of the contemporary young woman's champions defended her on the grounds that she was in fact obeying only too diligently the demands of her Galatea-role. If, an argument typically goes, there are those amongst the women of England who would seem to provide evidence for Lynn Linton's assertions, then the blame should be placed firmly with the men who, as Mary Braddon puts it, 'taught the girls of England this hateful slang [...and who] obtruded upon and paraded before them the odious women they take as their models'.[54] She goes on, apparently in the belief that the writer of the 'Girl of the Period' article is male, 'What cowards and hypocrites men must be too, when they can turn upon and assault the helpless woman who has meekly and dutifully copied the model they have set-up before her eyes, and at whose shrine she has seen them prostrate and worshipping!' (p. 215). In similar but more temperate vein, Henry James concludes an essay on 'Modern Women' with the assertion that when women 'present an ugly picture, therefore, we think it the part of wisdom for men to cast a glance at their own internal economy [...] They give the *ton* – they pitch the key.'[55] Like Pygmalion then, men are ceded the power to determine womanhood, to take the blame but also the responsibility for women's

behaviour. Rightly or wrongly reasoned, such a debate attests to the
readiness with which a Pygmalion-like figure might be effectively called
upon as a factor within, even in James's analysis a solution to, contemporary problems.

The group of women who are most liable to be constrained by the
Pygmalion-model of gender-division were female artists: writers, actresses, painters, and sculptors. The Latin poem, of course, inscribes
Galatea as muse and art-object, not creative herself but used rather to
sustain Pygmalion's creativity, and thus to be defined by the artist's
desires, as is the model of Christina Rossetti's 'In an Artist's Studio',
believed to be based upon Elizabeth Siddal:

> He feeds upon her face by day and night,
>   And she with true kind eyes looks back on him,
> Fair as the moon and joyful as the light:
>   Not wan with waiting, not with sorrow dim;
> Not as she is, but was when hope shone bright;
> Not as she is, but as she fills his dreams.[56]

Galatea provides the archetype for Siddal/the model's being subsumed
within D. G. Rossetti/the painter's work of art, and embodies the
latter's surrender of autonomy to the artist's vision. Christina Rossetti's
poem ruefully acknowledges the dimensions of nineteenth-century adaptations of Pygmalion's story which explicitly confirm the appropriate
male-ness of the artist, and his supremacy in matters of creativity even
over the goddess Venus. The work and reputation of Siddal herself were
clearly subject to this interpretative framing. Despite John Ruskin's
substantial support and more recent attempts to rejuvenate her reputation as an artist, she is still best known as Dante Gabriel Rossetti's muse.
In Victorian accounts of the couple, Siddal was treated as a lesser
Rossetti, and was described as showing 'brilliant promise as a colourist',
and having 'a wonderful eye for colour'.[57] But any extension of her
talents beyond this naive facility is credited to the influence of Rossetti
and his peers. Her works are variously described as 'small quasi-poetical
imitations of his work'; as 'beautiful, but without force. They were
feminine likenesses of his own.' She is also charged with having 'the
deficiencies of [Rossetti's] defects'.[58]

Women's creative success was particularly qualified by the charge that their work demonstrated a 'comparative lack of originality' which was the most conspicuous measure of their intellectual inferiority.[59] Individual artists might, for instance, be spoken of in terms of their relationship to their mentors: in a letter to Harriet Hosmer, Mrs Jameson acknowledges such a pattern in her reference to 'the malignant sarcasm of some of your rivals at Rome, as to your having Mr Gibson "at your elbow"' (quoted in Carr, *Harriet Hosmer*, p. 150). Even women's readily acknowledged success in writing novels might be put down to, 'the observing and imitating faculties [which] go for much in novel writing, even of the best kind; and observation and imitation are gifts, the possession of which in a peculiar degree by women no-one would dream of denying'.[60] Novelists, Alfred Austin concedes, may possess imagination, but suggests that it is of an inferior order, and one which is probably more common amongst women than men. Galatea was trapped within the bounds of Pygmalion's imagination. In *The Subjection of Women* (1869), John Stuart Mill agrees that women's inferiority in the arts may indeed be resolved into the material objection of a 'deficiency of originality' but goes on to add that,

Never since any considerable number of women have begun to cultivate serious thought, has originality been possible on easy terms. Nearly all the thoughts which can be reached by mere strength or original faculties, have long since been arrived at; and originality, in any high sense of the word, is now scarcely ever attained by minds which have undergone elaborate discipline, and are deeply versed in the results of previous thinking.[61]

He further added that men's chronological precedence in the field of the arts militated against women's achieving forms of their own. Mill thus reduced the question of women's achievement of an originality definable only by its unattainability to the material conditions of education and access to information which disadvantaged them. In only one art, as Mill recognises, were women readily accepted: 'The only one of the fine arts which women do follow, to any extent, as a profession, and an occupation for life, is the histrionic; and in that they are confessedly equal, if not superior to men' (p. 188).

Women achieved success as actresses in part through biological necessity, but also, I would argue, because in the theatre their work could most readily be made to fulfil two primary conditions of what I will term the Galatea-aesthetic. The actress was, first, necessarily imitative and derivative, necessarily speaking words given to her by a usually male author; and second, on the commercial Victorian stage, she was able, was indeed obliged, to fulfil the role of the isolated and desirable spectacle which was Galatea's first incarnation. Such an aesthetic, as we will see, also necessarily conditions the grounds upon which Victorian theatre functioned and was made acceptable to its audiences. The extent to which it can enable the negotiation of the illicit and the acceptable is shown in the narratives of Ellen Terry's personal and professional experiences during the nineteenth century.

'PYGMALION'S WIFE'

Theatrical, social, and artistic aspects of Pygmalionism forcefully coincide in the relationship between the young actress Ellen Terry and her first husband, G. F. Watts, one of the best known of the Victorian Classical painters.[62] Watts, along with Alma-Tadema, had casts of part of the Elgin Marbles in their studios, and it was in his early study of these marbles, and in the four years he spent as a young man in Florence that what Hugh Macmillan describes as Watts's devotion to the 'sculpturesque ideal of art' was born.[63] Macmillan goes on to suggest that Watts's paintings appealed to simple truths and primary emotions, as he believed did Classical sculpture. In 'Pygmalion's Wife' (plate 4), Watts tried to combine the two arts, as Swinburne noted in his comments on the painting, which was exhibited at the Royal Academy show of 1868. He also notes the consanguinity of woman and statue:

The soft severity of perfect beauty might serve alike for woman or statue, flesh or marble; but the eyes have opened already upon love, with a tender and grave wonder; her curving ripples of hair seem just warm from the touch and the breath of the goddess, moulded and quickened by lips and hands diviner than her sculptor's [...] her shapeliness and state, her sweet majesty and amorous chastity, recall the supreme Venus of Melos. In this 'translation' of a Greek statue into an English picture [...] we see how in the hands of a great artist painting and sculpture may become as sister arts.[64]

The painting was inspired by a bust from the Ashmolean museum, of which Watts kept a cast in his studio. In her biography of the painter, Watts's widow stresses that the painting was not a copy from the antique, but rather that his reverence for the bust he had found inspired Watts to paint Galatea's transformation from marble to life, rendering it thereby one of Watts's most imaginative works.[65] Of this painting, Macmillan writes that Watts, 'with a noble simplicity takes the whole myth for granted, and places before us the splendour of the animated

Plate 4   G. F. Watts, *Pygmalion's Wife* (1868)

state itself, leaving it to tell its own wonderful tale to the imagination. What her maker and lover was to her, every one that gazes upon that lovely countenance is compelled to become' (p. 138). As the painter of this image, Watts is particularly deeply implicated in the dynamics of spectating as set out by Macmillan, and in that act's apparently inevitable involvement in Pygmalionism.

Four years before this, on 20 February 1864, Watts had married the young Ellen Terry, an act similarly strongly imbued with emblems of the Pygmalion myth. Just before the wedding, the forty-six-year-old Watts wrote to inform his friend Lady Constance Leslie that:

I have determined to remove [Ellen Terry] from the temptations and abominations of the stage, giving her a [sic] education and if she continues to have the affection she now feels for me, marry her [...] whatever the future brings, I can hardly regret taking the poor child out of her present life and fitting her for a better [...]
I do not think I ought to be thought ill of [...] To make the poor Child what I wish her to be, will take a lot of time and most likely cost a great deal of trouble, and I shall want the sympathy and aid of all my friends so I hope none will look coldly on my endeavours.[66]

Watts is evidently uncomfortable with the extreme youth of a bride who was sixteen at the time of her marriage, and accurately anticipates the opposition which the match would provoke. However, just as Pygmalion is both repelled and inspired by the Propoetides, Watts is sufficiently moved by his distaste for the theatrical context in which he finds Ellen Terry to feel justified in desiring, and in assuming the right, to create something purer and more appropriate to her beauty. He also seems in some measure to be authorised by the dynamics of that theatrical context, and appropriates her as raw material, as Pygmalion does his marble. The painter tried to do this by remoulding Terry within his own art-form, and the bulk of their marriage was spent in Terry's modelling for Watts. The couple had met when Terry and her sister Kate posed for *The Sisters* (1862), a painting dominated by a yearning wistfulness on Terry's part which instils the image with a movement and tension unusual in Watts's work, but which was to become characteristic of the studies of Terry which Watts completed during their brief marriage.

Terry later noted in her autobiography that Watts wished to protect her, desiring for the young actress 'a solid social position', 'a noble place' in the history of her time, which he felt the theatre would not be able to give her (*Story of My Life*, p. 61). But as Graham Robertson commented in a letter: 'If Watts thought he could mould that vital and radiant creature into what he wished her to be, he did not show much intelligence.'[67] The failure of Watts's attempt to reshape Terry is chronicled in his divorce petition, drawn up in March 1877. In it the artist's bewilderment at the restlessness and lack of pliability of his *objet* is clear. The petition writes of Watts,

That although considerably older than his intended wife he admired her very much and hoped to influence, guide and cultivate a very artistic and peculiar nature and to remove an impulsive young girl from the dangers and temptations of the stage [...]

    That very soon after his marriage he found how great an error he had made. Linked to a most restless and impetuous nature accustomed from the very earliest childhood to the stage and forming her ideas of life from the exaggerated romance of sensational plays, from whose acquired habits a quiet life was intolerable and even impossible, demands were made upon him he could not meet without giving up all the professional aims his life had been devoted to.[68]

The roles of artist and husband clashed, as surely as did those of wife and actress for Terry, yet, in some of his works of art, Watts was able to acknowledge those disruptive energies which rendered the relationship incompatible with the Pygmalion and Galatea pattern he had initially envisaged.

    In the process of his disillusionment with Terry, Watts produced many of his greatest paintings, described a little unfairly by Edith Craig and Christopher St John as 'the only ones which have stood the test of time',[69] and by Ronald Chapman as having a 'lively warmth' lacking in his other works.[70] In her biography of Terry, Nina Auerbach skilfully evokes the tensions of Watts's portraits, particularly *Choosing* and *Ellen Terry*, in which Terry is 'mobile and brilliantly alive as she seems to struggle for more space than the canvas allows'.[71] The painter's own testimony to Terry is thus more eloquent and generous than those of his biographers, who largely omit any mention of Terry, but is ultimately still a baffled one. The story of Watts's fortunes as a would-be Pygmalion is, however, best and most appropriately told through the image of his sculpture *Clytie* (plate 5), casts of which were owned by Lord Leighton, who kept it in his studio, and by George Eliot amongst others. The bust, according to one of Watts's friends, represented 'an echo of the dramatic feeling' of Terry, which 'gave value to the conception and inspired the working of the marble, which Watts chiselled himself'.[72]

    This work was begun in the years immediately following Watts's estrangement from Terry, and his 'first essay' was exhibited, along with *Pygmalion's Wife*, in 1868. The story of Clytie, like that of Pygmalion, is found in Ovid's *Metamorphoses*. Clytie loves the Sun, but he is obsessed with the beautiful Leucothoe, whom he visits one day disguised as her mother. Although fearful when the Sun reveals his true identity, Leucothoe is 'vanquished by the glory of the god, / [And] With no complaint

Plate 5   G. F. Watts, *Clytie* (1868)

accepted his assault' (p. 81). So outraged is Clytie by this that she publishes the story far and wide, ensuring Leucothoe's father hears of it. He is so incensed that he buries his daughter alive, thus ridding Clytie of her rival. However, the Sun continues to shun Clytie, and in her neglect she pines, not eating or drinking, but 'only [gazing] / Upon her god's bright face as he rode by, / And [turning] her head to watch him cross the sky' (p. 82). It is at this point that the story's metamorphosis, the focus of Watts's sculpture, takes place:

> Her limbs, they say, stuck fast there in the soil;
> A greenish pallor spread, as part of her
> Changed to a bloodless plant, another part
> Was ruby red, and where her face had been
> A flower like a violet was seen.
> Though rooted fast, towards the sun she turns;
> Her shape is changed, but still her passion burns.   (p. 82)

The sensuousness of the resulting sculpture is described by an enthusiastic Swinburne thus:

Never was a divine legend translated into diviner likeness. Large, deep-bosomed, superb in arm and shoulder, as should be the woman growing from flesh into flower through a god-like agony, from fairness of body to fullness of flower, large-leaved and broad of bosom, splendid and sad – yearning with all the life of her lips and breasts after the receding light and the removing love – this is the Clytie indeed whom sculptors and poets have loved for her love of the Sun their God. ('Some Pictures of 1868', p. 363)

There is also, however, a darker struggle within the sculpture than Swinburne acknowledges. What might in another context pass for a loving glance over a bare shoulder appears here as part of Clytie's effort to writhe away from her spectator, from the sculptor, and from her immuring fate. Although the sculpture is technically beautifully 'finish-ed', it eludes being finally encompassed and stilled by Watts's art, so strongly are its struggles and claims to life asserted. The passion of Ovid's Clytie still burns, but within an impotent form; that of Watts's *Clytie* stubbornly struggles to elude her fate, and succeeds by sheer force of her irrepressible energy.

Something of the same quality of the subject's both enlarging and eluding the 'frame' of reference the artist seeks to impose, which holds the artefact poised in the moment of perpetual conflict, is also found in Watts's studies of Ellen Terry, and aptly prefigures Terry's own career-long negotiation with both the sculptural metaphor and a series of would-be Pygmalions. Watts wrote of his ambitions for 'Clytie' in a letter to Gladstone:

my aim in this my first essay has been to get flexibility, impression of colour, and largeness of character, rather than purity and gravity – qualities I own to be extremely necessary to sculpture, but which, being made as it seems to me, exclusively the objects of the modern sculptor, have deadened his senses to some other qualities making part – often glories – of ancient art, and this has resulted in bare and cold work.[73]

The terms of the artistic conflict outlined here find an appropriate counterpart in the story of the original Clytie, in Watts's impulse both to be the master of 'the live stone'[74] and its flexibility, and also perhaps in his recollection of his marriage with, and the character of, Ellen Terry. The energising dynamic in each instance is the opposition between the artist's claims to and desire for mastery, and the right of the object of his attention to its vitality and autonomy. In Clytie's case her desires are defeated, and she is subjugated within a form imposed upon her. That Watts was not so successful in containing Terry, his sculpture of Clytie seems ruefully to acknowledge. It may be significant that *Clytie* was ten years in the making, and was only finished in 1878, the year following Watts's divorce from Terry and her marriage to the actor Charles Kelly. Although the years intervening between their separation and divorce had included her lengthy affair with Edward William Godwin, she was still legally Ellen Watts until 1877, and in this troublesome capacity must have continued to baffle Watts as she did during their marriage. *Clytie* is Watts's testimony to Terry's untrammelled energy, and his witness of his own failed attempts to mould her into the demure form he had envisaged for her.

An incident often recounted as typifying Terry's position in her first marriage is the tale of her unpinning her luxuriant blonde hair in public, and the outrage this caused in her husband's circle:

Ellen Terry, as a bride, was brought over to luncheon with my aunt. My aunt described her as strikingly lovely, with brilliant eyes and very beautiful hair, but quite a schoolgirl and a decided tomboy. After luncheon, while my uncle and Watts paced to and fro in the garden talking, my aunt remained with Mrs Prinsep and Ellen in the drawing-room.

Suddenly the latter, with an air of supreme boredom, leant back over the arm of the chair in which she was seated, and, shaking her head to and fro, loosened the pins from her hair which tumbled about her shoulders like a cloak of shining gold. My aunt could only gaze in delight at the beauty of the girl as she sat there swaying her head gently from side to side while the mass of shimmering hair shrouded her and swept the floor. But Mrs Prinsep was horrified. 'Ellen! Ellen!' she cried, 'put up your hair!' And Ellen, flashing a wrathful glance at her tormentor, grasped the waving mass of gold, coiled it carelessly upon her head, and, stabbing it with pins, sat there looking lovelier than ever, a petulant, scolded child.[75]

Terry's defiant act recalls one of the commonest images of the Victorian Pygmalion-poems, where the statues' tumbling hair represents a simultaneous entry into life and sexual desirability. But the self-consciousness of her letting down her hair constitutes her seminal difference from the awakening Galateas of Victorian poetry whose hair fell at the command of their poets, whether they willed it or not. The vitality and radiance of Terry's act, her enjoyment of her own physicality and its impact, render the moment not one simply of social defiance or sexual enticement, but make it a claim on Terry's part to be seen, to capture and conquer the gaze of her audience, which she partially succeeds in doing.

However, when Terry later returned to the theatre, she found that the viewing conventions which structured the appreciation of her work mirrored the restrictive, admonitory attentions of Mrs Prinsep, and that audiences needed to be able to appreciate her as a Galatea if she was to achieve popular acclaim. She needed that is, as she petulantly recognised during her marriage, to pin up her hair, and once again to become, or at least to be taken for, a demure domesticated statue. Terry's success within the terms of Pygmalion's approval, despite her unconventional personal life, is part of the narrative to be recounted below, as is the extent to which her growing dissatisfaction with the stage by the end of the nineteenth century is most appropriately articulated through her explicit rejection of both the dimensions of Galatea's role, and the terms of the living statue's aesthetic. The assertion of this rejection was, however, only achieved after Terry had left the stage. While she was still being seen, the Galatea-trope proved almost inescapable.

CHAPTER 2

Acting Galatea, 'the ideal statuesque'

Victorian actresses' relationship with the Pygmalion and Galatea narrative has its roots in early-nineteenth-century manifestations of the relationship between sculpture and the English stage. Links between the Classical and contemporary stages were a critical commonplace in the late-eighteenth and first half of the nineteenth centuries, and in this conjunction Classical statuary plays an enabling part. Throughout *Stage Effect: or, the Principles which Command Dramatic Success in the Theatre* (1840), Edward Mayhew constantly refers to the Greek drama as the measure against which English theatre is to be set,[1] as does George Grant in *An Essay on the Science of Acting* (1828).[2] John Styles DD refers in 1838 to its roots in Greece and Rome, finding in that derivation the beginnings of the stage's dangerous character in ancient licentiousness.[3] The connection had earlier been embodied in William Cooke's *The Elements of Dramatic Criticism* (1775), which advocated a thorough education in the 'English classics' for actors, and a knowledge of 'translations of such of the antients as may be necessary'.[4] He also suggests that the actor's art may be assisted by the study of antique forms: for men he recommends that attention be paid to 'The two Antinouses. The Hercules Farnese. The Apollo Belvidere. The Apollo De Medicis. The Caracalla. The Fighting, and Dying Gladiators' (p. 200); and that women should study 'The Venus De Medicis. The Venus De Calipaedia. Diana, Flora, and The Graces' (p. 201). In the course of his advice, Cooke equates study of the antique with the observation and imitation of nature. In particular, he writes that a performer well studied in the Classical statues, in their 'inflexion of body, and composition of limbs', will be able to give an appearance 'of *grace*, and give that Je ne sai quoi, so much admired in the whole deportment of action' (p. 201). The Classical reference might almost seem then to justify, or to facilitate a form of 'not-acting' on stage, a tendency particularly marked in the actress, in whom, as Henry Siddons writes, 'being a woman, it was for her interest to look beautiful, and not to disfigure her face by distortions' (*Practical Illustrations*, p. 120). The worlds of the 'natural', or the 'every-day', and the Classical also coincide in the illustrations to Siddons's work which indiscriminately juxtapose Classical and contemporary costume in exemplary images of the representation of emotions such as 'Joy', 'Quietude', 'Enthusiasm', and 'Despair'.

The Classical world was an important part of the rhetoric of female beauty at this time. In *Beauties of the Modern Dramatists* (1829), a collection of aphorisms from recent plays under headings such as 'Chastity', 'Fashion', 'Innocence', 'Matrimony', those sayings under 'Beauty' make frequent reference to statuary.[5] Furthermore, the costume historian C. Willett Cunnington describes the early-nineteenth century in England as 'the Vertical Epoch', a term which derives its impetus from the classicising mode dominating fashion at that time. Although Classical motifs permeated the whole nineteenth century, and the lines identified by Cunnington as Classical make a reappearance in the 1880s and 1890s, the period from 1800–17 seems clearly to have been marked by a preference for white muslins which were chosen 'to suggest a resemblance to marble'.[6] So dedicated were young women to this fashion, that according to some commentators they risked their lives for it: '[Doctors] called catarrhal complaints the "muslin disease", and attributed the increase of consumption to the thinness of clothing. When the influenza broke out in Paris in 1803, as many as 60,000 fell ill daily, this high number being also put down to the account of muslin.'[7]

The popularity of this trend in fashion was undoubtedly promoted by the example of Emma Hamilton, whose own public image was an apparently conflicting mixture of the notorious and the classically ideal. As the mistress, and later wife, of the much older Sir William Hamilton, Britain's Envoy Extraordinary to the Court of Naples from 1764–98, she became known throughout Western Europe for her 'Attitudes', which were impersonations of Greek statues, vase-paintings, and mythological characters. The Attitudes themselves generated a variety of artistic responses, most notably perhaps Friedrich Rehberg's series of images of Emma in Classical drapery representing both figures from Classical mythology and such abstract figures as the 'Muse der Tankzkunst'. The series was published in 1794 under the title *Drawings Faithfully Copied from Nature at Naples*.

A spectator noted of Emma that 'she single-handedly created a living gallery of statues and paintings. I have never seen anything more fluid and graceful, more sublime and heroic.'[8] The Attitudes themselves have a complicated derivation, descending in part from the study of Classical antiquities carried out by the artist George Romney, and transmitted to Emma when, as a young woman new to London, she worked as a model for the painter. Romney travelled to Italy in 1773, where he studied women's dress in casts of ancient sculptures, and in the works of Michelangelo, making copious sketches which he may, as Kirsten Gram Holmström speculates, have used to instruct the then Emma Hart in his studio.[9] One of his paintings, of Emma as 'A Bacchante' (1785) was commissioned by Sir William, uncle of Hart's then-protector, Charles Greville. Inspiration was also taken from Sir William's extensive, pioneering collection of Greek vases.

It is with some surprise that Holmström goes on to note of Emma's Attitudes that 'the foundations for the paraphrases of classical art which enchanted aristocrats and artists in Naples were laid in England' (pp. 135–6). Holmström's surprise might be mitigated when we consider that, although the Classical referents and cultural practices which informed Emma Hart's performances were of course drawn from an Ancient European tradition, the impulse behind their contemporary manifestation in the Attitudes is in part determined by that impulse to Pygmalionism which was to become a prominent part of the practice of performance in Victorian England. Shortly after her arrival in Naples in 1786, Emma Hart herself writes Sir William into the part of Pygmalion: '[he is] constantly by me looking in my face. I can't stir a hand, leg, or foot; but he is marking [it] as graceful and fine [...] poor Sir William is never so happy as when he is pointing out my beautyies to [his friends...] he does nothing all day but look at me and sigh' (quoted in Jenkins (ed.), *Vases and Volcanoes*, p. 84), just as did Ovid's distraught Pygmalion before the 'birth' of Galatea.

Contemporary accounts of the Attitudes make explicit their audiences' investing in Sir William responsibility for his mistress's public incarnations. Hamilton was a noted connoisseur and collector, and was to become a major benefactor of the British Museum. In Emma he acquired, as Horace Walpole noted, a 'gallery of statues'.[10] The Comte d'Espinchal concurred when he wrote that 'If I were the chevalier Hamilton, I would review all Olympus; I would often see Hebe and Venus and the Graces, sometimes Juno, very rarely Minerva'.[11] Goethe wrote that in Emma, Sir William had 'found all the antiquities', and indeed treats her as the final, consummate acquisition of Sir William's collection:

Sir William Hamilton, who is still living here as English ambassador, has now,
after many years of devotion to the arts and the study of nature, found the acme
of these delights in the person of an English girl of twenty with a beautiful face
and a perfect figure. He has had a Greek costume made for her which becomes
her extremely. Dressed in this, she lets down her hair and, with a few shawls,
gives so much variety to her poses, gestures, expressions, etc., that the spectator
can hardly believe his eyes. He sees what thousands of artists would have liked
to express realized before him in movements and surprising transformations –
standing, kneeling, sitting, reclining, serious, sad, playful, ecstatic, contrite,
alluring, threatening, anxious, one pose follows another without a break. (*Italian
Journey*, p. 208)[12]

What none of these accounts explicitly allows for is the possibility that
Emma Hart/Hamilton may herself have decided that her future security lay in being complicit with her older admirer's Pygmalion fantasies.
Handed over, without her consent, by an impecunious nephew to his
uncle, when she believed herself only to be paying a brief visit to Naples,
she needed to find a means of securing Hamilton's support. Her Attitudes clearly helped her to do this, as is evidenced by the couple's
marriage in September 1791, a year when Emma took her performance
to some of Europe's capital cities, including London.

Like statues of Venus, Emma Hamilton attracted responses which
oscillated between uneasy perceptions of her overt sexuality, and appreciations of her taste in performance. In her own person, as the
Comtesse de Boigne recollects, 'Hors cet instinct pour les arts, rien
n'était plus vulgaire et plus commun que lady Hamilton. Lorsqu'elle
quittait la tunique antique pour porter le costume ordinaire, elle perdait
toute distinction.'[13] One Lady Betty similarly quoted in her journal
'Lord Bristol's remark [which] seems to me so just a one that I must end
with it: "Take her as anything but Mrs Hart and she is a superior being –
as herself she is always vulgar"' (quoted in Fraser, *Beloved Emma*, p. 163).
Clearly the conjunction of Emma Hamilton's talent and her classicising
robes (the latter believed to be authorised by Sir William's directions)
proved sufficient to erase, at least temporarily, the audience's awareness
of her class and of her disreputable past. The Classical habit seems then
to be a significantly persuasive cultural trope in the late-eighteenth and
early-nineteenth centuries, and to be capable in appropriate circumstances of facilitating a degree of personal display which might otherwise
be perceived as morally questionable. The line between respectability
and indecency, between decorum and the acknowledged play of desire,
seems, however, crucially to be bound up with the presence of an

appropriate Pygmalion figure. Once she had become known as Lord Nelson's mistress, contemporary satirical cartoons by such as James Gillray and Thomas Rowlandson demonstrate how the very sculptural Attitudes which had secured Emma Hamilton's fame and freedom from notoriety became the means by which she was condemned. The satirists make use of Emma's greatly increased weight: Gillray's 'Dido, in Despair!' (1801) shows an enormous Emma pining for the departing Nelson, whilst her aged husband sleeps beside her. A parodic version of Rehberg's images of Emma (which of course confirms the fame of the originals), appeared in 1807 and is attributed to Gillray. By its cruel emphasis of Emma's size, it confirms the sexual motivation and allure of the original Attitudes. Lady Hamilton's story ends then with the defeat of Classical restraint by contemporary gossip and scandal.

As a result of Emma Hamilton's influence, the statuesque, Classical register was adopted by actresses in a variety of types of theatre, and it is necessary to take a brief look at some of its less reputable manifestations in the early part of the century before going on to examine something of its influence on the legitimate stage, and its emergence there into the dynamics of a recognisable Pygmalion–Galatea trope. As we will see throughout this work, one of the subsidiary effects of the Galatea-aesthetic was the way in which it helped to define the legitimate theatre in which it was found. This is manifested most clearly in terms of its establishing that theatre's difference from, even opposition to, other kinds of theatre, most notably the music-hall, and the imported attractions of the Théâtre Français. For, whilst those stages made plentiful use of a Classical rhetoric on-stage, its connotations were carefully distanced from those of Galatea in the legitimate English theatre.

Early in the nineteenth century, as Richard D. Altick demonstrates in *The Shows of London*, spectacles of waxen, marble-like or otherwise immobilised women were plentiful in the public venues of the city. After thirty years of touring, Madame Tussaud established herself in premises in Baker Street in 1835, an early attraction in which was the waxen effigy of the singer Maria Malibran who died in 1836 (*Shows of London*, p. 333).[14] Entrepreneurs such as 'Professor' Keller and Madame Wharton provided spectacles of young women representing Canova's Graces and the goddesses in Rubens's *Judgement of Paris* (p. 346). Madame Wharton called a spurious connoisseurship to her aid in advertising her entertainments, which she suggested were put on by a 'troupe of Eminent Artistes, [who] had been favoured with admission to the studios of several celebrated painters and sculptors'.[15] Amongst the titles of Wharton's entertainments were 'A Night with Canova and Flaxman' and 'A Night with Titian', whilst the salacious potential of female display in Classical costume was exploited most explicitly by Mme Pauline's 'talented company of female artistes' at the Coal Hole Tavern, a notorious venue to which ladies might not be admitted.

It seems not to have been unusual at this period for men also to represent Classical figures. The most notable performers were 'The Great Belzoni', who combined feats of strength with appropriate Classical references to Achilles and the labours of Hercules, thus, as advertising declared, 'uniting Grace and Expression with Muscular Strength' (quoted in Altick, *Shows of London*, p. 343); and the equestrian Andrew Ducrow, who impersonated Mercury on horse-back, and who later appeared framed and on a pedestal as Achilles, Ajax, the Discobolus, and the Dying Gladiator.[16] Alongside these entertainments, which drew on the practice of *tableaux vivants* and *poses plastiques*, which the *Athenaeum* noted in 1830 had been 'the rage with the fashionable at Rome' (Altick, *Shows of London*, p. 345), and had their roots at least partly in Emma Hamilton's example, were the classically inspired burlesques and extravaganzas of James Robinson Planché, which were produced in partnership with Madame Vestris at the Olympic Theatre. The first result of their collaboration was the *Olympian Revels*, which opened Vestris's management at the Olympic in January 1831, and which featured the manageress as Pandora, a part in which, as John Coleman recollected, 'her youth, her beauty, her superbly symmetrical proportions, displayed to the utmost advantage by her classical costume [...] procured her a reception so enthusiastic and so overwhelming that she fairly broke down under it, and had to wipe away her tears before she could utter a single word'.[17] The collaboration of Planché and Vestris lasted until the middle of the century, and established the rhetoric of Classicism in the popular theatre.[18] However, Planché was also a student of costume, and it is perhaps in this respect that he achieved his greatest influence over the legitimate theatre. In his *History of British Costume* (1834), he argued that 'The historian, the poet, the novelist, the painter, and the actor have discovered in attention to costume a new spring of information and a fresh source of effect.'[19] In that work, he singles out for particular criticism the practice of having 'the heroes and sages of Greece and Rome [strut] upon the stage in flowing perukes and gold-laced waistcoats!' Planché advocates instead an antiquarian attention to costume which would 'introduce some hues and forms which otherwise had never entered into [the] imagination' of the artist (p. xvi).

As Planché notes, in his efforts to reform the theatre he was drawing in part on the evidence of other arts' successful accommodation of the Classical register, but was probably also influenced, as are the illustrations to Henry Siddons's work on gesture and action, by memories and etchings of Emma Hamilton; and by the well-established Classical tradition on the European stage. It is in this continental theatre that we find the first modern stage-adaptations of the Pygmalion and Galatea narrative. As J. L. Carr notes, in eighteenth-century France the story formed the inspiration for a series of comic adaptations which personified the statue as coquettish and fickle.[20] However, the legend's most significant appearance in the modern drama occurred in Rousseau's monodrama *Pygmalion*, in which the statue's post-Classical name is explained. Pygmalion states that it arose from his original conception for the statue: 'j'ai voulu vous faire nymphe, et je vous ai faite déesse. Vénus même est moins belle que vous.'[21] The play was first produced in Lyons in 1770, and shown later at the Comédie Française in 1775.[22] However, as Holmström shows in her study of late-eighteenth and early-nineteenth-century European theatre, this play, the first of its genre, was not performed in consistently Classical style. A contemporary illustration shows the Paris Pygmalion, Larive, wearing tunic and sandals, but with powdered hair and otherwise fashionable dress; his Galatea, Mlle Raucour, wore a richly decorated dress with paniers, was draped with garlands, and wore an elaborate wig (*Monodrama, Attitudes*, p. 45). *Pygmalion* also diverged in a variety of ways from its Classical literary source in Ovid.

No mention of the Propoetides is made, either as a reason for Galatea's coming into being, or as a threat to Pygmalion, and, for the greater part of the play, Pygmalion is troubled and emasculated by the work which he has created. His genius has vanished, along with his peace of mind, because of the insane passion he has conceived for his beautiful statue: 'Voilà donc la noble passion qui m'égare! c'est donc pour cet objet inanimé que je n'ose sortir d'ici! . . . un marbre! une pierre! une masse informe et dure, travaillée avec ce fer! . . . Insensé, rentre en toi-même; gémis sur toi; vois ton erreur, vois ta folie...' (*Pygmalion*, p. 234). Relief is only possible once Pygmalion has acknowledged Venus' supremacy, and has himself suggested that the goddess take and recycle half of his own life-source in order to animate the statue. The end of the brief drama sees Galatea awakening into a barely articulated life, Pygmalion united with her, and crucially reunited with his own sense of energy and life: 'Oui, cher et charmant objet, oui, digne chef-d'œuvre de mes mains, de mon cœur et des dieux, c'est toi, c'est toi seule: je t'ai donné tout mon être: je ne vivrai plus que par toi' (p. 236). Thus, Galatea's incarnation, as in later Victorian versions, signals a confirmation and strengthening of Pygmalion and the removal of a depleting force from his life. His inner unity and strength as a man and as an artist are reconfirmed through Galatea's living presence.

According to Holmström, although Rousseau's work remained popular in France until the beginning of the nineteenth century, it was in Germany that it achieved most influence, where it was championed by Goethe and produced in Weimar in 1772.[23] There, it served as an inspiration for the Classical dramas of I. C. Brandes' *Ariadne auf Naxos*, and his later *Medea* (*Monodrama, Attitudes*, p. 46). Unlike Rousseau's drama, these two plays adopted a more complete Grecian costume, which was replicated in 1778, in a production of Goethe's own *Der Triumpf der Empfindsamkeit*. The play concerns the love of Prince Oronaro for Mandandane, the faithful wife of King Andrason. So besotted is the Prince that he carries a doll (dressed in Grecian costume) in the form of Mandandane around with him in a box. The Prince is only cured of his infatuation when the King replaces the doll with his wife. When faced, unbeknownst to him, with the real woman, the Prince finds his love waning. When his power over the doll is lost, so is the Prince's passion. Thus he provides an early example of the symptoms of what Ellis would diagnose as Pygmalionism.

Goethe also made use of a statue device in his 1809 novel *Die Wahlverwandtschaften*, or *Elective Affinities*, which has been partially credited with generating the popularity of domestic *tableaux vivants*, such as those in which Arthur Hallam participated, in early-nineteenth-century England. In the novel, *tableaux vivants* are used twice, and on each occasion are enrolled as a significant means of designating a female character's moral standing and sensitivity. Luciane, the natural daughter of the central household is spoilt and vain, and uses the tableau for more effective self-advertisement:

Luciane quickly realised that she would be in her element. Her fine build and full figure, her regular yet impressive face, her light-brown braids, her slender neck, all was as if calculated for a portrait; and if she had only known that she looked better when she stood still than when she was in motion (for sometimes she accidentally made an oddly graceless movement), she would have devoted herself with increased zeal to this natural picture-making.[24]

By comparison, Ottilie, the retiring adopted daughter of the novel is called upon at a later date to impersonate the Virgin Mary in a Christmas crèche (the origin, Goethe suggests here, of the practice of *tableaux vivants*): 'And who can describe the expression of the newly created queen of heaven? The purest humility, the most charming air of modesty in the face of a great and undeserved honor, an incredible, unmeasurable bliss was written on her face, expressing both her own inner feelings and her conception of the role she was playing' (*Elective Affinities*, p. 204).

As Goethe most amply suggests here, and as Emma Hamilton had also shown, the invoking of a female sculptural image is a highly potent gesture, capable of challenging morality and actively determining the nature of an audience's ethical and aesthetic response. The invocation of the sculptural thus has to be carefully managed lest its more subversive potential be allowed to overcome its function of displaying appropriately configured feminine desirability. On the English stage, this meant that much critical attention was invested in insisting upon the 'naturalness' of the resort to the sculptural metaphor.

'WHEN IN REPOSE SHE WAS LIKE A MARBLE STATUE'

However, far from being natural, the connotations of the statue-image on the English stage can be shown to have been carefully constructed, rather than given. This is demonstrated in the broader context of the divide between the stages of London and Paris in the second half of the nineteenth century. The English theatre and its performers achieved definition by means of the construction of an opposition to the French theatre, and especially to its actresses: within this struggle for definition and precedence, the theatrical trope of sculpture was frequently enrolled. One of the best-known and most-admired figures of the mid-nineteenth-century stage in Europe was the French tragedienne Rachel Félix, an actress whose work, as Rachel M. Brownstein has noted, was particularly renowned for its sculptural qualities:

everyone compared Rachel to a marble statue – because of her pallor, and the sense perhaps of her bony body's hardness; because she was haloed by the aura of the ancient Greeks, whose statues were their most enduring legacy; because [...] her eloquent rare gestures were restrained [...] By embodying an ideal of classical art, and the hieratic power of a priestess or icon, she increased that trope's currency.[25]

The sculptural impression was peculiarly facilitated in Rachel's case by her status as the leading player, indeed the actress primarily responsible for the revival, of Classical French tragedy at the Théâtre Français from 1838 to 1855. Costumed for the Greek-inspired plays of Racine and Corneille, the actress provoked ready comparisons with classical statues:

Her beauty was not of that plastic order which we naturally associate with the ancient heroines; and yet no one ever more resembled the Panathenaic figures of Phidias [...] Her thinness was proverbial, but on the stage it was not noticed. Whether beneath the peplum or not, the angles of her shoulders and the prominent joints of her arms seemed in perfect harmony with the rest of her figure. When in repose she was like a marble statue; but the marble was full of life, breath, and passion.[26]

In this passage statuary and life are glancingly conjoined, but without in any way reducing Rachel's art, like that of Charlotte Sotheby, to her success in marmoreal imitation. Rather, Rachel's implicit reference to statuary functions as the measure of a condition which her art is bent on overcoming. De Calonne's recollections work to impress the reader with a sense of how far the actress exceeds the visual and still state of the statue, of her skill in imbuing the marble with life.

A similar impression is given in Charlotte Brontë's portrait of 'Vashti' in *Villette* (1853), which was inspired by Rachel, and which suggests that the actress is powerfully effective precisely because of her skilful, and often necessarily violent, fusion of passionate life with marbled restraint and regularity: 'Suffering had struck that stage empress; and she stood before her audience neither yielding to, nor enduring, nor in finite measure resenting it: she stood locked in struggle, rigid in resistance. She stood, not dressed, but draped in pale antique folds, long and regular like sculpture.'[27] Lucy Snowe's response to this spectacle mirrors its internal conflict: 'It was a marvellous sight: a mighty revelation. It was a spectacle low, horrible, immoral' (*Villette*, p. 339). In Rachel, marble and flesh were violently irreconcilable possibilities, elements which fought out their struggle through the vulnerability of her physicality. For G. H. Lewes, the realisation of such a struggle determines Rachel's greatness:

The finest of her performances was of Phèdre. Nothing I have ever seen surpassed this picture of a soul torn by the conflicts of incestuous passion and struggling conscience; the unutterable mournfulness of her look and tone as she recognised the guilt of her desires, yet felt herself so possessed by them that escape was impossible, are things never to be forgotten.[28]

Rachel's knowing assumption of the marble form facilitates a conscious realisation and exploitation of the struggle inherent in the 'living statue' metaphor, and results in some of her greatest and most characteristic performances.

This actress's adoption of the form of a statue on stage is not then an instinctive, 'natural' resource, the apotheosis of her femininity, as Jameson would have us believe, but may be a deliberate artistic and intellectual choice. Matthew Arnold suggests that it is on this quality of intellectualism that Rachel's artistry rests, and in this attribute that her claim to be seen as a 'radiant Greek-souled artist', one who imparts 'life renewed, old classic grace', resides.[29] In constructing a later comparison between Rachel and Sarah Bernhardt, it was the former's 'high intellectual power' which was the distinguishing factor: 'It was here that Rachel was so great; she began, one says to oneself as one recalls her image and dwells upon it – she began almost where Mdlle Sarah Bernhardt ends.'[30] For Arnold, Rachel's sculptural qualities signify her link with the severity of the Muses, her status as a self-conscious artist, and the extent of her self-awareness. A contemporary American drama critic wrote in confirmation of this that the part of Phèdre gave large opportunities for 'the display of the statuesque grace which is one of Rachel's most marvellous attributes [...] Rachel is certainly [...] the first of sculptors.'[31] Rachel is thus not simply an art-object, but is confirmed in her own person as an artist, self-consciously and deliberately fashioning herself, usurping the right of the sculptor, and as such defying the constraints of Galatea's situation, and the terms both of her reification and incarnation.

However, where Arnold celebrated, other English critics were ready to cite with distaste Rachel's artistic self-knowledge, regarding it as unbecoming, calculating, and thus contrary to feminine nature. Sir Theodore Martin was Rachel's most outspoken English critic, and one who crucially came to regard her sculptural poses as 'unnatural', and hence as peculiarly redolent of her shortcomings as a woman:

Attired in classical costume, and restricted to a style of action which masked that natural deportment which is ever eloquent of character, her hard and unsympathetic nature was for the time lost to view; and the eye was riveted by motions, graceful, stately, passionate, or eager, and the ear thrilled by the varied cadences or vehement declamation of her beautiful voice. But when her parts approached nearer to common life – when the emotions became more complex and less dignified – the want was more quickly felt. If, instead of Corneille and Racine, Rachel had been called upon to illustrate Shakespeare, with all the variety of inflection and subtlety of development which his heroines demand in the performer, she must, we believe, have utterly failed.[32]

Here, the deliberate resort to the statuesque becomes an attempt effectively to veil Rachel's inadequacies as a woman, and one which acts for Martin as a distracting, suspiciously captivating carapace which simultaneously signals her limitations as an artist.

Rachel's best-known parts and talents thus become in this interested and partial account, her downfall, both as an artist, and more particularly as a woman. Brontë's John Graham Bretton similarly judges Vashti as a 'woman, not an artist, it was a branding judgment' (*Villette*, p. 342). In Martin's account, typical in this respect of the tenor of much late-nineteenth-century English theatre criticism, these two aspects are similarly indivisible; or more precisely, the talent of the artist is determined by the moral virtue of the woman, the lack of which no amount of artistic intelligence or statuesque elegance can hide. Indeed, in this respect intelligence and statuary rather become measures of inadequacy. To excel on the stage, Martin wrote, 'something more than the accomplishment of art is necessary; and this something is a deep and sincere sensibility, and a moral nature which answers instinctively to the call of the nobler feelings' (p. 295). These qualities, which helped to constitute ideal femininity, were apparently lacking in Rachel, along with 'the finer and more tender graces of her sex' and 'true taste and right womanly feeling' (p. 295).

The actress with whom Martin seems implicitly to be contrasting Rachel is his own wife, Helena Faucit, an English actress who was a contemporary of Rachel's, and who was best known for her early-nineteenth-century appearances in Shakespeare. One of Faucit's most popular parts was Hermione, which she played to William Macready's Leontes at Drury Lane in 1837 and 1843.[33] In 1882, Faucit had long been retired from the stage, but was returning to public prominence with a series of articles on Shakespeare's women in *Blackwood's Magazine* in the 1880s.[34] Faucit began her career as an *ingénue* in the company of Macready, whose 'dominating desire to mould her performances to his own ideas' led to accusations that she had 'caught his manner and expression'.[35] Subsequently, however, Faucit was principally remembered for the womanliness and charm with which she 'opened up a world of poetry undreamed by [her audiences] – filled their eyes with visions of beauty and grace and dignity, living yet ideal'. In so doing, 'she won her way to the hearts of all by a gentleness and sweetness of aspect and demeanour, that spoke of the modesty and absorption of the true artist, who thought only of the work it was given to her to do'.[36] Not for Faucit then that artistic self-consciousness and intelligence that defined Rachel's work, but rather the forgetfulness of self which facilitates her oxymoronic 'living yet ideal' status, the status that was peculiarly the property of Galatea. I will argue below that it was very much in conservative social interests in the 1880s to assert the consanguinity of the actress and the woman. It was her particular interpretation of the symbiosis of these two parts which made Faucit an appropriate icon for the 1880s, for as Martin later recalled, 'she believed that the measure of her success was to make men forget the actress in the woman she represented' (*Helena Faucit*, p. 141).

Accounts of Faucit contrast explicitly, perhaps deliberately, with the egotism, ambition, and self-consciousness ascribed to Rachel.[37] However, in one crucial respect the work of Rachel and Faucit coincide: both draw for inspiration on Classical sculpture, and the work of both clearly demonstrates this source. Theodore Martin is, however, careful in his biography of his wife to assert that 'No attitude was ever studied or consciously assumed by the actress, or was what is understood by the phrase "statuesque"' (*Helena Faucit*, p. 340). In Faucit's case, then, it seems that we are to understand her invocation of images of Classical statuary as a 'natural', instinctive resort, and one which confirmed apprehensions of her 'pure womanly nature and high cultivation' (Stokes and Colmache, 'Helena Faucit', p. 760). In Rachel, however, the likeness to a statue-form could signal egotism and ambition, a suspicion confirmed by her wilful isolation on stage, her carelessness of other performers, and her invitation to the audience to concentrate on her individual spectacle: 'when she acted, the poet was only represented in one character, for she cared more for herself than the drama, and liked to be surrounded by mean performers'.[38] Rachel's physical isolation is thus made to figure the singularity also of her ambitions and of her moral estrangement. An examination of the processes whereby such very different readings of the statue-state may obtain reveals more precisely the weight accorded to the sculptural referent and the significance of its ascription.

GIVING 'CHASTE PERMISSION' TO DESIRE

In late 1844, Helena Faucit was on tour with Macready in Paris, and on Christmas Day of that year she visited the Louvre, where she later recollects that,

They have the glorious Venus of Milo [...] which to my mind far excels in beauty the Venus dei Medici. Never was anything so simply grand, and quietly yet eloquently graceful. The attitude, if so you may call it, is perfection. The figure is much larger than life, and yet loses nothing in delicacy and chasteness [...] If it did not seem presumptuous, I could say that I was conscious of a kindred spirit, which makes me open my heart to all beauty and nobleness. (quoted in Martin, *Helena Faucit*, p. 143)

In keeping with such a reverential response, she later slipped back alone to kiss 'the cold marble foot of the sublime work'. Faucit's act of veneration recalls that of Pygmalion, who similarly worshipped at his statue's feet, but Faucit's devotion prompts rather a desire to emulate than to liberate through animation. Reviews of her subsequent performances speak most highly of her when she most closely approximates to the idealised beauty and virtue embodied in Galatea and in (her version of) the Venus de Milo, as responses to her 1845 Antigone confirm. In this part, her likeness to a statue provokes worship rather than horror, and is allowed to complement rather than to contrast with appropriate dimensions of the part. The artist Sir Frederic Burton noted Faucit's capability of 'throwing herself at once into the spirit of Greek art' and of 'intuitively [divining] the Attic poet's intent' (quoted in Martin, *Helena Faucit*, pp. 150, 151), both activities which belie the actress's active intellectual participation in her art. Her talents were confirmed in Burton's appreciation and minute recollection of Faucit's 'pre-eminent physical advantages' which 'called vividly to mind the Greek ideal known to us in sculpture and in designs on the finer Athenian vases' (p. 151). Burton's conception of Faucit was later to prompt a drawing of her Antigone which he called 'The Greek Muse' (see plate 6), a title which appropriately confirms his act of distancing her from creativity, and making her into an artefact and inspiration, rather than an artist. Theodore Martin himself went further in his account of the extent to which Faucit embodied a sculptural ideal when he wrote that, 'twenty-three centuries after the poet who conceived [Antigone] has gone to his rest, it is presented to us fresh and beautiful, like some magnificent statue dug up from the ruins of Time, perfect as when it left the sculptor's hand' (p. 153). She presents 'the type of those beautiful forms which sculpture has made immortal, in the majestic form, the simple drapery, the serene and noble features of the actress' (p. 153). Faucit is, unlike Rachel, simply sculptural, not a sculptor. It is perhaps worth noting that the monument Martin raised to Faucit after her death in October 1898 bears an inscription from *The Winter's Tale*: 'The sweet'st companion, that e'er man / Bred his hopes out of', thus placing Faucit in death, as in life, as an idealised Muse figure, an inspirational icon.

Plate 6   Sir Frederic Burton, 'The Greek Muse' (Helen Faucit)

In Faucit's case, her likeness to sculpture is a measure of success which confirms rather than jeopardises her femininity, and which goes on to help to perfect her critics' perceptions of femininity. For some reviewers indeed, Faucit seems to epitomise feminine virtue as she becomes 'one of the most sympathetic actresses who ever walked the English stage'; 'She was not an actress, playing a part, so much as a woman, realising in the abstract the joys and sufferings of her sex.'[39] It is further notable that in their responses her critics feel at liberty to re-create Faucit, to mould her anew, into different cultural artefacts. The possibility of her own agency is denied as Faucit becomes the unconscious Galatea to her audience's Pygmalion, dependent on them, and on their desire for her reification. As Galatea lacks a voice, similarly little attention is paid to Faucit's vocal interpretation of her part, all efforts rather being directed at the appropriate inscription of her physical attributes.

De Quincey's appreciation of Faucit's Antigone gives the clearest indication of the extent to which the English actress's statuesque quality, and her likeness to Galatea, facilitate her popular success:

oh heavens! what a revelation of beauty! – forth stepped, walking in brightness, the most faultless of Grecian marbles, Miss Helen Faucit as Antigone. What perfection of Athenian sculpture! the noble figure, the lovely arms, the fluent drapery! What an unveiling of the ideal statuesque! is it Hebe? is it Aurora? is it a goddess that moves before us? Perfect she is in form; perfect in attitude [...]

Here was the redeeming jewel of the performance. It flattered one's patriotic feelings to see this noble young countrywoman realising so exquisitely, and restoring to our imaginations, the noblest of Grecian girls [...] One thing I regretted – viz., that from the indistinctness of my sight for distant faces, I could not accurately discriminate Miss Faucit's features; but I was told by my next neighbour that they were as true to the antique as her figure. (quoted in Martin, *Helena Faucit*, p. 154)

That to be desired is the actress's ultimate function is suggested in de Quincey's subsequent admission (notably omitted in Martin's quotation from him) that 'We critics [...] in the very teeth of duty and conscience all at one moment unanimously fell in love with Miss Faucit.'[40] Faucit's acting skills are not at issue in a review whose approbation is determined by her physical desirability, which is both conveyed and confirmed through its approximation to the statuesque. In this moment the statue-form becomes the ideal of desirability, and implicitly the ideal form of the 'natural' woman.

The principal difference then between Faucit and Rachel is that the former is enabled to convey her theatrical impression, even in some measure her availability to the audience's imagination, and crucially her desirability, apparently without self-consciousness, and with no resignation of her 'high moral qualities [as a] woman' or of 'her purity and honesty of heart'.[41] Rachel's triumphs, however, were held to be the result of calculation and training, of effort motivated by avarice and coloured by questionable morals. Further, whereas her own active sexuality was a prohibitive factor in Rachel's acting, and one which removed her from respectable society, Faucit's passive desirability is allowed to exist hand-in-hand with her modesty and virtue. Questions of sexual as well as creative agency are subsumed in the sculptural reference, and in this particular, Faucit succeeded in emulating the 'Venus de Milo, which to her was [...] the ideal of female beauty at its best' (Martin, *Helena Faucit*, p. 80). She too conveyed Venus' attractions whilst losing 'nothing in delicacy and chasteness'.

ACTING GALATEA: DESIRE AND DECORUM ON THE VICTORIAN STAGE

The allusion to conventions of Classical drapery and statuary was essential to this end. In his *Passages from the French and Italian Notebooks*, Hawthorne suggests precisely how the facilitation of desire might be achieved by Classical statuary. He recalls a conversation with the American sculptor Hiram Powers about Gibson's 'Tinted Venus'. As noted earlier, Gibson both believed that 'the Greek taste was right in colouring their sculpture. The warm glow is agreeable to the eye, and so is the variety obtained by it', and that 'this monotonous cold object' (that is, the conventional white marble statue), 'is out of harmony with everything that surrounds it' (Eastlake, *Life of John Gibson*, p. 212). Not all his contemporaries agreed, however. As Elizabeth Barrett Browning wrote to Mrs Jameson from Rome in December 1853:

We got to Gibson's studio, which is close by, and saw his coloured Venus. I don't like her. She has come out of her cloud of the ideal, and to my eyes is not too decent. Then in the long and slender throat, in the turn of it, and the setting on of the head, you have rather a grisette than a goddess.[42]

Early in the next year, she wrote to Miss Mitford that she had 'seldom, if ever, seen so indecent a statue. The colouring with an approximation to flesh tints produces that effect, to my apprehension' (vol. II, p. 155). In his response to the statue, Hawthorne reveals the way in which the more conventional statue might stimulate a more acceptable form of desire, and thus how the actress, in her approximation to the severity of a marble statue, might similarly excite her audience:

The best thing [Powers] said against the use of colour in marble was to the effect that the whiteness removed the object represented into a sort of spiritual region, and so gave chaste permission to those nudities which would otherwise suggest immodesty. I have myself felt the truth of this in a certain sense of shame as I looked at Gibson's tinted Venus. (*Passages from the Note-books*, vol. I, p. 371)

The adoption of Classical drapery on stage was similarly sexually potent, and seems to have enabled the actress to signal to her audiences a 'chaste permission' to desire. This type of costume was, of course, considerably more revealing of the body underneath than most Victorian couture, and confirmation of the effect of Classical drapery in the theatre is given in a passage ultimately omitted from the last of Ruskin's Oxford lectures on sculpture (the *Aratra Pentelici*), but which is reproduced in *The Works of John Ruskin*:

the subject of Greek art is the body only, and of Gothic art, the body as affected by the mind. Now, therefore, when a Greek sculptor uses drapery, he indeed uses it chiefly as a veil, for the sake of modesty or dignity, but his object in practically dealing with it is nevertheless to show as much of the bodily form as may be naturally (or even sometimes by violent artifice expressed beneath) [...] The folds of Greek drapery therefore, are, for the most part, used to express bodily form and motion. (vol. xx, p. 274)

The actress's body may thus be effectively cloaked and simultaneously revealed in classically derived implications of the ideal. Thus also might commercially necessary desire be invoked without compromising the equally necessary unselfconsciousness of the actress. This was the effect at which the theatre more generally aimed, an effect within which the body of the actress is rather at the behest of her spectators, and those who model her, her manager, playwright, costumier, than under her own control. Women's theatrical success, in England at least, depended upon the actress's ideally unconscious adoption of the sculptural mode which enabled their delicate negotiation of desire and decorum.

It was upon precisely such a negotiation that the success of W. S. Gilbert's blank-verse comedy *Pygmalion and Galatea* rested. Gilbert's play was highly popular with later-nineteenth-century audiences. Originally performed by Miss Robertson and Mr Kendal at the Haymarket in December 1871, the play had four major revivals, in 1877 (with Marion

Terry), and in 1883, 1884, and 1888 (all productions starring the American actress, Mary Anderson), and at least three other professional
performances by Julia Neilson, Lillie Langtry, and Janette Steer. Appropriately enough, Gilbert was a highly involved author in productions of
this play, and his patience was tried most strongly by his leading ladies'
own conceptions of Galatea. He even resorted at one point to threatening legal action against Janette Steer if she did not prove herself sufficiently malleable to his designs.[43]

Gilbert's play was probably inspired in part by the enforced visit of
the Théâtre Français to London in 1871, during the Prussian invasion of
Paris. In importing Classical French tragedies, they were seen to be
bringing a rigour and an independent artistry to the theatre which were
not possible on England's entirely commercial stages.[44] The English
theatre's invocation of Classical references at this time was rather
typified by Gilbert's profitable and popular pastiche. This play may be
further defined in comparison with a slightly earlier version of the
Pygmalion and Galatea story which was first performed at the Royal
Strand Theatre, under the management of Mrs Swanborough, in April
1867. William Brough's *Pygmalion; or, The Statue Fair* was advertised as
'An Original burlesque', and around the Pygmalion-plot, which is one
of several complicated love-stories in the play, are woven songs, dances,
and original music. Pygmalion and his statue's fortunes compete for the
audience's attention with the love-lorn Cupid and Psyche (who are
hounded by Venus); and with a complicated plot concerning social
climbing and marriage between Pygmalion's apprentice and the Princess Mandane, described in the dramatis personae as 'an Old Maid,
whose *pater* is anxious to *mate* her'.[45]

The comedy of the play derives from excruciating puns, from misunderstandings, the farce of social ambition, a ferocious representative of
mothers-in-law (here represented by a nagging Venus), and from the
way in which Pygmalion's relationship to his statue resembles that
between any love-lorn young man and an impervious woman:

VENUS: Of course – in vain you plead;
               She's *stone* deaf to your suit.
PYGMALION: Stone deaf, indeed.
VENUS: Her heart is hard as *marble*, and as cold.
PYGMALION: Marble!
VENUS: Her finely *chiselled* features—
PYGMALION: Hold!
               My fatal secret how could you discover?

VENUS: Secret! I but describe a hapless lover –
                They're all alike.   (p. 20)[46]

Later, when the statue has been animated, the parallels of language describing the rights of the sculptor and the expectations of the lover are again apparent:

PYGMALION: At least, say you're mine, and mine alone.
STATUE: Of course I'm yours, you carved me from the stone.

And later:

STATUE: Don't blame me Sir – you must see, sir,
                If aught's wrong with me, the fault's your own!   (p. 22)

The statue's coming to life is not unproblematic for, though Pygmalion has control over her, the statue cannot return his love as she does not have a soul. There is an interesting gap here between the implications of a purely physical incarnation and the birth into emotion, which is not acknowledged in other Victorian adaptations. Pygmalion's ardour is only reciprocated after Psyche breathes a soul into the statue. The latter is described in the dramatis personae as 'Pygmalion's most successful work, an unmistakable "hit", which afterwards becomes an equally unmistakable "miss", made for sale by the sculptor, but really *soul'd* by Psyche'.

The play ends with what its playbill describes as a 'Grand Allegorical Tableau, illustrating "Love's Triumph!" AND APOTHEOSIS OF THE STATUE'. But rather than focusing on the two figures of Pygmalion and Galatea who are at the centre of both the spectacular and the psychological attention in Gilbert's adaptation, the scene is a busy musical celebration of all the unions that have come about during the play. Both visual and textual emphases fall on the celebration of community rather than on the uniqueness and isolation of the statue. In this play, there is no return to stone, and the Pygmalion story simply becomes one among a number of comic vehicles for exhibiting the timeless vagaries of romance and its attendant complications. Links between Classical and Victorian Pygmalions are established, and the statue-device does, albeit very briefly, act as a means of displaying Miss A. Harland, who played the statue, in her first professional appearance. However, suggestions of stasis and the implications of an extended parallel between Classical and contemporary times are dispersed in this burlesque which, despite its title, moves far beyond the statue in its desire for humour, romance, and spectacle. Even the puns, which are the play's primary comic vehicle, extend beyond the mildly salacious connotations (on which W. S. Gilbert concentrates) and the remit of the Pygmalion story to draw on contemporary events: Brough makes the perhaps inevitable reference to the then leader of the Liberal party when the statue declares that 'I, a wretched sad stone; / Know nought of figures – I'm far from a Glad-stone' (p. 22).

Gilbert's play, by contrast, is aimed at a different, more ambitious kind of theatre and is much more single-minded in its pursuit of the Pygmalion and Galatea story, and in its focusing on the attractions of the statue. In Gilbert's version of the myth, Pygmalion is a professional Athenian sculptor, happily married to Cynisca, who also acts as his model, and who thus, the play goes on to imply, fulfils woman's most appropriate relation to artistry. 'Galatea' is Pygmalion's most recent work, and is an idealised version of his wife. Initially veiled behind a curtain at the rear of the stage, the statue is soon revealed, to the accompaniment of Cynisca's wistful account of the statue's loveliness, and of her own relative decline:

> Those outlines softened, angles smoothed away,
> The eyebrows arched, the head more truly poised,
> The forehead ten years smoother than mine own,
> Tell rather of Cynisca as she was.[47]

The play's comic business begins when Cynisca, who is leaving on a journey, bids her husband regard Galatea as her proxy:

> Be faithful unto her as unto me;
> Into her quietly attentive ear
> Pour all thy treasures of hyperbole,
> And give thy tongue full license, lest
> Disuse should rust its glib machinery.   (pp. 77–8)

Chaos reigns however, when, prompted by Pygmalion's naming her Galatea, the statue comes to life.

What ensues is a comedy of misunderstandings based largely on the incongruity of Galatea's existing as a fully formed adult whilst lacking adult knowledge of language and male–female relations, as was the case with Ovid's Galatea. Underlying this nineteenth-century situation, however, is the audience's knowledge of the potentially salacious situation in which Pygmalion and Galatea find themselves. Typical of the play's humour are the following two moments, in the first of which, Pygmalion explains what a man is to Galatea:

PYGMALION: A being strongly framed,
        To wait on woman, and protect her from
        All ills that strength and courage can avert;
        To work and toil for her, that she may rest;
        To weep and mourn for her, that she may laugh;
        To fight and die for her, that she may live!
GALATEA (after a pause):
        I'm glad I am a woman.
PYGMALION: So am I.   (pp. 81–2)

Similar bathos greets Galatea's wondering explanation of the symptoms of her love for Pygmalion, which are of course exactly synonymous with the conditions of the statue's relations to its sculptor:

GALATEA: A sense that I am made by thee for thee;
        That I've no will that is not wholly thine;
        That I've no thought, no hope, no enterprise
        That does not own thee as its sovereign;
        That I have life, that I may live for thee,
        That I am thine – that thou and I are one!
        What kind of love is that?
PYGMALION: A kind of love
        That I shall run some risk in dealing with!   (pp. 82–3)

The play proceeds through Galatea's chaotic encounters with other characters, until Cynisca returns to find Pygmalion in love with his statue. Enraged at his unfaithfulness, Cynisca invokes the power of a curse invested in her by Artemis to blind her erring husband. Once this has happened, Galatea is left bereft of the desiring gaze which was the motive for, and energy behind, her life. She begins to perceive the distress she has caused and seeks to right it by sacrificing herself. She pretends to be Cynisca before the blind Pygmalion, and manages to bring down her creator's curses upon her. Bereft of his desire to see her live, she thus has to return to her pedestal, and her marble state. Humbled by Galatea's selflessness, Cynisca lifts the curse on Pygmalion, whose final act in the play is to rush to the back of the stage and reveal once again the stony loveliness of Galatea, now known not only to be supremely beautiful, but also to be supremely good in her self-forgetfulness. In the final tableau, Galatea is both ethically as well as physically elevated, dominating the moral as well as the visual attention of her onlookers.

The crudity of the play's humour may seem, to modern readers, to sit uneasily with the sentimentality of its ending, but the whole was clearly successfully unified for its original audience through the desirability of the central spectacle of Galatea. The part, and indeed the whole play, rest heavily on an assumption of Galatea's beauty, and upon an ingenuousness which enabled a highly palatable display of modesty and sexuality conjoined. It was for these reasons, perhaps, that the part is remembered as being particularly attractive for beautiful actresses, and that the play made the considerable sum of £40,000 in fees for its author.[48] Published responses to Madge Robertson's original Galatea are scarce, but the *Athenaeum* reviewer judged that the play was received with 'signal favour, and seems likely to obtain a lasting popularity'.[49] The grounds of that popularity he cited as Galatea's beauty, the warmth of 'her frank and spontaneous avowal of her love for Pygmalion', and the naive 'confessions and inquiries of Galatea [...which] have so much of surprise in them that the audience is kept in continuous and uproarious laughter' (p. 803).

Miss Robertson's, later Dame Madge Kendal's, own rather indirect account of her performance is in keeping with the unselfconscious qualities of the character which are emphasised by the *Athenaeum*. In her memoirs, she makes most of Mary Anderson's 1880s success as Galatea, adding only later that she herself received the greatest ovation of her life in the part.[50] Kendal's conception of the part is, however, implicitly conveyed in an anecdote about the playwright Sydney Grundy's wedding-day. The actress was introduced to the new and very young Mrs Grundy on the afternoon of her wedding, and records that the couple spent part of their wedding-night watching *Pygmalion and Galatea*. Kendal recalls of the young bride, 'I doubt whether today such a creature could be met with. She was a moving, walking gallery of innocence, – a living Galatea' (p. 158). This recollection of a young, pure woman on the brink of sexual knowledge conjoins two possibilities similarly finely balanced in Galatea, a character replete with innocence, but whose position is defined by her unconscious embodiment of desire. As a later *Athenaeum* reviewer wrote of Marion Terry's Galatea, she was young, ingenuous, pure and earnest, her 'virginal charm [...] her distinguishing attribute', and though capable of arousing strong jealousy in Cynisca, 'It is a mistake to regard Galatea as endowed with passion' herself.[51] The conjunction of Galatea and Mrs Grundy, and the efforts of Mrs Kendal and Mr Grundy in effecting that conjunction suggest that much of the play's success may have been generated by the fact that, through what may be described as the 'Galatea-aesthetic', the difficulty of realising self-conscious female sexuality on stage may be overcome.

It was not, however, until the 1880s that the play, and the part of Galatea, upon whom rested 'the whole burden of interest' ('The Week', p. 127), achieved the zenith of their popularity. This was facilitated by a number of interdependent factors which include the peculiar constitution of gender-relations in England in the early 1880s, and the way in which the theatre responded to its social context. But it was also at this time that the part of Galatea was taken by its most fitting actress, the beautiful young American, Mary Anderson. Mrs Kendal wrote of Anderson that 'She was among the few, the very few, actresses I have known who have taken London by storm [...She] was an instant success and, for a time, threw into the background everybody else, no matter how great was their possession of beauty or talent' (*Dame Madge Kendal*, pp. 153, 154). Anderson's theatrical career was short but spectacular, her greatest strength proving to lie in playing statues. However, Anderson, like Galatea, may actually be simultaneously least powerful when she appears most desirable and influential, as the terms of Gilbert's play confirm. Galatea's pedestal (whether literal or figurative) is a peculiarly vulnerable and isolated place. No sooner does Galatea lose Pygmalion's love, and the animating power of his gaze, than she is reduced back to a marble form. In this respect, the situation of Galatea substantially resembles that of the nineteenth-century actress on the commercial English stage, one who depended on another's desire to see her in order to appear.

Other similarities between the actress and the figure of Galatea serve to heighten this sense of the former's actual vulnerability and lack of context when seeming most prominent on stage. Both actress and statue may, for instance, be said to exist outside historical time. Pygmalion's bringing a fully grown woman to life defies time's control, as does the moment of theatrical spectacle which occurs outside social time and is, for the audience, achieved equally spontaneously. Similarly, just as Pygmalion and Galatea's union comes about independently of the usual moral and socio-economic context surrounding a marriage, so part of the attraction of the theatrical spectacle is that it exists independently of the mundane and contingent world outside the theatre. Like Galatea, actresses' metamorphoses depended on a simultaneous metamorphosis not only of time, but also of space. The spatial isolation of the gazed-upon and desired female figures which literally occupy 'centre-stage' in Pygmalion's legend and the late-nineteenth-century theatre was the counterpart of their temporal isolation.

The conjunction of these two forms of isolation, when located within the gaze of the theatrical spectator, and particularly when nominally garbed in the remoteness of Classical antiquity, facilitates the realisation on stage of an idealised form of femininity. Combining both the timeless and the antique, the resulting figure naturalises the particular form of femininity it embodies, endowing it with a 'given-ness' which disarms criticism and enables belief. Two of the primary effects of this process were to deny the possibilities of agency, and of a self-conscious, transformative, creative capacity, on the part of the actress (as happened in responses to Emma Hamilton); and concomitantly to elide the distinction between the actress and her part, to heighten the sense of something naturally occurring on stage.

The Galatea-aesthetic places the actress at the heart of the cult of the 'natural' in the legitimate English theatre, a trend which flowered in the 1870s and particularly in the 1880s as part of the movement to encourage the middle classes to return to the theatre, and which coincided with the emergence of a neo-Classical visual rhetoric in the theatre. References to the 'natural' in the late-Victorian theatre perhaps more usually conjure up notions of the work of the Bancrofts, who sought to encourage the middle classes into the Prince of Wales theatre by bringing some of the trappings of the Victorian drawing-room into their auditorium, and thus diminishing the gap between the domestic and the theatrical experience.[52] However, so fundamental a part of the rhetoric of describing and embodying women was the recourse to the Classical and statuesque, and so profoundly concerned was this recourse with insisting upon the 'naturalness' of the woman thus described, that the Classical register became crucial to the conservative theatrical aesthetic of this period, one concerned with reflection rather than transformation. Thus in the later-nineteenth century, the actress might be perceived as being most contemporary when appearing most Classical.

CHAPTER 3

George Eliot, Daniel Deronda, *and the sculptural aesthetic*

On Victorian England's commercial stages, where audiences determined the theatrical spectacle as much as did actors and managers, the application of a statue-image to actresses implicitly recognised their role within a particularly female theatrical aesthetic, a Galatea-aesthetic, the terms of which have begun to emerge throughout the previous chapter. I coin this term not simply because of the popularity of dramatic versions of Pygmalion and Galatea's story in the theatre, nor because of the surprising number of productions where actresses play statues, or are reduced to sculptural forms, but rather because this term, and its specific connotations for the desirable actress performing before a commercial audience, is peculiarly appropriate as a descriptor for the female performer within the performance-context of late-Victorian theatre.

Matthew Arnold wrote in 'Bacchanalia; or, The New Age' (1864–7),

> The epoch ends, the world is still,
> The age has talked and worked its fill –
> The famous orators have shone,
> The famous poets have sung and gone,
> The famous men of war have fought,
> The famous speculators thought,
> The famous players, sculptors wrought,
> The famous painters filled their wall,
> The famous critics judged it all.   (*Poems,* p. 581)

In 'The famous players, sculptors wrought', Arnold links the skills of actors and sculptors as those artists most profoundly concerned to give material, plastic form to their conceptions. The medium shared by these artists was that of the human body. However, Arnold's line glances over the crucial difference between the two artists: the question of agency, and its implications for the relationship between artist and art-object. Arnold's account seems to imply that the two artists share equal status as originators of art, as moulders of their medium, and as active agents of creativity. However, the equivalence of actor and sculptor is complicated by the fact that the actor's medium is his or her own person, and by the oft-resorted-to metaphor of statuary to describe the actor's, or, more usually the actress's, stage-presence. Could the actress be both sculptor and sculpture?

The question of agency, of creative self-determination and autonomy, is precisely what is at stake within, and what is often concealed by, the ascription of the statue-image to actresses, and in this chapter I shall consider George Eliot's treatment of theatre and the sculptural aesthetic associated with it in *Daniel Deronda*. This novel is the century's most sustained fictional exploration of the figure of the statuesque actress, and it is worth considering at length not only because it raises crucial questions about the state of the English theatre in the early 1870s, the theatre that produced and fostered Gilbert's *Pygmalion and Galatea*, but more especially because in this text Eliot seems to envisage a way of negotiating the Galatea-aesthetic's restrictive implications.

In George Eliot's work we see an ever more engaged and sophisticated interrogation of the idealisation of social Galateas, of the assumptions of their Pygmalions, and of the ways in which this trope delimited the possibilities for creative women. The sculptural metaphor and its attendant dangers are most fully explored by Eliot in her dramatic poem 'Armgart' (1871) and in *Daniel Deronda*. These two works present Eliot's most considered portraits of the figure of the female performer, portraits which give profound insights into Eliot's sense of her own artistry, and the extent to which she, as a creative woman, had necessarily to encounter the prevalent descriptive potential inherent in the Pygmalion-metaphor. As we will see, it seems to be through her conception of the art of writing that Eliot, as a creative woman herself, is enabled to evade Galatea's fate, and through that art too that she envisages that actresses may also evade entrapment within the body.

'SUDDENLY ARRESTED LIFE'

The vulnerability of the body, and especially its susceptibility to ill-health, was never far from Eliot's own experience. 'Armgart' was begun in August 1870, when the Leweses had returned home briefly after two months of wandering from Cromer, to Harrogate, to Whitby, in an

attempt to improve G. H. Lewes's health.[1] Armgart's story, like that of
Daniel Deronda's Gwendolen Harleth, is largely told through encounters
with the sculptural metaphor, which here signal the extent and dangers
of her reliance upon the signifying capacity and public potential of her
body. She is an opera-singer, whom the reader meets on the first
evening of what promises to be a great career. But singing is more than
just a career, rather it is Armgart's life-force. She represents a life
without song, 'Without that voice for channel to her soul', as her maid
and cousin puts it, as a life crushed 'within a mould / Of theory called
Nature'.[2] Only in singing, does she have 'room / To breathe and grow
unstunted' (p. 98). This capacity would be denied were she to accept the
suit of her aristocratic lover Graf Dornberg. When she rejects him, she
also implicitly rejects the narcissistic, reflexive function she fears he
would exact. As she says, she will not be a woman,

> All grace, all goodness, who has not yet found
> A meaning in her life, nor any end
> Beyond fulfilling yours. The type abounds.   (p. 105)[3]

Singing enables her to evade such a fate. However, Armgart's fears of
a life without song seem to be fulfilled when, after an illness whose cure
has ruined her throat, she describes herself graphically as merely 'the
torso of a soul', and goes on:

> my song
> Was consecration, lifted me apart
> From the crowd chiselled like me, sister forms,
> But empty of divineness.   (p. 119)

Eliot thus suggests that part of Armgart's desire in singing has been to
achieve a distinction from other women, and from the sculptural metaphor which shows its dangerous side here in threatening so readily to
collapse their diversity into physiological synonymity.

In her early triumph, Armgart speaks of attaining a 'glory wide-
diffused', and of singing,

> for love of song and that renown
> Which is the spreading act, the world-wide share,
> Of good that I was born with.   (p. 92)

Her vision of a widely diffused good is reminiscent in its spatial dimensions of Dorothea's impact in *Middlemarch*, which Eliot memorably
describes as 'incalculably diffusive'[4] but unlike the latter Armgart does
not promise to be temporally diffusive, to exceed the moment of the

influence of the body upon which she relies. Eliot suggests elsewhere that such an event would be an impossibility:

the great poet or the great composer is sure that that sympathy will be given some day [...] so he can transport himself from the present and live by anticipation in that future time when he will be thrilling men's minds and ravishing their ears. But the artist whose genius can openly act through his physical presence has not this reversionary life; the memory of the prima donna scarcely outlives the flowers that are flung at her feet on her farewell night, and even the fame of a Garrick or a Siddons is simply a cold acquiescence in the verdict of the past.[5]

Armgart's sense of her effectiveness is defined by her awareness of her body's conditions, and she revels in its implications:

> Am I a sage whose words must fall like seed
> Silently buried towards a far-off spring?
> I sing to living men and my effect
> Is like the summer's sun, that ripens corn
> Or now or never. If the world brings me gifts,
> Gold, incense, myrrh – 'twill be the needful sign
> That I have stirred it as the high year stirs
> Before I sink to winter.   (pp. 86–7)

Thus, her reliance, as a performer, upon the vehicle of her body restricts Armgart's influence to her present.

However, alternative models of influence are offered in Leo and Walpurga, Armgart's teacher and her cousin. Walpurga contrasts the lofty and isolated lot of the singer with that of the woman standing amidst, and ready to help, the 'needy myriads' whom Armgart would brand as abject. These myriads throng, and as Walpurga goes on in words which would seem to answer Armgart's earlier question:

> you hardly stir
> But your act touches them. We touch afar.
> For did not swarthy slaves of yesterday
> Leap in their bondage at the Hebrews' flight,
> Which touched them through the thrice millennial dark? (p. 131)

Walpurga's topical reference to the abolition of slavery in America, and its link with the flight of the Hebrews, substitutes for Armgart's lofty ambitions an experience of temporal transcendence through service. Similarly Leo, in his old age, concerns himself with passing on his gifts to the young, scorning immediate impact for a temporally diffused form of serving others which Armgart too eventually takes up, as she comes to envisage a future passed,

> in some smaller town where I may bring
> The method you have taught me, pass your gift
> To others who can use it for delight.   (p. 138)

Eliot thus presents the reader with two radically different versions of vocation and artistry which are grounded in mutually exclusive experiences of historical time, one of which is concerned with the immediate gratification that attends performance, and is bound in and by the restrictions of the historical moment; while the other, being concerned with an impersonal service, can ultimately surpass that moment. The connotations for the female artist of this temporal distinction are informed by Eliot's use of the sculptural metaphor, and her own practice as a novelist. They may best be elucidated if we consider the interpretative potential the distinction connotes for works of sculpture, for, in its material aspect, sculpture is itself both a time-defying and time-bound art. It presents an image which can persist, in defiance of the transience of sculptor and model, as long as its concrete form endures; but it may also be bound always by the dimensions of the moment of creation, and condemned perpetually to repeat that same moment. Sculptures may likewise be commemorative by reinvesting a new era with its sense of relationship to particularities of the past; or by simply marking the past-ness, the temporal limitation and antiquity of the past event. The sculpture may thus be either perpetually inspiring, linking and focusing sympathetic moments across the centuries, or it may be bound in temporal sterility, captured and closed, a fate which Armgart risked.

This tension of temporal possibilities forcibly struck George Eliot on her first visit to the Vatican in April 1860. Recalling her stay in Rome, Eliot meticulously recorded her appreciation of the sculptures she and G. H. Lewes saw. Though unimpressed by her visit to John Gibson's studio, where with one exception she saw 'nothing but feeble imitations of the antique – no spontaneity and no vigour' (Cross, *George Eliot's Life*, vol. II, p. 158),[6] Eliot responded warmly to those examples of Classical sculpture which she saw elsewhere, appreciating in particular the Belvedere Apollo, the Dying Gladiator and the Lateran Antinous. She goes on, 'After these I delighted in the Venus of the Capitol, and the Kissing Children in the same room; the Sophocles at the Lateran museum; the Nile; the black laughing Centaur at the Capitol; the Laughing Faun in the Vatican; and the Sauroktonos, or Boy with the

Lizard, and the sitting statue called Menander' (vol. II, p. 152). Eliot's diligent enumeration (to borrow Henry James's term[7]) of her perceptions breaks down, however, in her vital and excited recollection of her 'greatest treat':

Perhaps the greatest treat we had at the Vatican was the sight of a few statues, including the Apollo, by torchlight – all the more impressive because it was our first sight of the Vatican. Even the mere hurrying along the vast halls, with the fitful torchlight falling on the innumerable statues, and busts, and bas-reliefs, and sarcophagi, would have left a sense of awe at these crowded silent forms which have the solemnity of suddenly arrested life. (vol. II, p. 153)

The passage progresses from a sense of the lambency with which the torchlight played in reinvigorating the Apollo, to an awareness of the stark contrast with which Eliot is struck between her own swift progress and rapid assimilation of perceptions, and the 'suddenly arrested life' of the statues. There is in this final perception no sense of Keats's apprehension of the figures on a Grecian Urn as 'For ever warm and still to be enjoy'd, / For ever panting, and for ever young', rather an absolute time-bound, rather than time-conquering, stillness. In this visit to the Vatican I would suggest that Eliot experienced the distinction between the temporal and representational possibilities which arguably form the generative and sustaining 'systole and diastole'[8] of some of her later work, and which offer her the chance to recuperate both the sculptural metaphor, and the representations of women's artistry which had been grounded in, and restricted by the recourse to that descriptive device.

In *Daniel Deronda*, Eliot gives her fullest exploration of the statue metaphor and of the temporal distinction I have outlined, and applies both to a consideration of the contemporary theatre and the place of women within it. The conjunction of the three elements of statuary, time, and the theatre offers insights into Eliot's aesthetic practice as a woman writer, and ultimately into the way in which women's use of language interferes with the imposition of the Galatea-model. The opposing groups into which the characters of *Daniel Deronda* fall are most accurately defined by their differing experiences of, and existence in, their own historical time.[9] This distinction cuts across the more readily available, but ultimately inadequate, lines of racial and national identity, and thus provides the means, for instance, of recuperating the English but enlightened Meyricks, and of correctly placing the Jewish but transgressive Lapidoth and Alcharisi. The 'good' and 'bad' characters in the novel, to borrow Leavis's terminology, are divided according to whether they see their existence as qualified and determined by their racial and cultural heritage and future, as well as their own personal present; or whether they literally gamble all on the importance of the present moment, living only in that, and trusting to its transient resources, in particular to the physical body, for their personal fulfilment through isolated and short-lived gain. As we will see, the novel goes on to associate the latter tendency most readily with the work of the actress.

Gwendolen Harleth's living through and making herself known by her physical body epitomises the tendency to live solely in and for one's own historical moment. This proclivity is most fully demonstrated in the novel's charade scene, when Gwendolen chooses to impersonate a statue, and is tempted to use the power wielded by the spectacle of her body to elicit her audience's admiration, and their acquiescence in a system of values grounded in her physicality. As we will see, Gwendolen is further likened to a statue at several moments throughout the novel which chart her diminishing belief in the capacity of her way of life fully to encompass and still her 'fits of spiritual dread' (vol. 1, p. 90). But the statue-image is also used in Eliot's first description of the Jewish singer Mirah Cohen, where its use has different temporal connotations:

a girl hardly more than eighteen, of low slim figure, with most delicate little face, her dark curls pushed behind her ears under a large black hat, a long woollen cloak over her shoulders. Her hands were hanging down clasped before her, and her eyes were fixed on the river with a look of immovable, statue-like despair. (vol. 1, pp. 279–80)

The moment is not deliberately contrived by Mirah, as Gwendolen's is, nor is she at all enamoured by, or even aware of, her position before an audience. She is neither enclosed by, nor does she seek to close, her moment of 'statue-like despair', with the result that the image of the spiritually and racially estranged woman resonates from this moment through the rest of the text, linking Mirah's mother, Mrs Glasher, Alcharisi, and Gwendolen, and the legendary figures of Berenice, Hermione, and Medea. This unselfconscious moment links Mirah to, and embeds her within, a tradition of despairing, abandoned women, spanning centuries and cultures in going beyond the dimensions of her own grief to evoke theirs. Even within the contemporary moment of her experience, unbeknown to her, Mirah's image is connecting with a sympathetic capacity in Daniel Deronda, through whose eyes she is presented to the reader. Mirah unconsciously surpasses and exceeds her temporal and physical limits, while these bounds are precisely what Gwendolen seeks to reinforce.

In their experiences of performance, and their concomitant realisation of the vulnerability of the public female body, Mirah and Gwendolen are both linked to the novel's professional female performer, the
Jewish opera-singer and actress, Alcharisi. Eliot uses the figure of Alcharisi to dispute the legacy of female performance, displaying in her a
flame burnt out by its energies and delusive desires. Further, through
this actress and the novel's series of fractured families, Eliot also resists
the recourse to pregnancy as a woman's means of effecting a link with
future generations, and of thus surpassing the time-bound body.
Pygmalion's statue is of course initially confined to its material conditions, but in coming to life it is transformed from something still and
lifeless into a female being, within the straitened circumstances of whose
mute subjection, pregnancy becomes the means whereby the 'statue'
may exceed the limits set on her existence by her creator and her own
body. Her achievement is, however, ambiguous, for while she has
literally created something beyond herself, in so doing she paradoxically
acknowledges that the means by which she is enabled to do so is also that
which constitutes the bounds of her existence. Pregnancy thus becomes
a compromising, rather than a personally aggrandising state.

In *Daniel Deronda*, Eliot responds to this dilemma of female figuration,
and the restriction to the body's resources by questioning the desirability
of playing Galatea and by interrogating the oxymoronic implications of
the 'living marble' image. In these processes, she effectively challenges
the biological aesthetic which would see women's opportunities for
creativity determined and delimited by their bodies. In both the texture
and narrative of her novel, Eliot counters such restrictions with a form of
creativity which can be described as 'bodyless' (although firmly gendered) and which, as we will see, can refute the implications of
Pygmalion's gaze.

SPECTACLES AND SPECULATIONS

Eliot's examination of theatre, and her novel's exploitation of the
theatrical metaphor are central to her achieving this end, for, as we have
seen, it was in this arena that women were both most vulnerable to the
restraints of sculpture, and were most readily accepted as artistic figures.
Daniel Deronda was written shortly before the later-Victorian theatre's
regenerative efforts came to be widely acknowledged, and before Henry
Irving's success at the Lyceum (which he took over in 1878) had confirmed the middle classes' return to the theatre. The newly inaugurated

Nineteenth Century, which first appeared in 1877, contained articles by Irving himself on textual questions in Shakespeare,[10] and *Macmillan's* first theatre review was Juliet Pollock's 1881 article on Irving's Lyceum production of Tennyson's *The Cup.*[11] At the beginning of the decade, however, when Gilbert wrote *Pygmalion and Galatea,* the few theatrical articles which appeared in mainstream periodicals had all railed against the prevailing condition of the English theatre.

They were largely prompted by the Théâtre Français's 1871 visit to London. The appearance of this subsidised company focused critics' minds on two principal blights of the commercial English stage: the star-system, whereby one principal actor or actress carried the production regardless of the play or other players; and the long runs which were necessary to recoup high production costs. As a commercial business, the English theatre had necessarily to put financial before artistic interests, even to the extent that plays might be re-written to fit the dimensions of the leading player's capacities. Thus artistic timidity was encouraged, as was a reliance upon proven formulae which would ensure long runs. Hamilton Fyfe summed up the long-term effects of the commercial theatre thus:

It has deprived playgoers of the opportunity of seeing constantly acted the finest plays of the past along with the most interesting of the works of modern authors. It has made the dramatic author merely a component part in a complicated piece of money-getting machinery. It has placed the greatest obstacles in the way of the actor and actress who want to become efficient in their art by means of constant practice in fresh parts.[12]

By contrast, the French company's artistic success was credited almost entirely to its being a state-subsidised body, which had a wealth of fully trained talent to draw on in its own *conservatoire.*[13] Writing in 1875 of the then-postponed threat that the post-war French government might have had to arrest funding of the company, Juliet Pollock suggests that, 'Had such a measure been adopted the *Théâtre Français* [...] must have gradually assumed the conditions which attach to a playhouse existing as a mere money speculation' ('The *"Théâtre Français"'*, p. 139), having earlier written elsewhere that, 'no theatre which is a mere money speculation, will ever become a great school of art'.[14] This was, however, precisely the state of the English theatre of the time, 'a mere speculation [...wherein] the best ambition of the player is at an end, and is replaced by a restless vanity or a greed for gain'.[15] Alfred Austin similarly concludes that 'speculation has invaded the green-room' and, likening theatre-lessees to members of the Stock Exchange, concludes that 'it seems to have come to be pretty generally acknowledged that the best artist [...] is he who, like the best grocer, can make the largest amount of money'.[16] In such a context, a well-acted drama becomes simply a speculation sufficiently dangerous for none to be able to afford.[17]

English theatres did not share the status of those of Paris which Pollock believed constituted part of the 'national pride of the people' ('The French Stage', p. 402), and whose Academicians were often highly respected national personalities. Bernard Shaw spelt out the thrall of the commercial theatre at the end of the nineteenth century bluntly:

all but the merest fraction [of theatrical costs] may be, and very frequently is, entirely lost. On the other hand, success may mean a fortune of fifty thousand pounds accumulated within a single year. Very few forms of gambling are as hazardous as this [...] in the theatre you must play a desperate game for high stakes, or not play at all.[18]

This venturesome aspect of the contemporary theatre lies behind Eliot's employment of theatre and the theatrical metaphor in *Daniel Deronda*, partly because in this aspect the English theatre was an appropriate compendium of the prevailing scourges of its parent society. *The Game of Speculation*, a highly popular comedy loosely based on the French play *Mercadet*, opened in London in 1851 and satirised 'the trading, speculative spirit of England'.[19] Dickens had written in *Bleak House* (1853) of the 'many handsome English ladies in India who went out on speculation', looking for husbands;[20] and had scattered *Nicholas Nickleby* (1839), his novel most concerned with the theatre, with references to speculation. In *The Way We Live Now* (1875), Trollope describes a society diseased throughout by the urge to accumulate vast, easily won sums of money, and which is consequently rotting away at its very core. Eliot's adoption of the motif of 'speculation' is, however, much more elaborate than these earlier uses, and embraced not only the term's contemporary and degraded aspects, but also its archaic and more sublime forms. Speculation, in its various forms, is adopted as the central vehicle of the novel's emotional as well as financial transactions, and the figure of the statuesque actress is implicated in both.

The *OED* offers ten definitions for 'speculation', many archaic or obsolete, which taken together effect an appropriate frame of reference within which to plot the mobility of Eliot's characters. This framework implies the hierarchies of a conventional morality, but it is also responsive to the dimensions of activity and interaction peculiar to this novel. Mordecai Cohen's and Daniel's intellectual pursuits and visionary endeavours are encompassed by some of the rarer definitions of speculation as the faculty of seeing, especially a comprehending or intelligent vision; as contemplation or profound study of a far-reaching, or subtle character; and abstract or hypothetical reasoning on subjects of an abstruse or conjectural nature. These characters are untainted by the financial implications of the word which first emerged with Adam Smith's *An Inquiry into the Nature and Causes of the Wealth of Nations* (1776): Mordecai is content to rely on charity, and Daniel is rich enough to be cushioned from financial cares in their efforts to transmit the lessons of Judaism's past. Not for Gwendolen such cogitative, intellectual 'speculations': '[she] was as inwardly rebellious against the restraints of family conditions, and as ready to look through obligations into her own fundamental want of feeling for them, as if she had been sustained by the boldest speculations; but she really had no such speculations' (vol. 1, p. 74). Financial speculations are ironically implied here too, of course, for Gwendolen's activities are encompassed by the financially opportunistic implications of 'speculation' which apply also to the theatres of the 1870s. The range of such activities in the novel embraces each tier of society, and varying levels of legitimacy, including the figures of the Jewish pawn-brokers and of the consummate gambler, Lapidoth, who is also of course an actor. Given the state of the English theatre of the 1870s, we may now see his compulsive gambling as actually intrinsic to, and a habitual activity of, one engaged in that theatre, rather than as an aberration in the artist.

The activities of gambling and theatricality mingle repeatedly throughout the novel, doing so first of all in the compact and resonant opening tableau. The tawdry auditorium of the Leubronn casino, whose 'gilt mouldings, dark-toned colour and chubby nudities' (vol. 1, p. 4) call to mind the ornateness of Victorian theatres, provides an abundantly speculative opening to the novel, the theatricality of which is heightened by being filtered through the gaze of a soon-to-be personified spectator, as was the start of *Adam Bede*. Gwendolen is intriguingly presented as the central focus of the tableau through Daniel Deronda's eyes, and through a series of questions which uneasily interrogate her beauty:

Was she beautiful or not beautiful? and what was the secret of form or expression which gave the dynamic quality to her glance? Was the good or the evil genius dominant in those beams? Probably the evil; else why was the effect that of unrest rather than of undisturbed charm? Why was the wish to look again felt as coercion and not as a longing in which the whole being consents? (vol. i, p. 3)

Gwendolen is then left suspended in mid-action while Deronda's gaze roams around the casino's *pose plastique*, which is shattered only when he re-focuses on the spectacle of her betting, when 'suddenly he felt the moment become dramatic' (vol. i, p. 7).

Gwendolen is from the start engrossed in, and enclosed by, her desire to be seen, and her theatrical self-exhibition itself becomes part of the gambling and speculation in the casino. So absorbed is she in the potential of her physical spectacle, that she makes it the basis of her ensuing financial, as well as social and emotional transactions, both in the casino and in the rest of the novel. Gwendolen may then exemplify 'the identity of eroticism and money' in women's involvement with gambling.[21] The capacities of her body and her 'looks', are the capital she gambles with, and, like the actress, who may be both artist and lucrative art-object, Gwendolen combines gambler and betting-capital within the single unit of her own body. Thus, when her attempt to wager the spectacle of her body for the return of influence and financial stability misfires, first in the casino and then in her calculated marriage, her stake is lost and she becomes subject to the control of her gambling opponent, her spectator, so compromising has been her speculation, and so total her reliance on her ultimately transient physical attractions. Only in her narcissistic mirror-gazing can Gwendolen control the spectator's gaze. In this novel, for a woman to offer herself up to be seen is to relinquish control over her personations.

This scene draws also on one final and crucial aspect of the meaning of 'speculation', which establishes the centrality of the activities of seeing and watching in the novel, and which demonstrates the commercial mechanisms determining women's function on the later-Victorian spectacular stage. In an obsolete usage, speculation also meant a spectacle, and it is this meaning, concomitantly with that of financial gaming, which Gwendolen could be said to restore when we first see her. In the Victorian theatre, female performers were deeply and impotently implicated in speculation. Their bodies, and not those of male actors, were the stakes, the spectacle, upon which their theatres' fortunes relied. Financial pressures meant that the theatrical speculation had to pay off handsomely and quickly, and one of the surest ways to guarantee a prompt return was to fill the stage with the sight of pretty women, to institute the 'reign of legs'.[22] Hence, the presence of certain types of women came to be identified with the degraded state of the English theatre: 'the presence of young ladies more and more ravishingly the opposite of spiritual', as Austin rather lasciviously describes them (Austin, 'Present State of the Stage', p. 456), came to signify, as well as to constitute, the theatre's speculative basis in a decade increasingly conscious of its theatrical shortcomings.

This emphasis on spectacle, conveyed through the female body, foregrounds the visual aspect of the theatre rather than its narrative impulse, as the actress, like Galatea, is isolated in the viewer's gaze. Gambling similarly privileges the isolated moment of speculation above the moment of deserving dependent upon its contingent position within a tradition or continuing narrative structure. The practice of *tableaux vivants* works in the same way, and Gwendolen repeatedly seeks through this means to play the trump-card of her body which she hopes will disrupt and supersede the moral imperatives of her moment. Eliot's earlier fictional actress, the French Laure, acts in a similar manner to exploit her winning physical presence on stage. Lydgate as a spectator is, of course, entirely taken in by the Provençale's 'dark eyes', 'Greek profile, and rounded majestic form' (vol. 1, p. 228): 'She talked little; but that was an additional charm [...] her presence was enough' (vol. 1, p. 230). But she goes on to use her physical charms in order that she may escape the consequences of murdering her husband, a fatal disruption to the narrative of her marriage.

Within the theatre, George Eliot's own experiences had shown her how damaging concentration on the visual aspect of performance could be. Her letters are imbued with her distrust of the very nature of performance and physical display, and of the theatrical project as it was conceived during her time. She wrote to W. L. Bicknell on 9 October 1879, of his project to adapt *Romola* for the theatre: 'the state of our stage would make me shudder at the prospect of its characters being represented there'.[23] In particular, Eliot's letters are full of her apprehensions of the body's potential for detracting from, even denying, the art of the playwright given prevailing performance-conditions, and of the way in which the static moment of spectacle can detract from narrative momentum. It was perhaps such a perception that led her to write from Surrey to John Blackwood, 'I came down here half-poisoned by the French theatre, but I am flourishing now, and am brewing my future big book [*Daniel Deronda*]' (16 June 1874, *Letters of George Eliot*, vol. vi, p. 58). Such a view is very far from the innocence with which the younger Miss

Evans regaled Mr and Mrs Bray with news of her stay in London in 1846: 'We have been to town only once, and are saving all our strength to "rake" with you; but we are as ignorant as Primitive Methodists about any of the amusements that are going [...] Please to come in a very mischievous, unconscientious, theatre-loving humour' (1 June 1846, vol. I, p. 219).

For the older Eliot, theatrical success seems to have rested on the actor's ability to go beyond the resources of the physical, to surpass or transcend the limits of corporeality, and to appeal to a discrimination which would embed the performance within an aesthetic and literary tradition, rather than remaining fixed in a moment of spectacle. Eliot's letters often speak in anticipation of a theatrical visit in the familiar colloquial form of going to see a performer: 'I am going next Thursday to see Grisi in *Norma*. She is quite beautiful this season, thinner than she was and really younger looking' (24 May 1852, vol. II, p. 28). But letters which also recollect theatre visits only in the same visual terms record disappointed expectations. She describes her reaction to watching Rachel (an occasion she recalls in terms of seeing) in such a way as to reveal the necessity of the transformation of reactions to the purely physical, of movement between registers of experience which the theatre ought to entail. Having seen Rachel in *Adrienne Lecouvreur* in the actress's last London season in 1853, Eliot wrote to Caroline Bray and Sara Hennell on 17 June that, 'When the drop-scene fell, we [i.e. Eliot and G. H. Lewes] walked about and saw the green room and all the dingy, dusty paraphernalia that make up theatrical splendour' (*Letters of George Eliot*, vol. II, p. 104). Eliot discovered the mechanics of transformation on this occasion, but did not experience them in Rachel. For her, the 'theatrical splendour' of Charlotte Brontë's 'Vashti' was not to be found.[24]

Eliot's 1869 trip to the continent brought greater, although not entirely favourable, theatrical returns. In Rome, she writes to John Blackwood, she and Lewes 'went to see', and the verb is once again telling, 'Ristori as Judith, this being advertised as her Farewell performance'. Even with the considerable deduction of 'shivering discomfort, and the worst company imaginable to act with her, it was a gain to see again a nobly beautiful woman, grand and graceful in her attitudes and movements, and with a delicious, deep voice' (6 April 1869, vol. V, p. 24). However, she continues, it is painful that one whose glory can only be in being a great artist, should show so miserable, stupid an egoism as to select a cheap company that turns the ensemble into a farce or burlesque which makes an incongruous and often fatally neutralising background to her own figure. (vol. v, p. 24)

Lewes similarly wrote in his Journal that: 'Ristori herself was worth going to see for the beauty of her person and her voice and the statuesqueness of her attitudes', but, 'as a performance it never moved us and seemed far too much like a group of poses plastiques' (quoted in *Letters of George Eliot*, vol. v, p. 25). Ristori's self-consciously statuesque, physical qualities embody her egoism, and defeat her aspirations, and in these respects she is emulated by Gwendolen Harleth. The statuesque was widely appreciated, and may be approved in an initial register of visual appreciation, but too great an emphasis on spectacle militates against the absorption of both moment and actress into the play's disrupted narrative.

Only the French actor Got and the Italian Tommaso Salvini seem to have merited Eliot's unqualified enthusiasm. She saw Salvini play Otello twice in April 1875, and Lewes's journal records that 'Polly came home in a fever of excitement' (quoted in *Letters of George Eliot*, vol. vi, p. 142) from one of the performances. She herself writes to Alexander Main of Salvini in terms which show how far beyond the spectacular and physical the performance took her. Her record is rather one of emotional than visual impact: 'Great art, in any kind, inspirits me and makes me feel the worth of devoted effort, but from bad pictures, bad books, vulgar music, I come away with a paralyzing depression' (26 May 1875, vol. vi, p. 147). Eliot's recognition of Salvini's greatness testifies to the limitations which their physiology variously imposed on male and female performers. Despite the fact that she records more extensively her impressions of the female artists of her day, it is notably a male actor who is the one performer credited with moving Eliot unequivocally to rapture. Whether the reason for this lies with the ambitious desires of the female performer, who exploited her body for most of her impact, or in the peculiarities and prejudices of the audience's gaze, remains ambiguous. Here, as in *Daniel Deronda*, both seem equally symptoms of the society they designate and witness, in which women are more likely to be both defined by and beguiled by the opportunities apparently inherent in the physical, and in particular, in the resort to the statuesque. These tendencies are, however, challenged in a novel which plays with the very concept of seeing itself, and in particular with the gaze which would restrict femininity to its statuesque potential.

BREAKING THE MOULD

Eliot's adoption of statue-imagery in *Daniel Deronda* is partly used to figure Gwendolen's attempts at self-determination through sexual manipulation. Gwendolen demonstrates her limited awareness of the sexual and 'political' possibilities of her body within the public gaze in her readiness to adopt the public status, the value as spectacle, of a sculptured image. The full extent of her mistake is revealed only when Gwendolen's marriage to the eligible Henleigh Grandcourt is achieved, for her marriage sees her ironically petrified into precisely the public spectacle and monument she aspired to be; a spectacle which fatally combines references to all the visual art forms in which even Gwendolen could desire to be represented: 'the scene was as good as a theatrical representation for all beholders [...] it was a thing to go out and see, a thing to paint. The husband's chest, back, and arms, showed very well in his close-fitting dress, and the wife was declared to be like a statue' (vol. III, p. 207).

This moment is the culmination of Gwendolen's obsessive self-awareness (even when alone she 'automatically looked in the glass' (vol. I, p. 17)), and her persistent will to occupy centre-stage. But, as the reader is by then aware, rather than being a confirmation of her power to charm through her body, the moment most fully realises instead the limitation of Gwendolen's powers by the strategies she has invoked. Eventually Gwendolen is forced to adopt the actress's life of pretence and the isolation of the statue as a means of defending herself against her husband's taunts and the well-meaning pity of her companions: 'Gwendolen, indeed, with all that gnawing trouble in her consciousness, had hardly for a moment dropped the sense that it was her part to bear herself with dignity, and appear what is called happy. In disclosure of disappointment or sorrow she saw nothing but a humiliation which would have been vinegar to her wounds' (vol. II, p. 226). From desiring to captivate and enthral the audience's gaze, she is finally moved to seek to evade and fool it.

The fate of Gwendolen's aspirations is amply foretold in the charades at Diplow, an episode which also indicates Eliot's response as an author to the perceived tendencies of contemporary theatrical performances.[25] Gwendolen's impersonation of Hermione is a complex cultural event, which draws on diverse strands of literary, artistic, and dramatic reference, and which thus crucially contrasts Gwendolen's belief in the moment of spectacle and the potency of her statuesque physicality, with the author's commitment to the narrative process in which her characters are always, if reluctantly, embedded.

The charades are originally conceived in the aftermath of Herr Klesmer's denigration of Gwendolen's singing and of the society which encourages her. He tells her:

> you are not quite without gifts. You sing in tune, and you have a pretty fair organ. But you produce your notes badly; and that music which you sing is beneath you. It is a form of melody which expresses a puerile state of culture – a dandling, canting, see-saw kind of stuff – the passion and thought of people without any breadth of horizon. There is a sort of self-satisfied folly about every phrase of such melody; no cries of deep, mysterious passion – no conflict – no sense of the universal. It makes men small as they listen to it. (vol. 1, pp. 67–8)

Wounded by this unwonted criticism, Gwendolen has to find a means both of regaining a sense of her own supremacy, of re-consolidating in as public a manner as possible 'the effect of her beauty on a first presentation' (vol. 1, p. 75), and, more importantly, of reinstating the criteria of physical attractiveness by which she sets such store. The statue-scene from *The Winter's Tale* is chosen for performance because Gwendolen wanted to get 'a statuesque pose in [her] favourite costume' (vol. 1, p. 82) of Greek dress. The statue-scene gives ample opportunity for Gwendolen's self-display: 'her arm resting on a pillar, [she] was elevated by about six inches, which she counted on as a means of showing her pretty foot and instep' (vol. 1, p. 85). This desire draws on the aptly petrifying tradition of commemorative etchings of great actors in famous parts. As Hugh Witemeyer has pointed out, Gwendolen's pose exactly replicates an etching of Mrs Siddons as Hermione; it was common practice for society women to draw on actresses' poses for their tableaux vivants (*Eliot and Visual Arts*, p. 94).

Gwendolen desires to turn Shakespeare's scene of reconciliation and reunification into a display of her power over her family, her spectators, and the text, but in blindly manipulating the drama for her own ends, in exalting one moment of the whole play, and denying its context and implications, Gwendolen is linked with the egotistical actresses Eliot had watched, as well as being indicted by the terms in which England's commercial, spectacular theatres were being condemned. Eliot and her contemporaries recognised the disease of egotistical motivation as fatal to the theatre, and injurious to the renown of the playwright. Eliot had seen it in Ristori's surrounding herself with the mediocre in Rome, and H. B. Baker noted the tendency again in her London performances of

1873 ('The Theatres', p. 550). Juliet Pollock wrote of Rachel in 1875 that, 'when she acted, the poet was only represented in one character, for she cared more for herself than the drama, and liked to be surrounded by mean performers' ('The *"Théâtre Français"*', p. 166). In the event, Gwendolen's scheme backfires. Her dignity is surrendered as her fear is excited by the apparition of the painted panel of the dead face and fleeing figure she had previously had locked away, and she ironically and unintentionally turns into 'a statue into which a soul of Fear had entered' (vol. I, p. 86). Gwendolen's belief in her own moment cannot sustain her, and like the professional actress, she is trapped by and ironically immured within the implications of the statue-analogy.

Furthermore, her attempts to evade the descended imperatives of the narratives she takes up are countered as Eliot reinstates the implications of the stories Gwendolen manipulates. Gwendolen's Hermione resembles in some respects that of Helena Faucit.[26] When she played Hermione to Macready's Leontes, like Gwendolen and Siddons, Faucit was raised on a low dais, with one arm resting on a pedestal by her side. In line with her type of acting, however, she rejects a 'rigidly statuesque' pose, as Leontes has to be struck with her natural posture (Faucit Martin, 'Hermione', p. 34). Faucit recalls the 'startling, magnetic effect' upon actors and audience alike when the statue descends. Macready was strongly affected: 'Oh, can I ever forget Mr Macready at this point! At first he stood speechless, as if turned to stone; his face with an awe-struck look upon it' (p. 35). But then he embraces Faucit with such passion and emotion that her horror is as uncontrolled as Gwendolen's when the panel springs open:

His passionate joy at finding Hermione really alive seemed beyond control. Now he was prostrate at her feet, then enfolding her in his arms. I had a slight veil or covering over my head and neck, supposed to make the statue look older. This fell off in an instant. The hair, which came unbound, and fell on my shoulders, was reverently kissed and caressed. The whole change was so sudden, so overwhelming, that I suppose I cried out hysterically, for he whispered to me, 'Don't be frightened, my child! don't be frightened! Control yourself.' (p. 35)

Gwendolen has tried to guard against precisely such overtones of control, to avoid playing Galatea, but her means of doing so leave her isolated and vulnerable.

Gwendolen's seeking to absorb herself and others in the immediate present of her physicality is amply revealed by the sculptural metaphor.

However, the use of this image shifts from complacent celebration to the tension underlying the smooth carapace of Gwendolen's self-display when her desire to see her husband dead eventually fractures her marbled surface. This desire is foretold in the charade scene's submerged allusions to a play which, more precisely than *The Winter's Tale*, presages the psychological shifts which underlie Gwendolen's figuration as a statue. The scene evokes the story of another Hermione, in Racine's *Andromaque* (first performed in 1667). This play barely surfaces in the text, being, like Gwendolen's 'fits of dread', the subject of veiled allusions and suppressions which assert the status of narrative, context, and tradition against the will of those who would deny them. Attracted initially by a simple coincidence of names in Shakespeare and Racine, the reader soon discovers a matrix of allusions to Racine and to Rachel, one of his most celebrated interpreters.[27] Rachel appeared as Hermione rather than in the title-role when she acted in *Andromaque* in London in 1850. Although there is no record of Eliot's having seen Rachel in this part, she could certainly have known of it, for G. H. Lewes reviewed her performance for the *Leader*.[28] The figure of Rachel surfaces in connection with Alcharisi later in the novel, but her link with Gwendolen is established by the latter's belief that she could easily rival the mythic head of the French stage, despite her lack of acting experience. Her mother's recollections of Rachel, and her own 'one or two' visits to the Théâtre Français, convince Gwendolen that she could surpass Rachel, because 'she was more beautiful than that thin Jewess' (vol. I, p. 75), and specifically because she has better arms.

Gwendolen's desire to act in a Greek dress awakens the idea of Racine in her mind: 'No word for a charade would occur to her either waking or dreaming that suited her purpose of getting a statuesque pose in this favourite costume. To choose a motive from Racine was of no use, since Rex and the others could not declaim French verse' (vol. I, pp. 82–3). But this attractive idea is not easily dispelled from Gwendolen's mind: '"Something pleasant, children, I beseech you," said Mrs Davilow; "I can't have any Greek wickedness." "It is no worse than Christian wickedness, mamma," said Gwendolen, whose mention of Rachelesque heroines had called forth that remark' (vol. I, p. 83). Moments later, Rex suggests the statue-scene from *The Winter's Tale*. In order to please Gwendolen, and to satisfy contemporary expectations, the actors adopt Greek costume, but once invoked, the terms of Classical Greek and French tragedy are not easily subdued. Appearing nominally as Shakespeare's Hermione, Gwendolen unwittingly provokes thoughts of the future of Racine's character, and her own.

Gwendolen and Racine's Hermione pass through similar experiences of humiliation at the hands of men they believe love them. They see that love denied and what should be theirs – in Grandcourt, a financial duty, in Pyrrhus, his passion – pass to their rivals Mrs Glasher and Andromaque, rivals who had previously pleaded with them on behalf of their sons' futures. Gwendolen initially resolves to observe Mrs Glasher's wishes, and not marry Grandcourt, but self-interest eventually prevails, and, like Hermione, she absolves herself of responsibility for her competitor. Both heroines' reaction to their subsequent desertion is the same 'ominous calm'. Cleone, Hermione's confidante, describes her mistress's state thus:

> Non, je ne puis assez admirer ce silence.
> Vous vous taisez, Madame, et ce cruel mépris
> N'a pas du moindre trouble agité vos esprits?
> Vous soutenez en paix une si rude attaque [...]
>
> Et votre bouche encore muette à tant d'ennui,
> N'a pas daigné s'ouvrir pour plaindre de lui?
> Ah! que je crains, Madame, une calme si funeste![29]

When Lush reveals the terms of Grandcourt's will to Gwendolen, her whole frame is bent on defeating her husband's expectations of hysteria; she will not flinch, even though Lush's 'speech was like a sharp knife-edge drawn across her skin' (vol. III, p. 84).[30]

It is true that the Victorian novel and the French tragedy move apart in their resolutions. Hermione determines to effect Pyrrhus' death, but when her orders are fulfilled, she rushes to Pyrrhus' corpse and stabs herself before it. Gwendolen, however, despite her fascination with her coveted dagger – 'small and sharp, like a long willow leaf in a silver sheath' (vol. III, p. 224), language which deadens the potential violence of its subject – resists the murderous solution it promises. When Grandcourt drowns, Gwendolen finds in Daniel Deronda a vehicle for redeeming her own narrative. She exchanges her pedestalled position – now she only 'looked like a melancholy statue of the Gwendolen whose laughter had once been so ready when others were grave' (vol. III, p. 347) – for the intimacy signalled by Daniel's sympathetic touches and looks, and most powerfully demonstrated shortly after Grandcourt's death. Unable to answer Gwendolen's plea,

He took one of her hands, and clasped it as if they were going to walk together like two children: it was the only way in which he could answer, 'I will not forsake you' [...]

That grasp was an entirely new experience to Gwendolen: she had never before had from any man a sign of tenderness which her own being had needed. (vol. III, pp. 222–3)

Gwendolen's imprisonment within the physical isolation she has embraced is unequivocally shattered in her and Daniel's final meeting which, as Adrian Poole has noted, re-enacts elements of *The Winter's Tale* episode.[31] In this scene, Gwendolen 'sat like a statue with her wrists lying over each other and her eyes fixed' (vol. III, p. 400) at the news of Deronda's impending marriage, looking 'before her with dilated eyes'. But rather than being entrapped by a 'horrible vision' (vol. III, p. 401), the analogue of the charade scene's painted panel, the power of that vision is defeated by Daniel's touch, and his sympathetic look of sorrow. The warmth of a human touch dispels the cold isolation of the statue, just as Leontes' 'O, she's warm!' (*The Winter's Tale*, v.3.109) confirms Shakespeare's Hermione's return to life.

THE ACTRESS, THE SINGER, AND THE SAGE

Gwendolen eventually comes to reciprocate Daniel's tenderness, pressing away the tears from his eyes as he had done hers (vol. III, p. 402). This detail gains particular resonance from its comparison with a similar moment in Daniel's long-awaited meeting with his mother, the Princess Halm-Eberstein, and erstwhile opera-singer Alcharisi. On this occasion, Alcharisi too is moved to tears, and allows Daniel to take both her hands, as Gwendolen does. But she then presses away her own tears, and leans her cheek on Daniel's brow, avoiding his eyes (vol. III, p. 143). Alcharisi maintains the distance which has enabled her to achieve her ambition, her shunning of mediocrity, her desire to avoid marriage, and thus to usurp the family structures in which she was brought up. Gwendolen, who shares some of these desires, finally supersedes her physical isolation, but Alcharisi remains trapped in and by the decaying form which was the vehicle of her earlier success.

Deronda's meetings with his mother bring into sterile and discrete proximity the two modes of action which direct the novel. In them, Eliot contrasts the individual who seeks his duty and responsibility in his racial past and future, with one who resists being made what she terms a 'makeshift link' (vol. III, p. 132) between generations, concentrating her energies instead on securing present fame. Typically the moments intervening between Daniel's speech plunge us back into his past, embroil us in his efforts to comprehend and sympathise: he '[recalls] his sensibilities to what life had been and actually was for her whose best years were gone, and who [...] was now exerting herself to tell him of a past which was not his alone but also hers' (vol. III, p. 126). Alcharisi, however, never escapes the present of her body: when shaken by anger, her shaking 'was visibly physical' (vol. III, p. 125). Eliot writes of Alcharisi that 'each nucleus of pain or pleasure had a deep atmosphere of the excitement or spiritual intoxication which at once exalts and deadens' (vol. III, p. 128). Her intoxication with her own spectacle, her 'sincere acting' both deadens and contains the impulses of the moment: her feeling 'immediately became matter of conscious representation: experience immediately passed into drama, and she acted her own emotions' (vol. III, p. 128). She thus surrenders her emotions to her auditor or spectator, draining herself gradually of emotional resources. As Thomas P. Wolfe puts it: 'The performed self is finally a prostitution of, in Feuerbachian terms, the essential, the generic communal self.'[32]

Thus Alcharisi, the actress, singer, and woman who seeks her fulfilment in the fallacious attempt to control the mechanisms and public inscriptions of her body, becomes the paradigm of those characters who privilege their own historical moment above the narrative and inheritance of their communities. It is not enough to say that Alcharisi's emotional history is mirrored in the corroding disease of her body, for Eliot shows that it is precisely her dependence upon the physical which constitutes Alcharisi's treachery. In a moment of impassioned self-justification, Alcharisi shows Daniel a portrait of herself 'in all the fire of youth' and asks, 'Had I not a rightful claim to be something more than a mere daughter and mother? The voice and the genius matched the face. Whatever else was wrong, acknowledge that I had a right to be an artist, though my father's will was against it. My nature gave me a charter' (vol. III, p. 183). But she ultimately finds herself trapped within those bodily resources by which she hoped to subject others to her. Alcharisi's wasting disease confirms her lack of control and, combined with the black and fiery details of her clothing, suggests that her life and energy will be completely eradicated by her death, if indeed 'in her dusky flame-coloured garment' she is not already 'a dreamed visitant from some region of departed mortals' (vol. III, p. 186).[33] The arts are not, in Eliot's fiction, an appropriate resort for rebels who would make of them rather the means than the end of their revolt.

In *Daniel Deronda* a more redemptive hope is expressed through Mirah, who demonstrates Eliot's effort to create a space for the female artist in which the body will not be the primary means of determination. In so far as it is possible to conceive of a body-less performer Mirah achieves that status, albeit outside the theatre, for there even her purity is exposed to the sexualised categorisation and commercialisation of the audience's desire. Mirah's body becomes merely a necessary tool, or channel, for the singing voice in which her relationships are grounded. She thus fulfils Eliot's perception that music 'blends everything into harmony – makes one feel part of one whole which one loves all alike, losing the sense of a separate self'.[34] Her relationship with Daniel is initiated, and its seminal stages marked, by music which by-passes the necessity of dramatic representation. They meet first through Daniel's singing the Gondolier's song from Rossini's *Otello* ('his voice had entered her inner world without her having taken any note of whence it came' (vol. i, p. 280)). Later, at Lady Mallinger's evening-party, as he listens to Mirah's self-effacing singing ('which had that essential of perfect singing, the making one oblivious of art or manner, and only possessing one with the song' (vol. ii, p. 144)), Daniel 'began by looking at [Mirah], but felt himself presently covering his eyes with his hand, wanting to seclude the melody in darkness' (vol. ii, p. 145). Neither Daniel nor Mirah obtrudes the physical self, but testifies in music to the power of that medium to surpass the time-bound particularities of speech and physical spectacle.

Despite her art's lack of physiological definition, Mirah is still a strongly gendered character, but rather than deriving from a merely physical foundation, her female identity is founded instead in a culturally constructed definition of gender. This forms the counterpart of the body as an instrument of personal definition in the novel's structural series of transient and transtemporal dichotomies. The novel as a whole suggests that it is only through being responsive to, and further perpetuating, culturally descended concepts such as gender that these concepts might evolve to accommodate present needs. George Eliot writes of this process to John Morley,

as a fact of mere zoological evolution, woman seems to me to have the worse share in existence. But for that very reason I would the more contend that in the moral evolution we have 'an art which does mend nature'. It is the function of love in the largest sense, to mitigate the harshness of all fatalities. And in the thorough recognition of that worse share, I think there is a basis for a sublimer recognition in women and a more regenerating tenderness in man. (14 May 1867, *Letters of George Eliot*, vol. iv, p. 364)

The quotation is from *The Winter's Tale* (IV.4.95–6) and, like the rest of the letter, recalls Deronda and his 'acts by which he bound himself to others' (*Daniel Deronda*, vol. III, p. 186). As a novelist, Eliot worked from within patterns of experience offered by her own culture, seeking amelioration and change through participating within these patterns so as truthfully to reveal their shortcomings. As she writes in 'The Natural History of German Life':

Appeals founded on generalizations and statistics require a sympathy ready-made, a moral sentiment already in activity; but a picture of human life such as a great artist can give, surprises even the trivial and selfish into that attention to what is apart from themselves, which may be called the raw material of moral sentiment.[35]

George Eliot was undoubtedly fascinated by the phenomena of performance, and Nina Auerbach has gone so far as to personify her as 'an actress for whom the role of Great Author is merely the culmination of a life of continual self-creation and self-display', as a 'Diva' herself whose receptions of audiences at the Priory 'exude theatricality'.[36] However, this approach risks conflating the discrete performance spaces of the stage and drawing-room. It seems unlikely that Eliot was personally attracted to the isolated possibilities of the performer. In her portraits of the opera-singers Armgart and Alcharisi, it is precisely this element of performance which shapes their professional arts, and which makes their own stories cautionary rather than celebratory. They tell of the female artists' desires and ambitions, but reveal also the iniquities and ultimate delusion involved in pursuing those desires in the public gaze. They reveal George Eliot's clear-sighted apprehension of the dangerous limitations of female creativity in the contemporary theatre, and of the female body in that arena.

The immediacy of an audience's response might have appealed to Eliot but, as Julia Wedgwood reports in her obituary of Eliot, it was not the unmediated status of the performer which attracted her: 'She once said, in referring to Mendelssohn's visit to England, that the musician's power to move the crowd with a visible thrill of enthusiasm would have been the object of her aspiration, had she been allowed her choice of the form her genius might have taken.'[37] Rather, 'George Eliot' was, like Mirah, a 'body-less' artist. 'Her' name was coined when the difficulties of appearing publicly and being received, either in print or in person, as Marian Evans Lewes became apparent. The body which attempted to absorb within itself the unofficial conjunction of Evans and Lewes was subject to infrequent and carefully controlled public displays. Edith Simcox writes that Eliot was reluctant to have her likeness taken, due to her fear that it would mean that her 'private person [was] made to a certain extent public property'.[38] She never went out unaccompanied, perhaps fearing people's 'speculations' if they saw her without Lewes, and her Sunday afternoons at the Priory were effectively open only to those guests who were prepared to accept 'Evans Lewes' and not to those wishing simply to worship 'George Eliot'. The author's deliberate attempt largely to conceal her body from public sight meant that, on the whole, her fiction was not easily compromised by that body's implications.

Like Mirah, Eliot attempts to accommodate herself and her work within an ongoing tradition, largely composed of the work of male artists. Eliot's place within this tradition has been a highly malleable one in the hands of critics,[39] but her own sense of her place within literary history may be detected in her use of earlier authors in *Daniel Deronda*. It is clearly not Eliot's intention to plumb absolutely the analogic resources of the three plays which figure most prominently in her novel. Rather she participates in the tradition of literary cross-fertilisation, adaptation, and intertextuality which was practised by the playwrights she draws on in her allusions to *The Winter's Tale*, *Andromaque*, and *Medée*. Shakespeare, Racine, Corneille, and Euripides all adapted earlier literary sources for their own dramatic ends, necessarily re-investing those sources with modern pertinence, but not thereby obliterating their provenance and autonomy. (For instance, the triangle of relationships between Gwendolen, Grandcourt, and Deronda initially shadows, but is not foreclosed by nor does it supersede the relations between Hermione, Pyrrhus, and Oreste.) These authors place themselves, as Eliot does herself, within a literary heritage which successively enriches each coming generation according to its recognition of both its own place within the descent of literature and ideas, and the rightful place of its predecessors. Eliot's appropriation of elements of the work of her literary forebears within *Daniel Deronda* is creative and therefore selective. They exist therein allusively, and all the more suggestively because they evade incorporation within what Adrian Poole calls a 'too rigid interpretation' ('Hidden Afinities', p. 305) of the novel's allusions. In her practice of allusion, Eliot thus participates in the perpetually commemorative and time-defying, rather than temporally bound, part of the temporal distinction upon which *Daniel Deronda* rests as, she believed, did the greatest sculpture:

the greatest painters and sculptors have surely not been those who have been inspired through their intellect, who have first thought and then chosen a plastic symbol for their thought; rather the symbol rushes in on their imagination before their slower reflection has seized any abstract idea embodied in it. Maybe, perhaps the artist himself never seizes that idea, but his picture or his statue stands there an immortal symbol nevertheless. ('Liszt, Wagner, and Weimar', p. 104)

Her allusions are thus a form of testimony to perennial human concerns, and to the writer's capacity perpetually to address those concerns. Thus, Eliot triumphs over the material, physical constraints of the present, and of the body in that present. Unlike that of the actress, Eliot's work is physiologically defined neither in its form nor in its function.

The inspiration behind her aesthetic may have lain in Eliot's perception of how Classical authors, like sculpture, were able to defy time. Writing in 1856 of an earlier successful production of Sophocles' *Antigone* at Drury Lane, Eliot marvels: 'so completely did the poet triumph over the disadvantages of his medium, and of a dramatic motive foreign to modern sympathies, that the Pit was electrified, and Sophocles, over a chasm of two thousand years, once more swayed the emotions of a popular audience'.[40] Eliot goes on to suggest that Sophocles triumphs by successfully manipulating a form of emotional allusion, by appealing 'to perennial human nature' ('The Antigone and its Moral', p. 262) rather than by allowing himself to be restricted to 'the Greek point of view' (p. 264). She writes, 'Wherever the strength of a man's intellect, or moral sense, or affection brings him into opposition with the rules which society has sanctioned, there is renewed the conflict between Antigone and Creon' (p. 265). In her practice of allusion, the author has then to seek that nodal moment, which is 'for ever young' and for ever alive for a succession of audiences, just as the greatest sculpture transcends its moment of instantiation. It is in this most profoundly allusive moment that Eliot locates the 'highest Form of art': 'the highest organism [...] the most varied group of relations bound together in a wholeness which again has the most varied relations with all other phenomena'.[41] 'Artistic form', she continues, 'as distinguished from mere imitation, begins in sculpture & painting with composition or the selection of attitudes and the formation of groups, let the objects be of what order they may' (p. 434). Eliot then goes on to argue for sculpture as a persistent source of definition for the use of language, and in particular, I would argue, for her practice of allusion: 'The old phrases should not give way to scientific explanation, for speech is to a great extent like sculpture, expressing observed phenomena & remaining true in spite of Harvey and Bichat' ('Notes on Form', p. 436).

The representational mode of sculpture is thus recuperated in its providing a foundation and exemplary model for Eliot's art, an aesthetic practice determined on transmitting the moment of most profound Form, the moment most varied and whole, the moment that retains its truth, and is best capable of linking its recipients, as Daniel and Mirah are linked through a moment of song. Such moments are what Eliot seeks in other writers, the substance that she then rewrites for her present readers. All this, sculpture provides a prototype for, but a prototype which necessarily involves the artist's commitment to going beyond the partial, transient, isolated form of the body within which Alcharisi and Galatea are trapped, to embrace the representational possibilities of language. In going beyond this form, and in her manipulation of language, Eliot becomes in some measure a Pygmalion-figure and an inspiration for those women, as James describes them, 'for whom the "development" of woman is the hope of the future' (James, 'George Eliot's Life', p. 677). One of those women was the pioneering actress Elizabeth Robins who later described George Eliot as 'my idol', and who went on in her own career to become a distinguished writer and translater, as well as a performer.[42]

CHAPTER 4

Very lovely Greek statues: the London stage in the 1880s

Eliot's recuperation of the linguistic flexibilities and potential of the sculptural metaphor, and the challenge she offered to the orthodoxies of Pygmalion's position did not bear immediate fruit. The gendered assumptions which shaped the ascription of roles of sculptor and sculpted, of the one being moulded and the one to be moulded, were not readily to be overturned, as contemporary responses to Eliot's death demonstrate. George Eliot's death on 22 December 1880 prompted a number of extended memorial articles in early 1881, most of which concentrated, as the *Blackwood's* article put it, on the 'public George Eliot', on her works rather than her life, and sought to establish 'a fairly accurate idea of how the genius of George Eliot was moulded'.[1] The obituary articles also considered the implications for literature of the death of 'the greatest woman who ever won literary fame' as Leslie Stephen described her, 'and one of the very few writers of our day to whom the name "great" could be conceded with any plausibility'.[2] Stephen describes her demise as marking 'the termination of the great period of English fiction which began with Scott' (p. 152), thus already associating her implicitly with the act of commemoration, of looking backward.

Stephen is trying actively to mould Eliot's memory, and to delimit its potential. The metaphor of moulding emerges in the obituary articles in a number of ways. It may invoke the creative process;[3] or it may provide the metaphorical authority for the activity of the obituaries' authors in their concern appropriately to shape Eliot's legacy, to fashion her literary memorial and monument. That activity seems to be generated by an anxiety about Eliot's own capacities to influence her readers. In 'The Moral Influence of George Eliot', Julia Wedgwood recalls as most emphatic the novelist's 'vehement recoil from that spirit which identifies what is excellent with what is exceptional' (p. 177). Wedgwood cites the degree and intimacy of Eliot's involvement with her contemporaries, writing that 'no preacher of our day, we believe, has done so much to

91

mould the moral aspirations of her contemporaries as she has, for none other had both the opportunity and the power' (p. 176). As a corollary of this approach she confers upon Eliot a form of 'democratic Pygmalion' status whose power to influence is generated by, or rests upon, the spirit of the novelist's intimate engagement with her readers, a group who, in this account, seem crucially not to be restricted to the already established confines of the past.

Such a dangerous status is not articulated by Stephen, but the fear of it nonetheless informs his article, which ends with an uncomfortable assessment of Dorothea Brooke's powers of influence. He invokes what he describes as the 'rather depressing' image of 'anonymous Dorotheas feeling about vaguely for some worthy outlet of their energies [...] condescending to put up with a very commonplace life in a vague hope that somehow or other they will do some good' ('George Eliot', p. 168). This image is, of course, at the heart of *Middlemarch*, and of Eliot's belief in the inheritance of influence. *Daniel Deronda*, the novel which most fully exemplifies Eliot's notion of influence, is barely mentioned in the obituaries. Stephen ends his memorial by consigning Eliot to an already vanished past, and thus curtailing her influence: 'we feel her to be one who [...] has brought great intellectual powers to setting before us a lofty moral ideal, and, in spite of manifest shortcomings, has shown certain aspects of a vanishing social phase with a power and delicacy unsurpassed in her own sphere' (p. 168). Stephen's Eliot is a time-bound icon, an image bound by reminiscence, and already out-dated. Iconographically, Stephen substitutes for the diffusiveness of Dorothea an image of Eliot as exceptional, isolated, and elevated. He writes that Eliot 'stands out as superior to her rivals' (p. 155), that she is 'set apart'; set 'at an intellectual elevation high enough to be beyond the illusion of the city fashion' in literature (p. 158). Stephen's apparently laudatory sense of her position as 'the last great sovereign of a literary dynasty' (p. 152) similarly conveys Eliot to a position of temporal isolation, notably one which does not allow of the possibility of a sustained influence, of successors. Her 'exceptional' qualities put Eliot on a pedestal, a position which is rather one of limitation and isolation than of inspiration. This curtailment of Eliot was symptomatic of aspects of the treatment of women in the coming decade, which was one of tremendous gender-anxiety, generated by fears about homosexuality, and about the implications of women entering into new professional arenas.

As a cartoon from *Punch* helps to demonstrate (see plate 7), the early part of the 1880s saw the emergence of publicly expressed anxieties

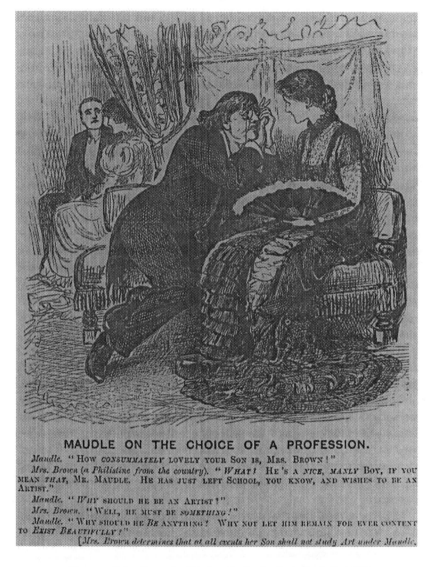

MAUDLE ON THE CHOICE OF A PROFESSION.

Maudle. "How CONSUMMATELY LOVELY YOUR SON IS, MRS. BROWN!"

Mrs. Brown (a Philistine from the country). "WHAT! HE'S A NICE, MANLY BOY, IF YOU MEAN THAT, MR. MAUDLE. HE HAS JUST LEFT SCHOOL, YOU KNOW, AND WISHES TO BE AN ARTIST."

Maudle. "WHY SHOULD HE BE AN ARTIST?"

Mrs. Brown. "WELL, HE MUST BE SOMETHING!"

Maudle. "WHY SHOULD HE BE ANYTHING? WHY NOT LET HIM REMAIN FOR EVER CONTENT TO EXIST BEAUTIFULLY?"

[*Mrs. Brown determines that at all events her Son shall not study Art under Maudle.*

Plate 7 'Maudle on the Choice of a Profession', *Punch*, 80 (1881)

about male effeminacy and homosexuality. It was a period which also experienced a drop in the birthrate (following the proliferation of birth-control information in the late-'seventies[4]), and subsequent fears about national defence in years which witnessed electoral agitation (resulting in the Third Reform Act of 1884), and the fall of General Gordon in Khartoum, an event which shook British belief in the security of the Empire.[5] In this context, homosexuality came to take on the status of a threat to the nation, and was publicly countered by the Criminal Law Amendment Act, the so-called Labouchère Amendment. Amongst other measures, this act raised the age of consent from thirteen to sixteen, made procuration a criminal offence, and introduced new penalties for private as well as public homosexual behaviour. Alongside this narrative ran a parallel move to extend the range of sexual discourses to include the explicit articulation of female sexual desire. In 1884, Eleanor Marx and Edward Aveling published a devastating attack on female chastity and late marriages. Chastity, they wrote, was 'unhealthy and unholy', and was just one of the social diseases springing up due to unnatural dealing with sex relations.[6] Also in that year, the pioneering woman doctor, Elizabeth Blackwell, asserted the strength of female sexual desire without reference to the usual pretext of a desire for children, even writing that in women the sexual passion might be of a profounder character than in men.[7] The memory of the childless, but not celibate, and for the greater part of her life, unmarried 'George Eliot', was an important, even an inspirational factor.

At this time, the alliance between theatre and the social good proved unprecedentedly felicitous, for in a society experiencing the fear of gender instability, the actress could function as a paradigm of female virtue, which at this time might embrace the ability to excite, although not self-consciously to represent, heterosexual desire. Qualms about female self-exhibition, and the actress's professional status, were subdued by the need to publicise feminine virtues and desirability in an appropriately determined context. This, the theatre could do, and this, as I hope to show, the Galatea-aesthetic significantly both enabled and confirmed.

To some extent, those writers who embraced the theatre of the early 1880s were making a virtue out of necessity. As Hamilton Aïdé wrote in 1885: 'The number of our theatres has more than doubled in the last five-and-twenty years; consequently it is clear that the taste for dramatic performances in this country is on the increase. Great and good men recognise more and more that the theatre may be fully as potent a factor for morality as the pulpit.'[8] Similarly, given that the theatre provided numerous employment opportunities for women, and especially since middle-class women were increasingly attracted to the apparent freedoms of the stage, Aïdé suggested that that arena for women's work could profitably be drawn into a select range of approved professional openings: 'I feel very sure that there is a number of well-educated, high-principled girls, with an aptitude for representation, who run no greater risks here than they do in any other arena where prudence and vigilance are needed' (p. 526). Even Eliza Lynn Linton questions whether acting is necessarily any more injurious to 'the modesty of her sex' than other professions. Carefully selecting her dramatic examples, of sexuality invoked but doomed, she suggests that, 'to act Ophelia or Juliet, or even La Dame aux Camellias [sic], does not seem to us, outside buffaloes, so likely to damage the inherent modesties of woman's nature as the discussion of doubtful subjects before a mixed audience, which more than one of our lady-lecturers has done'.9 While she concedes that appearing *en maillot*, in 'a gold cord and a pointed cap' may give the moral nature a shock, it is no less a shock than that administered 'in medical classes and mixed life-schools' (p. 12), and given that 'there is not a house, a husband, and a child for every woman in England' the stage is as good a place as any other in which to earn a living for 'the poor unmated and unsupported surplus female population afloat in the world' (p. 14). In addition, the stage was ultimately under the control of the playwright, 'who has it in his power to elevate the theatre into the grandest and purest of all the pulpits whence men and women are exhorted to become pure, brave, generous, and magnanimous' (p. 13); and carefully to manage and direct female public appearances.10

In the early 1880s, a new variety of 'public woman' had emerged, the so-called 'platform woman', such as Annie Besant, or the suffrage campaigner Millicent Garrett Fawcett, who could most powerfully promote her own opinions by the persuasive spectacle of 'her personal attractiveness' and 'her charm of voice and manner'.11 Kathleen Fitzpatrick would later make of Lady Henry Somerset, the nineteenth-century philanthropist and one-time President of the British Women's Temperance Association, a statuesque and influential figure in describing the terms of the latter's influence: 'Bareheaded, in a black dress, standing quite still, without one gesture, she could hold an audience of thousands for an hour on what had been considered till then the dullest subject on earth.'12 Powerful and potentially radical on a speaker's platform, precisely these attributes could, however, make the actress a sexually conservative figure. Writers surveying the burgeoning employment and educational possibilities for women feared that 'beauty [might] die on the altar of female independence'; that 'higher occupations [than the domestic] are spoiling women's looks'.13 But, as Lynn

Linton writes, the occupation of the actress was crucially 'not un-feminine' ('The Stage as a Profession', p. 14): the English actress could advertise the persistence of desirable femininity in the midst of fears about women's masculinisation through professionalisation, and could thus be enrolled as a conservative social force.

The actress's social redemption occurred within the broader framework of the theatre's growing social prominence. In 1883 the playwright Frederick Wedmore wrote that 'by action and reaction the change has been wrought; the London world has acted on the theatre, and the theatre has acted on the London world'.[14] In the same year, Theodore Martin set out more explicitly the reciprocal conditions of this union: if the theatre could attract men and women with 'the true histrionic gift' and 'dramatists of true poetic power [...it] might again become, what it ought to be, not only the best recreation, but a moral teacher of the age, only less potent than the sacred influences of religion'.[15] Inspired partly by Helena Faucit's writings, the novelist Mrs Craik suggests that by stirring or refreshing an audience, the great actor may be 'among the best benefactors of society'.[16] By reciprocating society's applause with a stabilising moral force akin to that of religion, Martin argues, performers might gain entry into the society of their audience. At this time, the extent to which actresses were allowed into the best society was effectively the marker of the enhanced prestige of the theatre and the definitive sign of its new identity. T. H. S. Escott writes in 1885 that actors 'insist on making themselves seen and heard' in society, and this not as actors,

but *quâ* gentlemen or ladies of fashion [...] assuming the airs of people of the highest social consideration, the actors are perpetually asking themselves what their position is. As a matter of fact, it is, with the exception of their woman-kind, what it always was. The actress in society is a novel feature. Madame Christine Nilsson, the *prima donna*, visits Lady Salisbury. Mrs Bancroft – Marie Wilton – visits Lady Hayter.[17]

However, Escott goes on to suggest that such social advances were not in fact facilitated by the actress's increased respectability, but rather by society's being 'in a sense, stage-struck'; and further that, 'There is a certain prurient prudishness, a salacious inquisitiveness about London society. It loves to hover over, or alight on, the borderland which separates conventional respectability from downright dissoluteness. There is nothing which it so dearly loves as a soupçon of naughtiness' (p. 296). Escott dares to articulate what other commentators ostensibly distance themselves from, that is, the persistence of the actress's sexual desirability. During this decade it was precisely this 'soupçon of naughtiness' which determined the actress's 'respectability', and confirmed her as an ally of commentators like Lynn Linton who wished to deflect the anxieties generated by gender-inversion.[18]

To suggest, as I am doing, that the actress could be a highly conservative social figure is to run counter to the prevalent current view of the Victorian actress as a woman of positively transgressive and liberating sexual energies. Tracy C. Davis, for instance, writes that 'the gorgeous actresses overturn the hegemony of false feminine propriety'.[19] However, such a view fails to make a distinction between an actress's own active sexuality, and the desirability that might be imposed upon her on stage. An unusual professional standing and questionable twentieth-century hindsight collapse this distinction into a reading of actresses' sexual 'freedom' which makes that state a laudable achievement and an advancement of women's claims. Such an account fails to recognise that women could not necessarily control the spectacle of their desirability in the hierarchised, public world of the English commercial theatre, as George Eliot shows in *Daniel Deronda*, and that any sexual freedom actresses had might rather be used as a mechanism of the society they lived in than in actresses' own interests. The peculiarities of this decade enabled critics to absorb and recycle English actresses' sexuality, as well as their on-stage assumption of more conventionally virtuous parts, in the interests of social stability, and as I hope to show, it was the actress's participation in the Galatea-aesthetic which provided the medium through which that sexuality could safely be displayed.

'SHE MOVED LIKE A VERY LOVELY GREEK STATUE'

The demand for Classicism on the English stage was well established in the 1880s. In 1883, Frederick Wedmore wrote testily of those 'to whom a story, if it deals with Ancient Greece, appeals as matter to be reverenced'.[20] He was referring to a fashion which unexpectedly united in enthusiasm the educated middle classes and the newly burgeoning group of aesthetes, but which also generated popular manifestations which signalled the cultural proliferation of this theatrical phenomenon. In London in 1886 there were at least three neo-Classical productions to be seen, two of which were in part the responsibility of Edward Godwin, who was a disciple of Planché, and Ellen Terry's erstwhile lover. He was described by Louise Jopling as having a soul which 'must have been the reincarnation of a Greek sculptor'.[21] John Todhunter's *Helena in Troas* was designed by Godwin in a reproduction of a Classical stage at Hengler's Circus in Regent's Park, profits from which were to go to the British School of Archaeology at Athens; Wilson Barrett's production of Sydney Grundy's *Clito*, a story about a Classical sculptor which was given at the Princess's, was also designed by Godwin; and two plays, 'The Tale of Troy' and 'The Story of Orestes', were presented at the Prince's Hall by Professor Warr, under the patronage of the Prince and Princess of Wales, in order to raise funds for the University Endowment Fund, a charity which was concerned to extend the benefits of a university education to the middle classes in London. Designers of the latter production included Leighton, Poynter, Watts, and Professor Newton of the British Museum.[22]

These productions were all fully reported, and often visually represented, in the pages of the popular illustrated newspaper *The Graphic*. Alongside its accounts of these productions the paper also carried advertisements which demonstrated the extent of the influence of the Classical mode. In the same number in which it gives an account of 'The Story of Orestes', and a full-page illustration of Clytemnestra awakening a group of improbably languorous Furies (plate 8), *The Graphic* also carries an advertisement for Mr Beecham's pills which shows the eponymous manufacturer backed up by the authority and desirable vigour of Athena.[23] Two weeks later an advertisement for 'Bridal Bouquet Bloom' appears which irresistibly promises to '[impart] exquisite beauty'. This beauty is described as having 'a natural brilliancy, purity, and charming fragrance. It removes freckles and sunburn.'[24] Thus, it enables young women the more readily to emulate the Classical beauties currently to be seen on the stage.

The chief value of many of these neo-Classical productions seems to have been as spectacle rather than as effective drama: as John Stokes notes, 'Historical accuracy, picturesque staging, and effective drama' do not 'necessarily coincide'.[25] Indeed, for some of the young women involved in *Helena in Troas*, they did not even have to move, let alone act. According to Louise Jopling, she was instructed by Godwin 'to drape, and seat, half a dozen figures in the same attitudes as those on the frieze of the Parthenon. The poor things had to remain without moving during the whole time the play was in progress! They were attired in unbleached calico draperies, which simulated the white marble, just tinged with age, wonderfully well' (*Twenty Years*, p. 290). Of Wilson Barrett's *Claudian*, the *Athenaeum* writes that as a spectacle it was beauti-

Plate 8   'Clytemnestra and the Furies', *Graphic*, (1886)

ful, and that 'the effect of the pictures is delightful'.[26] Some anxiety is felt
as to the extent to which the play seems not to enable 'the display of
individual capacity in the actors', but that is quickly submerged within
the general satisfaction afforded by the spectacle. Frederick Wedmore in
The Academy celebrates the 'luxurious and engaging' visual effects of the
play. He suggests that Miss Eastlake, the play's leading actress, is
unequal to her part, but subsumes that suggestion within his observation
that on the grounds of her resemblance to the 'large nobility of the Elgin
Marbles' she is 'thoroughly worth seeing'. He congratulates Miss
Ormsby, who plays a Greek slave, on the grounds of her acting, but the
terms of her success are revealing in that they too partake of a version of
the sculptural-aesthetic. Wedmore evokes Emma Hamilton in writing of
Miss Ormsby that 'Her attitudes, rapidly changing, and "statuesque"
only in their beauty – for they are never immobile – are not merely
studied with admirable care, but must be due to a temperament that
instinctively understands expressiveness in action.' Wedmore suggests
that the inspiration behind her acting derives from the antique forms
which she studies, for it is in those forms that the principle of 'expressive-

ness in action' resides, that quality which Ruskin celebrates in the
sculpture of the fifth century BC. However, rather than the analytical
skills of a Ruskin, the actress is notably accorded the powers of an
'instinctive temperament', and the ability simply to emulate.

A similar emphasis on the authority of the antique, mediated through
its contemporary male proponents, is apparent in responses to Ellen
Terry's performance in *The Cup*, a rather turgid, although attractively
presented neo-Classical drama by Tennyson, which was produced at
the Lyceum in 1881. The *Pall Mall Gazette* wrote in reviewing this 'New
Drama of the Laureate', that 'If anything can reconcile to the modern
stage that small section of the cultivated public which has hitherto held
aloof, it is the class of entertainment now to be seen at the Lyceum.'[27]
There was in that theatre, and in the eyes of its audiences, little room for
the conservatoire-trained actress of France, for art was valued less than
the appearance of the artless. In earlier remarks on Ellen Terry, Henry
James had revealed the way in which 'nature', or its conventional
signifiers, had come to take over from 'art' as the criterion by which
actresses were judged:

By many intelligent persons she is regarded as an actress of exquisite genius,
and is supposed to impart an extraordinary interest to everything that she
touches. This is not, in our opinion, the truth, and yet to gainsay the assertion
too broadly is to fall into an extreme of injustice. The difficulty is that Miss
Terry has charm – remarkable charm; and this beguiles people into thinking
her an accomplished actress. There is a natural quality about her that is
extremely pleasing – something wholesome and English and womanly which
often touches easily where art, to touch, has to be finer than we often see it.
('The London Theaters', p. 361)

But most of James's fellow critics were as willingly beguiled by Terry as
the rest of her audiences. Mowbray Morris, perhaps taking a dig at
James, wrote that Terry alone had 'that rare and precious gift of charm,
that gift to which the dullest of us can never be insensible, which the
cleverest can never analyse or define'.[28]

Terry's charm was inseparable from her statuesque grace, and in no
production is this more apparent than in *The Cup*, where she plays
Camma, wife of the Tetrarch Sinnatus, and later Priestess of the
Temple of Artemis. In this play, the noble and virtuous Camma is
desired by Synorix, played by Irving, who is Sinnatus' great enemy. Left
widowed by Synorix' hand, Camma devotes her life to revenge on
Synorix, and to worship of Artemis. She poisons him by offering him the
eponymous cup, and when sure of his death, kills herself too. The

production was notable chiefly as a 'dramatic spectacle',[29] much of the success of which was due to the play's numerous Priestesses and female Attendants, and to Terry, whose merits, according to *The Theatre* reviewer, had 'never before been so happily and fully exhibited'.[30] The *Pall Mall Gazette* likewise wrote that, 'To the grace, distinction, and breadth of style of Miss Terry as Camma the success of the representation is chiefly attributable. Wearing with exquisite grace the Grecian costume, Miss Terry gave the early scenes all the charm of which they are capable. In the later and stronger act her gestures were superb' ('New Drama', p. 11). The play itself insists on the sculptural derivation of Camma's beauty: 'The bust of Juno and the brows and eyes / Of Venus; face and form unmatchable!',[31] and the play's reviewers took their lead from this guide, and from her costume, which was designed by Edward Godwin.

From the first, the relationship between Godwin and Terry had overtones of the Pygmalion–Galatea narrative.[32] Godwin's biographer writes the designer into the role of Terry's Pygmalion, describing the actress as 'his major experiment, [who] had been allowed no corsets, hats, or cosmetics' (*Conscious Stone*, p. 162). For Godwin was also an enthusiast for dress reform, and Terry in some respects acted as a model for Godwin's ideas, both in private and in public. The couple's first collaboration had been on a dress for Terry's role as Titania in Bath in 1862. In his role as local journalist, Godwin had attacked the theatre company's Classical burlesques 'on the grounds that they were ugly' (Terry, *Story of My Life*, p. 46). His efforts to beautify the stage along Classical lines began with Terry's dress, which must have resembled the clinging simplicity of the dresses of Burne-Jones's women in 'The Golden Stairs' (1866–80):

Mr Godwin designed my dress, and we made it in his house at Bristol. He showed me how to damp it and 'wring' it while it was wet, tying up the material as the orientals do in their 'tie and dry' process, so that when it was dry and untied, it was all crinkled and clinging. This was the first lovely dress that I ever wore, and I learned a great deal from it. (Terry, *Story of My Life*, p. 46)

Mrs Oliphant was provoked to respond to dress reformers such as Godwin who were blinded by the 'learned folly of Classicism', and to their 'ingenious notion' that the Greek *chyton* should be adapted for general wear by English women. She writes: 'The French revolution was nothing to it; in our own opinion it would be more possible to disestablish the Church, abolish the House of Lords, and cut the sacred vesture of the British Constitution into little pieces, than to transform English garments into Greek.'[33] In fact, English society proved more malleable to the concept of Greek attire than Mrs Oliphant anticipated. Curiously perhaps, reviews do not mention Godwin's responsibility for Terry's costumes, and for her poses,[34] although the designer, described by Max Beerbohm as 'the greatest aesthete of them all',[35] would have been implicitly included in *Punch*'s criticism, in its review of *The Cup*, of 'all the Burne-Jonesians and the aesthetic pagans [who] will rave about her in her classic drapery as "consummate"'.[36]

This drapery enabled 'the display of her particular gifts': 'Under her thin, sea-green raiment of lissome stuff, the movement and the arrested movement of the actress are equally perfect. Aided by draperies arranged with the most singular skill, the figure, in its freedom and suavity, recalls the Elgin Marbles and the designs of the artist who has learnt the best from them – Mr Albert Moore' ('Mr Tennyson's New Play', p. 36). In his review, Clement Scott restricts Terry's impact to the Classical allusions of her costume: 'We seem to see before us the concentrated essence of such fascinating art as that of Sir Frederic Leighton, and Mr Alma Tadema, in a breathing and tangible form. Not only do the grapes grow before us [...] but in the midst of all this scenic allurement glide the classical draperies of Miss Ellen Terry'.[37] She is reduced to the signification of robes designed by Godwin, which achieve their meaning within a context created by the work of Leighton, Alma-Tadema, and G. F. Watts. As Clement Scott notes elsewhere, reviewers study 'the acting of Mr Henry Irving and the inimitable picturesqueness of Miss Ellen Terry' ('*The Cup*', p. 193). Thus, where Irving is 'most memorable', Terry is 'most delightful'.[38] Insufficiencies in her speech, noted by the *Academy* and *Punch*, are more than compensated for by the sight of her.

In her early-twentieth-century autobiography, Terry claims for herself the status of collaborator with Godwin and Watts both in their artistic work, and in her appearances on stage.[39] She writes of Watts and Godwin as two of the artists from whom she learnt 'Judgment about colours, clothes, and lighting' (*Story of My Life*, p. 150), and of Godwin as the designer of her dresses in Tennyson's *The Cup*: 'My dresses, designed by Mr Godwin [...] were simple, fine and free' (p. 198). However, as we have seen, reviews of Terry in *The Cup* ascribe to the actress a simple picturesqueness deriving from the terms of the play, and are largely devoid of any notice of her own creative skills. Within the concatenation of artistic authorities set up by her reviewers, the self-knowing autonomy and scenic authority evidenced in Terry's own writing on the play

MISS ANDERSON as GALATEA.
Copyright 1883, by Napoleon Sarony,
37 UNION SQR., N.Y.

Plate 9   Mary Anderson as Galatea (1883)

(pp. 194–9) have little chance of being acknowledged. To do so would be to credit the statue with life beyond its appearance of simple desirability, and of malleability: as Virginia Woolf has the character of Nell in *Freshwater* ingenuously respond when asked her name, 'Sometimes I'm Modesty. Sometimes I'm Poetry. Sometimes I'm Chastity. Sometimes, generally before breakfast, I'm merely Nell.'[40]

In Mary Anderson's two productions of *Pygmalion and Galatea*, in December 1883 and September 1884, and in the differences between them, we see revealed most conclusively the terms upon which the popular actress successfully occupied the stage at this time, and the statue came to life. Anderson's first Galatea was determined by her perception that 'some remnant of the inanimate marble would inevitably linger about [the statue], giving to her movements a plastic grace, and to her thoughts and their expression a touch of the ethereal'.[41] Publicity photographs for the American tour of this production insist on the stillness of the statue (plate 9). Critics were only mildly enthusiastic about this Galatea, who was perceived as lovely but chaste, perhaps too much so.[42] Her performance was felt to retain 'the coldness and purity of the marble from which she is freed',[43] and as such was unable to dislodge from the mind of the playgoer the memories of Mrs Kendal's 'flesh and blood' Galatea, in whom, 'every attribute of the woman is pronounced, every feeling fully possessed'.[44]

An intriguing by-product of this production is the controversy over who arranged Anderson's Greek robes, over who was responsible for 'moulding' the 'very graceful, very Greek'[45] image she presents. It had been suggested that Lawrence Alma-Tadema had taken charge of this matter, and indeed he was responsible for suggesting that Anderson should appear as a Tanagra statuette with drapery around her head. However, this idea was rejected, presumably because, although in Alma-Tadema's view it was more 'authentic', in terms of a modern audience's appreciation, it would have interfered with their view of Anderson. In fact, Alma-Tadema relates, Anderson was dressed to a design by the New York painter, Frank D. Millet, although her robes were adjusted by Alma-Tadema in the play's two intervals. At no point in the article is it suggested that Anderson might have organised her own costume, although she herself makes such a claim in her autobiography. Anderson records that Alma-Tadema's Tanagra suggestion was unsuitable: 'The author insisted that Galatea looked like a stiff mediaeval saint; so the Tanagra idea was abandoned. At the last full dress rehearsal, matters grew worse. Pose after pose was tried, but the judges in front had something to say against each [...] I resolved to make my statue in my own way' (*A Few Memories*, p. 150).

Alma-Tadema's final satisfaction, indeed his only one in a play which he dismisses as 'clumsy and silly' and as having 'no archaeological pretensions at all', is in Anderson's dress and appearance: 'She moved like a very lovely Greek statue, taking successive and evidently studied attitudes that reminded the eye of the Venus of Milo, the daughters of Niobe, and other standard works of antiquity.' *Punch* is similarly happy to consign Anderson to the status of a statue in its last number of 1883, where she is depicted as a cross between a Greek statue and an embryonic statue of liberty (see plate 10).[46] *Punch*'s caption runs:

> Miss Anderson, by Jove! Jaun-
> -Diced critics may frown at you,
> But you're the lovely statue,
> Miss Anderson, by Jove![47]

The following year, however, the *Athenaeum*'s 'Dramatic Gossip' column reported that in her new production of the play, 'A noteworthy improvement is apparent in the acting of Miss Anderson, whose method seems now to be formed. Apart from the statuesque beauty by which it was at first characterised and which it still retains, her Galatea is now supremely tender and womanly.'[48] The reason for her success seems to have consisted in her finding a way in which to combine statuesque beauty with the tender and womanly. It was with this production that Anderson opened her most successful season in London, and this which gave the key-note for that success. For the *Pall Mall Gazette*'s representative it suggested that there could 'be little doubt that the great success which the beautiful American actress has already achieved will be enduring'.[49] In this season she went on to perform, to great popular if not critical acclaim, the part of Juliet. This prompted one critic to question querulously 'why any trouble should be taken to mount "Romeo and Juliet" when Miss Mary Anderson looks just as well, if not better, on a pedestal as Galatea'.[50]

JULIETS, 'LOTTIES', AND 'TOTTIES'

It might be objected that this analysis of the position of the actress on the stage of the 1880s and of the Galatea-aesthetic is insufficient in that it has concentrated so far on those plays which explicitly embrace the representation of the Classical world. However, as the professional narratives

Plate 10 'The American Evening Star' (Mary Anderson), *Punch*, 85 (1883)

of Anderson and Terry demonstrate, their performances in other parts, even the choice of those parts, were not immune from the considerations more usually attaching to Galatea. As Juliet for instance, Terry simply becomes her appearance. For Clement Scott, the minutely detailed first sighting of Terry was enough to determine his judgement of her performance: 'Attired in pale primrose satin, with light-brown hair falling unfettered over one shoulder, Miss Ellen Terry was surely a Juliet that enchanted every eye.'[51] In the first years of the 1880s there were three well-known productions of *Romeo and Juliet* on the London stage, the terms of the reception of which proclaim the persistence of the Galatea-aesthetic even in non-Classical plays.

Juliet was played by the eminent Polish actress Helena Modjeska at the Court Theatre in 1881, by Ellen Terry at the Lyceum in 1882, and by Mary Anderson also at the Lyceum in late-1884. In 1882, Theodore Martin commented on the part of Phèdre that this 'character, like Juliet on our stage, has always been regarded in France as the best touchstone of an actress's tragic powers' ('Rachel', p. 288). Such a consideration, however, seems to have been far from uppermost in the minds of contemporary actresses and reviewers. More important for all, including the illustrators of *Punch* and *The Theatre*, seem to have been the play's visual qualities, as George Rowell notes:

In the Victorian period *Romeo and Juliet* was widely regarded as the most pictorial of the tragedies. Irving spoke for his fellow actor-managers when he told Ellen Terry: '*Hamlet* could be played anywhere on its acting merits. It marches from situation to situation. But *Romeo and Juliet* proceeds from picture to picture. Every line suggests a picture. It is a dramatic poem rather than a drama, and I mean to treat it from that point of view.'[52]

The play also had the advantage that, like Victorian adaptations of Pygmalion and Galatea's story, that of Romeo and Juliet enabled the display of, and contained its own solution to the problems raised by, theatrical representations of female sexuality. Juliet's youthfully unconscious desirability is invoked by others only to be obliterated by death, when it becomes part of the mechanism which effects a peaceable alliance between powerful political forces. The unselfconscious nature of that desirability is aptly demonstrated in the illustration which immediately followed *The Theatre*'s review of the Irving–Terry production and showed Juliet's slumbering, unselfconscious form, implicitly offered up to the reader's view (plate 11). Juliet's sexual awakening is amply contained by the dimensions of the tragedy, thus making the part the

Plate 11   'Juliet', *The Theatre*, 5 (1882)

perfect vehicle for conveying the attractively malleable sexuality of the actress.

This was an aspect of the part not fully appreciated by Helena Modjeska. She came to London with a well-established reputation in her home country and in America, and used *Romeo and Juliet* as one of the plays with which she sought to conquer London. Modjeska fell foul of some critics who were more concerned with the accuracy than with the spirit of her pronunciation, but a graver fault lay in her conception of her heroine. She recalls in her autobiography that:

It was my belief that in that poetic scene [III.5] Shakespeare had not intended to give an impression of sensuousness. These two children are unconscious of their passion. They meet because they love, because they want to be together, to hear each other's voices and to look in each other's eyes, and cherish and kiss or die. If they succumb to the natural law and the calling of their southern blood, it is not done with premeditation. There is no necessity, either, to remind the audience what had just happened in Juliet's room by such naturalistic details as a disarranged four-posted bed, or the turning of the key of a locked door at the nurse's entrance, or Romeo's lacing his jerkin, and a dishevelled Juliet in a *crêpe de chine* nightgown. Such details are cheap illustrations and unworthy of a true artist. Shakespeare's plays do not require such commonplace interpretations in order to produce a genuine, vivid, and refining impression upon the audience.[33]

Modjeska's failure to win over London was due in some part to her scrupulousness in refusing to give her audience quite the attractive vision it desired, and also to her self-conscious artistry which was all too transparently plain: '[Madame Modjeska's] art is evident; she is all actress; self-conscious, inconsistent, disappointing.'[54]

The same could not be said of Ellen Terry's Juliet. For her the part was held to enable the display of 'the graciousness of her presence [...] the litheness of her attitudes' (Scott, 'Romeo and Juliet', p. 235). Clement Scott continued:

in the balcony scene it would have been difficult to find a fuller expression of natural grace, a more comely figure, attitudes more picturesque, or manner more tender [...] The parting with Romeo again was instinct with charm, and consistently natural. It was not acting at all, so true was it to the nature of such a Juliet at that moment. (pp. 239, 240)

A few critics quibbled briefly about Terry's relatively mature Juliet (she was in her mid-thirties at the time), but most were prepared to be swayed by her attractions. Only Henry James held out against the popular acclaim which kept *Romeo and Juliet* running for twenty-four weeks.[55] He found Ellen Terry 'too voluminous, too deliberate, too prosaic, too English, too unversed in the utterance of poetry', too emphatically 'not Juliet'.[56]

The tenor of critical responses seem determined largely by the extent to which critics privilege the visual over the auditory or intellectual impression, the extent to which they are themselves prepared to inhabit Pygmalion's place, and to be flattered into exercising his desiring gaze. Distressed by Terry's speech, James clearly was not prepared to submit his critical faculties to be overcome by her appearance, but in the Lyceum, Terry was almost inevitably subject to theatrical judgements based on visual appreciation. In *Romeo and Juliet*, as Frederick Wedmore records, the visual effect was paramount, 'the scenery and appointments are such that they would draw the public for several months even if the Romeo and Juliet were little short of ludicrous'.[57] Irving and Terry were hardly that, but they were subject to, and perceived as constituent objects within, the stage-set: 'it would have taken not only genius, but faultless genius, to dominate over such surroundings' (Wedmore, 'Romeo and Juliet', p. 201). In *Romeo and Juliet* the actress could achieve notable success because the terms of her part of unselfconscious young lover could be made consistent with both the mechanisms of the spectacular stage, and with the Pygmalion-like activities of audience and critics. These terms of success were confirmed by Mary Anderson's 1884 Juliet. In the previous year, Oscar Wilde had written to Anderson of his desire that she should play the Duchess of Padua in his play of that name. Anderson's suitability for the role is clear when he writes that the Duchess's 'first effect is that of pure Beauty merely: she passes across the stage and says nothing'.[58] He goes on to suggest to the actress that 'the essence of art is to produce the modern idea under an antique form'. However, Anderson turned down his role, and the aspirations that it represented, preferring instead to succeed as Galatea through the less demanding medium of the visual spectacle which the stage more readily made of its appeal to the 'antique form'.

Her production of *Romeo and Juliet* (designed by Lewis Wingfield), and her mediocre performance in the leading role, seem to have provoked in critics an unprecedentedly strong realisation of the terms upon which success on the London stage was achieved, and of the implications of those terms for the theatre. On this occasion, there was a perceptible gap between responses to the spectacle, and to Anderson, who is described as 'graceful, painstaking, but ineffectual'.[59] Anderson is 'nothing if not statuesque: she looks well standing in an attitude, she looks well asleep in the Tomb Scene; she is best when posing, or reposing'; for of poetry, 'impulse and passion', and the 'essentials' of performance, she has none.[60] Most appropriately, Anderson chose to end her production with Juliet's death, and with her being carried, like a votive image, off the stage.[61] Despite its perceived shortcomings however, Anderson's production of *Romeo and Juliet* was a great popular success, on terms that even William Archer was moved to concede: '[Miss Anderson's Juliet] is so far from being a good performance, that she does not even speak her lines correctly, far less musically; yet it is so instinct with mere physical grace that we watch it without indignation, and sometimes with positive pleasure'.[62] The danger of such a response is that, as Archer noted, melodrama becomes the ruling spirit of the stage, and poetry is banished. William Terriss's Romeo, he suggests, would offer 'considerable gratification' to a deaf audience and is a 'good fighting Romeo', appropriate to melodrama if not to the 'mythic love-song in action' ('Myths of Romeo and Juliet', pp. 449, 450) that is Shakespeare's play.

The most significant aspect of the success of this production was the extent to which it challenged the boundaries between different kinds of theatre, and hinted at the elision of a distinction between legitimate theatre and the burlesque and music-hall stages. It is arguable, I think, that much of the critical disapproval of Anderson was prompted by the transparency with which she revealed the terms of the actress's popular success, and by critics' desire to forestall that revelation, which threatened to collapse theatrical boundaries, carefully maintained until now in the interests of respectable theatre and theatre-goers. *The Theatre*'s review of Anderson's Juliet describes her as

An ambitious, popular, beautiful, self-confident lady, but as far from Juliet as darkness from dawn. What is it then? A most excellent representation of Miss Mary Anderson, the favourite of the hour. She has never come out of herself. She appears as Parthenia, Pauline, Galatea, the French actress in 'Comedy and Tragedy', but she is always Miss Mary Anderson. Never once is she anyone else. The best of it is, the public does not want her to be anyone else. ('Our Omnibus-Box', p. 311)

These terms suggest that there is little difference between the purely personal success of the burlesque performer and that of the actress. Later in the same year and prompted in part by Mary Anderson's success, a *Punch* columnist wondered whether, in the interest of modest self-effacement, Miss Mary Anderson might

suppress those classic studies of the female form divine between which and those of the LOTTIES and TOTTIES of our extravaganzas and pantos we see very little distinction, except what there is in the name of the Actress. For, let it be once known far and wide that a lively woman, exhibiting in classical drapery the exquisite gifts of Nature touched up for Stage purposes by theatrical Art, is in her private life a model of all the virtues, and this will serve as an attractive advertisement to many goody-goody people who might otherwise have avoided what would have appeared to them, when forming their opinion of the piece and Actress from the photographs, to be merely the assumption of a certain character on account of the opportunity afforded by it for suggestive display. Then let it be bruited about that she has refused offers of marriage from a Lord Chancellor, a Lord Chief Justice, two or three Dukes, an Archbishop, and half-a-score or so of Lordlings, and all the best parts of the theatre will be crowded for weeks.[63]

Punch thus provides a uniquely frank appraisal of the terms upon which theatrical success is accorded, and an appraisal which notably elides the Galatea-aesthetic's emphasis on physical attractions with the burlesque stage.

In 'Our Dramatists and Their Literature' (1889) George Moore suggests that for some audiences burlesque theatre and light fiction enjoyed the same cultural status,[64] and it is to some of the popular theatrical narratives of the decade that I would now like to turn, for in that class of fiction we see evidence both of the extent of the Pygmalion–Galatea story's influence; and of the way in which narratives of the elevation of the lower classes (for instance, of the actress–protégée being carefully moulded by a theatrical manager) are made skilfully to straddle both legitimate and illegitimate theatres. This professional trajectory seems to be enabled precisely by the extent of the actresses' capacity literally to embody Galatea's virtues and desirability, and to use those attractions to effect a bridge between different kinds of theatre.

Lottie Fane, the heroine of Harriett Jay's *Through the Stage Door* (1883), is the embodiment of unusual virtue on the burlesque stage, despite the fact that she is 'not above wearing tights, and exposing her shapely limbs to the common public gaze'.[65] So modest and womanly is she that she attracts the honourable devotion of one Colonel Sedgemore. The end of the novel sees her eventually married to the Colonel, but not until she has confirmed her womanliness and worth by making the transition into the legitimate theatre by playing Shakespeare. Lottie's 'grace and lissomeness', the 'pretty tone' of her voice, and her 'naïveté and charm' (vol. I, p. 120) form the basis of her success, and in the novel's terms, signal a coterminous modesty which is not sullied by the burlesque, but which is actually fulfilled in Shakespeare. Similar trajectories are plotted in Edith Drewry's *Only An Actress* (1883), and in the actress Florence Marryat's *My Sister the Actress* (1881), in both of which novels the actresses' artistic respectability is confirmed in their renditions of Juliet. In Mrs Humphry Ward's *Miss Bretherton* (1884), whose heroine was inspired by Mary Anderson, the eponymous actress also acts Juliet, although without an initial apprenticeship spent in burlesque.

These fictional heroines are of the same physical type as Lottie Fane. Marryat writes of her character Betha Durant that she has 'bright hair [...] the colour of ripe corn at the roots [which] gleams as if the sun shone on it at the tips [...] pale cheeks [...and] dark lashes',[66] as well as delicate, thin hands. Even after she has taken to the stage she retains these moral tokens intact: 'Her soft golden hair, her pure complexion, her dewy grey eyes, the bloom upon her cheek, all betoken the glow and elasticity of sweet seventeen' (*My Sister the Actress*, vol. I, p. 238). Such descriptions would, of course, be consistent also with critics' descriptions of Terry and particularly of Mary Anderson, but devoid of an immediate referent in the stage actress's physical presence the fictional actresses can seem almost sexless presences, and certainly lack any suggestion of a conscious, adult sexuality. In their physicality, they resemble rather the statuesque women of contemporary paintings by Burne-Jones, Puvis de Chavannes, Leighton, Moore, and Watts, who share the actresses' cool, androgynous, sculptured loveliness, rather than the appeal of female maturity. The smooth purity and marble-like shades and contours of their boyish bodies appropriately deflect rather than signify the presence of active female sexuality.

In the Pygmalion-narrative and its Victorian adaptations, the statue is transformed by the force of the sculptor's desiring gaze, its pallid stillness taking on the warm colours of blushing skin, its shape relaxing into the slightly more rounded contours of conventional desirability. It is the desire and gaze of the male, the act of witnessing performance, which seems to activate and determine the sexual potential of the inanimate body, rather than the woman's own willing: the very 'blank-ness' of the canvas offered by the actress which excites desire.[67] In 'Sexual Agency in Manet's *Olympia*', Lisa Moore writes that in paintings 'the represented woman is not sexual because she herself exudes or exemplifies or enacts her own desire, but because there exist in the painting conventions, including that of a naked female body, through which (male) desire can be enacted'.[68] Theatre-fictions suggest that similar conventions shape the theatre audience's sexualisation of the actress, whether on the burlesque or on the legitimate stage.

It was, of course, a more usual critical practice for commentators to establish a mutually insulating distinction between the two different types of theatre. However, there is a tangible continuity of interest, audience, and function which links actresses of the burlesque and legitimate stages and which, as *Punch* demonstrates, is effected in part by precisely that Classical drapery which is ostensibly a primary signifier of the respectable theatre. The aesthetic function of the Classical reference on-stage overlaps substantially with the *raison d'être* of more popular theatres, where 'personal charms, very liberally displayed, are the main ingredient to success' (Aïdé, 'The Actor's Calling', p. 525); and whose actresses are described as those 'who come on the stage to show their diamonds and their fine dresses [...] creatures who court the glare of the foot-lights to enable them to display as much of their persons and as little of their costumes as certain managers will permit'.[69] It is in contemporary popular fiction, rather than in theatrical reviews and periodical articles that the potential overlap between the musical and legitimate theatres, and the fragility of the distinction between them, is articulated. It is suggested, for instance, that the audience for the burlesque was not made up simply of young swells and the lower classes, but attracted a politer audience too. As a burlesque actress, Lottie Fane's performances elicit both 'roars of hoarse laughter from the pit' and 'gentler sounds of applause from boxes and stalls' (*Through the Stage Door*, vol. 1, p. 32). Further, like that of many fictional actresses of this time, Lottie's innate virtue, marked principally by her inability to walk (she can only trip lightly and run merrily), means that she is able eventually to cross over into straight theatre, and to perform in Shakespeare. But the theatre she performs in is that in which she gained her earlier triumphs. Although Sarah Bernhardt also shared the same theatrical space as chorus girls in making her London début at the Gaiety Theatre in 1879 when that theatre, notorious in the nineties for its Gaiety Girls, was already advertising itself by means of posters including 'leg motifs' (Davis, *Actresses as Working Women*, p. 135), it was not generally the case that legitimate English and burlesque theatre shared the same space. The fictional detail thus seems particularly significant.

These common features are the grounds of a functional link between actresses of the musical and dramatic theatres with which some commentators seem ill at ease, perhaps because burlesque actresses signified much more blatantly than did their colleagues the underlying, and perhaps indelicate, terms of their work and audiences' reception of it. Dramatic actresses could be absorbed more easily into the middle-class society critics and audiences would have them bolster, and as we have seen, their theatrical success could be mediated in terms of less exceptionable feminine charms. The success of the burlesque actress flagrantly exposed the element of prescriptive sexuality in female performance – its sexualised display was its end and justification.

Its irrepressibility, and possibly also its scope for exposing the hypocrisy of Victorian audiences, led the burlesque to be adopted in fiction by two novelists and theatre-critics, and later playwrights, George Bernard Shaw and George Moore, who resisted what they saw as the theatre's pacification through its increased respectability. In Lalage Virtue and Kate Ede, Shaw and Moore respectively create attractive heroines whose sexual charms, rather than their pretension to dramatic skills, justify their occupation of the stage. Their sexuality also determines their social position, for Lalage as the mistress of the aristocratic Marmaduke Lind, and for Kate as an actress at the centre of the stage's commercial business: 'Was she not the living reality of the figures posted over the hammocks in oil-smelling cabins, the prototype of the short-skirted damsels that decorated the empty match-boxes which [sailors] preserved and gazed at under the light of the stars?'[70] Lalage plays a similar role in that, far from disrupting Marmaduke's place in the aristocracy, their relationship enables him to sow his wild oats, as his future mother-in-law puts it,[71] and facilitates his reconciliation to the insipid bride chosen for him. Shaw and Moore do not, therefore, dispute the qualities which determine the actress's stage presence, rather they are keen to ensure that that presence is not simply absorbed into the scheme of its parent society, its actual dimensions diminished within a reflectionist ethic. Both uphold the stage as ideally apart from its audience, and seek to enforce that positioning in the actresses' early, and graphically reported, deaths from drink and poverty. However, Shaw and Moore are aberrant voices in this period, whose other novelists were concerned to use and then to supersede the burlesque as part of an apologia for the actress, and a plea for her respectability.

FRENCH MASKS OR ENGLISH FACES?

There was, however, at least one highly popular actress who defied the Pygmalion-attentions of critics and audiences, choosing rather to be seen as explicitly controlling her own stage appearances through her self-conscious artistry. The French actress had perennially been associated with a trained art and, particularly since Rachel, with sexual immorality. In the 1880s, these two aspects forcibly converged in the person of Sarah Bernhardt, and were fostered by two contemporary literary events: the publication of Zola's *Nana* (1880), which was translated into English in 1884; and a new translation of Diderot's *Paradoxe sur le comédien* in 1883, with a disapprobatory foreword by Henry Irving. Bernhardt made her first appearance in London in June 1879, when she opened with *Phèdre*, in the part most closely associated with her predecessor, Rachel. Matthew Arnold's famous plea for the theatre, prompted by the visit of Sarah Bernhardt and the Théâtre Français, is written through the actress's voice: 'when I pass along the Strand and come opposite to the Gaiety Theatre, I see a fugitive vision of delicate features under a shower of hair and a cloud of lace, and hear the voice of Mdlle Sarah Bernhardt saying in its most caressing tones to the Londoners: *The theatre is irresistible; organise the theatre!*' ('The French Play', p. 243). Arnold wrote further that the Théâtre Français had shown the middle class 'the sure truth that the human spirit cannot live right if it lives by one point only, that it can and ought to live by several points at the same time', and that the theatre might succour its concomitant need 'for expansion, for intellect and knowledge, for beauty' (p. 240). Bernhardt's own attractions played an integral part in Arnold's theatrical desire, as they did for English audiences throughout the 1880s.[72]

Alongside the exhibition of her acting, Bernhardt mounted a show of her paintings and sculptures during her stay in England. Its launch party was a major social event, and attracted such figures as Gladstone, with whom she discussed the morality of *Phèdre*, and Leighton, both of whom were seen to have extended conversations with the actress. The *Art Journal* wrote warmly of the collection of art-works, describing them as worthy of 'respectful attention' even had their author been other than who she was.[73] The *Journal* added further that it would never have dreamt of ascribing the works to a female hand had their origin been unknown. Bernhardt's own account of her lucrative sculpting career, which included a commission for the Casino at Monte Carlo, makes of her sculpture a clear alternative to her life on stage. She writes of the period immediately preceding her visit to London, that sculpture would have provided a very adequate means of earning a living and that, 'Discouraged and disgusted with the theatre, my passion for sculpture increased.'[74] It would seem that Bernhardt envisaged the two careers as distinct but complementary, that each provided a repository for a similar kind of artistic energy. For Bernhardt, the stage could be a venue for the kind of self-sculpting activity which was largely denied to her American and English contemporaries.

It was perhaps a growing awareness of the actress's desire for autonomy which meant that, as the next decade progressed, and especially after Bernhardt left the Français in 1880, a new, more critical appreciation of her developed alongside her evident popularity, for she came to be seen as threatening precisely that relationship between theatre and its middle-class audience which, according to Arnold, she had helped to initiate. The complacency of this relationship was imperilled particularly by her 1884 Lady Macbeth, who threatened to rob her lord of the initiatory power within the play. Rather than confirming her as a Galatea, the dynamics of Bernhardt's performance meant that the 'pleated white garment which clung mysteriously to [her] figure' in this part, rendered her rather a Delilah or a siren.[75]

Another French import of that year was Zola's novel *Nana*, translated and published in England by Henry Vizetelly. Zola's courtesan initially advertises herself through the theatre, where she ironically appears as the 'Blonde Venus', in a rendition which restores the sensuality to a character purified by Faucit. Nana's qualifications for the part are exclusively the physical ones of the courtesan. She herself laughingly acknowledges this on stage as her lack of a singing voice becomes clear. But as the theatre-manager Bordenave realises, talent is immaterial in a theatre which he angrily insists should rather be called a brothel. However, it is not the sexuality of the actress which is most at odds with English theatre of the 1880s. Rather, Zola's most shocking innovation is to introduce the sexual self-consciousness which is Nana's greatest weapon. The scene of her undressing before her mirror, watched by her most abject lover, Comte Muffat, and by her own eyes, effectively realises Nana's consciousness of her sexual power through her own spectating.[76] This moment in the novel was inspired by Manet's *Nana* (1877; plate 12). The painting was prompted by the appearance of the adolescent Nana in the final stages of *L'Assommoir* (1877), and then incorporated into Zola's fiction in his later work. Nana's stare in the painting is, like that of the earlier *Olympia*, directed out of the painting, challenging the viewer both to acknowledge complicity in Nana's self-knowledge and the mechanisms of her power, and to avoid identification with the male admirer in the painting who is oblivious to Nana's self-conscious revelling in her influence. In Zola's text the reader is in some measure forced to risk this identification, reading through the eyes of Comte Muffat, as the actress fulfils the knowledge and self-possession revealed by Manet in embracing herself before her mirror, delighting in the vehicle of her power. Muffat is disturbed and exasperated by this 'solitary self-indulgence',[77] but rather than alienating him, the sight acts to confirm further his subservience by his inability to escape. Nana's self-awareness and self-conscious manipulation of her audience are at the heart of her danger, and are most profoundly opposed to the unselfconsciousness that is Galatea's primary characteristic and function.

In the early 1880s the material distinction between self-aware and unselfconscious representations of an actress's sexuality was played out on the London stage in the diversity of responses to Bernhardt. In 1881, she gave the London première of what would become a stock play in her repertoire, Dumas *fils*'s *La Dame aux camélias* (first performed in 1852), the story of a courtesan's self-sacrificing love for a young man. For many members of her audience, Bernhardt simply became Marguerite Gautier, her success achieved through the coincidence of the demands of Bernhardt's part and the bent of what were perceived by some as her

Plate 12   Edouard Manet, *Nana* (1877)

'natural' talents: 'The abandoned behaviour which had always been the
dominant trait of Bernhardt's love-stricken heroines, but which had
sometimes seemed exaggerated, was completely suited to the role of
Marguerite' (Aston, *Sarah Bernhardt*, p. 50).[78] However, for those members of her audience who discerned in Bernhardt's style evidence of the

more rigorously trained, and hence necessarily palpably self-aware, school of French acting, her performances were not so readily acclaimed. In his 1886 article on Sarah Bernhardt, 'A Well-Graced Actress', William Archer writes of how theatrical training may supplement an actress's 'natural' gifts, and crucially enable her to confound the inherent moral prejudices of an English audience. Archer suggests that despite the narrow range of her parts and the pecuniary necessity which prompted her 'excessive professional toils' and exhausting tours, Bernhardt managed to retain, 'All the essentials of her talent [...] well-nigh unimpaired'; and still to be arguably 'the foremost figure on the contemporary stage'.[79] He suggests that the competence of her art outweighs her narrow limits and renders her 'vehemently sensational parts' ('A Well-Graced Actress', p. 772) palatable to an English audience: 'so perfect are her methods, so exquisitely does she move and speak, so various and beautiful are her gestures, her poses, her intonations, that we see her with never-failing pleasure and pay her willing allegiance as to the queen of the modern stage' (p. 775). Some might have doubted her right to such a title, claiming it rather for Ellen Terry, but none would have denied Bernhardt's astonishing success in popularising the sensational heroines of Sardou and Dumas *fils* in England. Bernhardt might indeed seem, in the words of Henry James, 'a sort of fantastically impertinent *victrix* poised upon a perfect pyramid of ruins – the ruins of a hundred British prejudices and proprieties'.[80]

The nature of the actress's moral disruptiveness, and the extent to which it could be put down to the training which set Bernhardt apart from English actresses' more easily assimilable constructions of 'naturalness' on stage, is explored in Mrs Ward's *Miss Bretherton*. This novel, by Matthew Arnold's niece, sets up a comparison between French and English stage-traditions which emphatically establishes the latter as an agent of moral stability through being a vehicle for the publicising of unselfconscious female loveliness. The French tradition is enmeshed rather in invidious notions of the actor's lack of sensibility (an idea inspired by Diderot), and produces 'thin, French, snake-like creatures who have nothing but their *art* [...] nothing but what they have been carefully taught, nothing but what they have laboriously learnt with time and trouble, to depend upon'.[81] The serpentine Bernhardt is the most obvious target of this attack. *Miss Bretherton* was the author's first work of fiction and is the story of the exceptionally beautiful, but dramatically crude, Isabel Bretherton, her theatrical education and subsequent success, and her love for the critic Eustace Kendal, whose influence, we are led to believe, will probably result in her leaving the stage. In a letter to Mrs Ward, Henry James accuses the author of sacrificing Isabel Bretherton's artistry to the interest of her relationship with the reclusive Kendal. This sacrifice, however, was precisely what audiences and critics other than James demanded of the theatre:

You have endeavoured to make us feel [Isabel's] 'respectability' at the same time as her talent, her artistic nature, but in taking care to preserve the former, you have rather sacrificed the latter. Then granting that she cared to marry Kendal, you overlook too much, I think (but this I said to you), the problem of a union between two such opposed lives, and how her blaze etc., with all its vulgarities, would appear to him, keep him off. Also how the concessions she would have to make to his tone and his *type* would alarm her, hungry for more fame and success. I should have made her pass away from him – with hopes (on his part perhaps) of catching up with her later. I think your end has a little too much of the conventional love-story: though granted your view it is very pretty indeed.[82]

Ward's portrait of Bretherton was inspired by Mary Anderson, the climax over the debate of whose success, of course, occurred in 1884, the year of *Miss Bretherton*'s publication and Anderson's Lyceum Juliet. Along with Henry James, the Wards had entertained Mary Anderson at their home in January 1884. Charmed by her, they accepted an invitation to see her act in W. S. Gilbert's *Comedy and Tragedy*. The party was disappointed with what they saw, finding that Anderson over-played her part, and lacked dignity, self-control, and self-expression.[83] A few days later, however, Mrs Ward told her sister-in-law that the experience had given her the idea for a novel, which was hurriedly written during August and September of that year, and published at the end of November. Mrs Ward subsequently denied that her novel had anything to do with Anderson, perhaps, as John Sutherland suggests, out of pique at reviewers' concentrating on this aspect of her novel (*Mrs Humphry Ward*, p. 104). At least half of *The Academy*'s review of the novel is taken up with a consideration of how far Miss Bretherton resembles Mary Anderson, although the reviewer goes on to suggest that this matter is of little consequence. He stresses above all that they are alike physically: 'Isabel Bretherton is of a tall and graceful presence, with Greek lineaments.'[84]

The novel opens at a Royal Academy private viewing, a setting also used by Edith Drewry and Shaw, and one which confirms the extent to which the actress may be a visual art-object, a modest and unselfconscious social icon. The impact of Bretherton's grace and charm at the gallery exactly replicates the terms of her, and Anderson's, theatrical success. As the American playwright Edward Wallace predicts:

Oh, she's not much of an actress; she has no training, no *finesse*. But you'll see, she'll be the great success of the season. She has wonderful grace on the stage, and a fine voice in spite of tricks [...] she is such a frank, unspoilt, good-hearted creature. Her audience falls in love with her, and that goes a long way. (*Miss Bretherton*, p. 10)

However, Ward's disillusionment when she saw Anderson gives a new degree of scepticism to the familiar fiction of the actress who easily and gracefully wins the hearts of her audience. In the person of the fastidious critic, Eustace Kendal, Ward shows how Bretherton's lack of subtlety and her muted artistic sense destroy the 'sympathetic relation between him and the actress which the first scene [a dance and dumb-show] had produced' (p. 50). Once she speaks, her spell is 'irrevocably broken, and [Kendal] seemed to himself to have passed from a state of sensitiveness to all that was exquisite and rare in her to a state of mere irritable consciousness of her defects' (p. 50), thus provoking reminiscences of the difficulties Mrs Jameson described as attendant upon Hermione's incarnation.

That Miss Bretherton's defects prosper on the London stage is a measure of the crudity of the English theatre, which Kendal explicitly opposes, showing Ward's debts to James and her uncle, with his sense that 'The French would no more tolerate such acting as this because of the beauty of the actress than they would judge a picture by its frame' (p. 52). Thus Ward initiates her own sense of the opposition between the well-trained, stylised French school of acting, and the less technically rigorous English tradition which relied heavily for effect and technique on the visual and moral continuum between stage and society. But the ensuing novel attempts to legitimise English audiences' instinctive theatrical preferences by showing how their judgements are borne out even when Miss Bretherton has received and benefited from a properly conceived theatrical education. That is, Ward seeks to demonstrate that the actress's inherent taste and modesty remain the factors which determine her popularity.

Like James, Archer, and Matthew Arnold, Mrs Ward seems to have realised that the legitimate English theatre, in all its aspects, needed better to organise itself in order to compete with the visiting French companies, to satisfy the increasingly fastidious and educated tastes of a regular theatre-going clientele, and thus more competently to advertise female English modesty. Miss Bretherton accordingly undergoes an informal training from Kendal's French brother-in-law who, like James's Peter Sherringham in *The Tragic Muse* (1890), is a diplomat and well-informed aficionado of the Théâtre Français. But her training simply enables her the better to convey the 'natural' attractions of the pure, graceful woman first perceived by Kendal. It does not disrupt the relationship between the personal and social aspect of the woman and the type of her attraction as an actress. Amidst all the changes occasioned by her tremendous success, 'One thing was unchanged – the sweetness and spontaneity of [her] rich womanly nature' (p. 245). It is this sustained womanliness which is the mark of her success, and which is confirmed by the willingness with which she welcomes being 'moulded' in her training, being newly created by the shaping consciousness of her French master.

In making a distinction between the art of the French actress and the apparently artless charm of Miss Bretherton, Ward was not only commenting on Bernhardt's success, but was also participating in the controversy prompted by Walter Herries Pollock's translation of Denis Diderot's eighteenth-century manuscript *Paradoxe sur le comédien*, published as *The Paradox of Acting*. At the heart of the dialogue which makes up the *Paradox* is the issue of sensibility, and specifically whether the work of the actor ought to be the result rather of careful observation and mimicry, or of the actor's personal experience of the emotions to be acted. Diderot writes thus of the actor, 'He must have in himself an unmoved and disinterested onlooker. He must have, consequently, penetration and no sensibility; the art of mimicking everything, or, which comes to the same thing, the same aptitude for every sort of character and part.'[85] Mrs Ward has Isabel Bretherton demur from this description of the actor's art ('Diderot is wrong, wrong, wrong!' (p. 202)), as she believes rather that to feel is the secret of success: 'When I could once reach the feeling of the Tybalt speech, when I could once hate him for killing Tybalt in the same breath in which I loved him for being Romeo, all was easy; gesture and movement came to me' (pp. 202–3). Thus the quality of her art was rather determined by her womanly sensibility and sympathy, which her training the better brings out, than by the cold calculations which, it is implied, lie at the heart of Diderot's soulless French performer, and which in Ward's text are embodied in the character of the novel's French actress, Mme Desforêts. It is Miss Bretherton herself who raises objections to this actress, on specifically moral grounds. She objects to the capacity which training gives Mme

Desforêts to override moral criteria by means of her talent. She declares, 'It makes my blood boil to hear the way people – especially men – talk about Mme Desforêts; there is not one of you who would let your wife or your sister shake hands with her, and yet how you rave about her, how you talk as if there were nothing in the world but genius – and French genius!' (pp. 89–90).

The case manufactured against Diderot in this novel, and echoed in Henry Irving's preface to the *Paradox*, was in fact a travesty of his position, and fails to take account of the contradictions in a manuscript left unrevised and unpublished at Diderot's death in 1784. Rather the *Paradox* is reconstructed in a form in which it can participate in 1880s debates on theatrical transformation and the morality of the stage. Far from suggesting that the actor is an immoral rogue whose performances are supremely self-conscious and deceitful representations of emotion, Diderot implies that off-stage the actor must be sufficiently sensitive either to his own or to others' emotions to garner material for his impersonations. However, he suggests that when acting the emotional propensity has to be brought under control, for it is when the extreme of sensibility has passed that 'memory and imagination unite' (*Paradox*, p. 44) and creativity takes place. If one can derive a consistent position from the *Paradox* it seems to be that sensibility has no place on the stage, where it can disrupt the measured representation of emotion, but that the actor or actress must at least be sensitive enough to appreciate sensibility in others off-stage.[86]

This is a reading not dissimilar to that of Diderot's self-appointed nineteenth-century opponents. But they saw their opposition as necessary in order to counteract the implication in Diderot that the best actor might be a calculating creature whose theatrical standing relied on a lack of common humanity. This was an implication particularly unbecoming to the actress and one which had to be refuted if she was to remain desirable in, and subject to, the audience's gaze. Further, if Diderot's contention is allowed to stand, it makes of the actress one capable of manipulating her audiences, controlling rather than being subject to their desire, and hence wresting the power of dramatic determination from them and the playwright. Such a possibility was strongly resisted.

Henry Irving's preface to Pollock's translation made of sensibility an explicitly moral attribute, and defended the actor's right to it. He suggests that the French philosopher's account of sensibility on the stage was only appropriate to a stage lacking in prestige, whose actors were by

definition rogues. Irving draws for evidence on this extract from the
Paradox:

I find [actors] polished, caustic, and cold; proud, light of behaviour, spend-
thrifts, self-interested; struck rather by our absurdities than touched by our
misfortunes; masters of themselves at the spectacle of an untoward incident or
the recital of a pathetic story; isolated, vagabonds, at the command of the great;
little conduct, no friends, scarce any of those holy and tender ties which
associate us in the pains and pleasures of another, who in turn shares our own.
(p. 63)

We should note, as Irving fails to, the hyperbolic and humorous vein
which Diderot falls into here, and which is not typical of the whole; and
that the dialogue form enables a degree of playful exaggeration. Also,
shortly before the last quotation, Diderot gives an account of the actor's
profession which qualifies implications of disrepute, although not in
such a way as to placate Irving, for this statement too reinforces the
actor's standing outside common social attitudes and experience.
Diderot writes:

I have no thought of calumniating a profession I like and esteem – I mean, the
actor's. I should be in despair if a misunderstanding of my observations cast a
shade of contempt on men of a rare talent and a true usefulness, on the scourges
of absurdity and vice, on the most eloquent preachers of honesty and virtue, on
the rod which the man of genius wields to chastise knaves and fools. (p. 62)

For Diderot, as for Shaw and Moore, it was part of the condition of the
actor and actress that they remain outside society's sway in order the
better to represent, entertain, and enlighten it.

Irving, however, could not accept a position which advocated that the
actor worked from without his or her society, and thus cites instances of
actors whose performances owe something to their emotional and social
circumstances. But here Irving unwittingly demonstrates how closely he
is in agreement with Diderot by writing that it is quite possible for the
actor,

to feel all the excitement of the situation and yet be perfectly self-possessed. This
is art which the actor who loses his head has not mastered. It is necessary to this
art that the mind should have, as it were, a double consciousness, in which all
the emotions proper to the occasion may have full sway, while the actor is all
the time on the alert for every detail of his method. (*Paradox*, pp. xv–xvi)

In fact this concurs remarkably closely with parts of the *Paradox*, with
Diderot's contention that 'The man of sensibility obeys the impulse of

Nature, and gives nothing more or less than the cry of his very heart; the moment he moderates or strengthens this cry he is no longer himself, he is an actor' (p. 46). But clearly the imputation of vagabondage, and the practice of deceit, no matter how playfully implicit, had to be countered by the leading exponent of the respectable stage.

Irving's lead was followed by the actors and actresses who responded to William Archer's questionnaire survey on responses to Diderot, a survey which he reports came to be known as 'the "Actor's Catechism"'.[87] Mr and Mrs Kendal, reports Archer, 'are strongly of the opinion that the emotional effect they produce upon their audience varies in accordance with the greater or lesser emotional effect experienced by them in their own persons' (p. 276). Their response elides categories of personal and professional, making the potential quality of their acting concomitant with their personal sensibility. In the case of the actress the witness to sensibility was even more necessary, although it had crucially to be tempered by a degree of self-control which itself seemed a force of delicacy and modesty on stage, as Mary Anderson's testimony to Archer confirms.

The re-circulation of Diderot then only serves to confirm the practitioners of English theatre in their elision of stage and society at this time, an elision which, for the actress, confirmed the appropriateness of the statue's revealing elegance, coupled with Galatea's desirability and malleability. In *Miss Bretherton*, Isabel fulfils the function of being a lovely woman and exciting a healthy desire in the reclusive critic, and the organicism of the relationship between theatre and society is cemented by the most likely end of the heroine's leaving the stage to marry one of her audience. This is, of course, precisely what James objects to in Mrs Ward's novel, and what he resists in his own *The Tragic Muse*, where his actress-heroine's Juliet confirms that her talent is an element which will keep her on the theatrical stage, rather than one which enables her removal to the domestic sphere. Thus, as we will see, Miriam Rooth comes to invite the epithet of Gorgon, rather than Galatea, one threatening to subvert rather than to submit to an admiring gaze.

'BE DAMNED CHARMING'

James's novel signals a shift in perceptions of the actress in the late-1880s, and in her relationship to the Galatea-model, but perhaps even more significant in opening up a range of new creative possibilities both for actress and audience was Ellen Terry's 1888 performance of Lady

Macbeth. The part is a far cry from the remit of her earlier roles, and is now best remembered through John Singer Sargent's full-length portrait of the actress as Lady Macbeth (1888). This image, and the performance it commemorated, are significant in signalling a shift away from the mutually dependent malleability and desirability hitherto so fully expressed in Terry's appearance and appearances. For the black-and-white studio photographs of Terry was substituted the violence of the lurid, Pre-Raphaelite colours of Terry's shimmering, beetle-strewn green robe, and her flaming knee-length red hair. Terry herself wrote of the portrait: 'The whole thing is Rossetti – rich stained-glass effects' (*Story of My Life*, p. 307). Thus, Terry is linked rather to the temptresses and wanton women of the Pre-Raphaelites than the self-sacrificing heroines of Classical tragedy. In the painting Terry is poised at the moment (unacted upon the stage) when Lady Macbeth raises a crown above her own head, and suggests, as Terry writes, 'all that I should have liked to be able to convey in my acting as Lady Macbeth' (p. 306). The figure, towering in the stillness of its almost sculptural presence, instantaneously re-writes the significatory possibilities of Terry's body. Ironically once again partially defined by its costume (designed by Mrs Comyns Carr), her body is, however, no longer immediately available and amenable to the designs and desires of her audience, and necessarily undermines the assumptions of the given-ness and naturalness of the interpretative 'certainties' previously associated with the desirable female body on stage. This same body is now the vehicle of dissimulation and treachery, the means by which Terry sought to convey her belief that Lady Macbeth was no fiend, but really loved her husband, thus confusing irrefutably the moralities that the actress had seemed to confirm.

The most frequently used adjective for Terry throughout her career so far had been 'charming'. It was clearly felt by the protective Edy Craig and Christopher St John, Terry's daughter and the latter's female partner, to be a belittling expression, for they praise Winston Churchill's speech at Terry's Jubilee in 1906 expressly for not employing the term. It is, however, I think, possible to read Terry's Lady Macbeth as recuperating a less accommodating sense of the term. In this part she could be, in her own ambivalent term, 'damned Charming', bewitching, captivating, and self-conscious. In a marginal note in Terry's copy of *Macbeth*, she gives herself instructions to 'Play with his hands and *charm* him.'[88] The actress's annotations reveal not only the considerable imaginative intuition Terry brought to the part, but also the extent of her stage-craft and professionalism, none of which was usually credited by her re-viewers. Appropriately, Terry was later to record with some delight of this production of *Macbeth*, that 'the critics differ, and discuss it hotly, which in itself is my best success of all' (*Story of My Life*, p. 306).

Terry's appearance as Lady Macbeth signalled the commencement of a process of development and mutation in her own career which was echoed in the theatre as a whole with the advent of Ibsen on the English stage. As we will see, Ibsen's plays and the work of a new generation of actresses in them effectively re-wrote Galatea's position in the English theatre. But this development did not happen in isolation, and it is important to note the complementary changes which came about in the popular Terry's more visible role and activities, and in the new kind of inspiration she was providing for her contemporaries.

CHAPTER 5

Living statues and the literary drama

The 1890s witnessed the proliferation of the Classical female figure in an increasing variety of social and cultural locations. The banner heading of *The Daily Graphic* featured a female artist, dressed in a *chyton* delicately slipped from one shoulder, and a similarly draped female scribe, joined together by an arc of cupids. Its daily weather reports were accompanied by illustrations of a Classical maiden, whose pose altered with the weather, but whose dress, as *Punch* noted in 1894 in its 'Verses to the Weather Maiden', remained a constant delight to her 'thousand fond admirers':

> Your classical costume a true delight is
> To all who study you from day to day,
> And even if it hastens on bronchitis
> It serves your graceful figure to display.[1]

Earlier in the same year, *The Sketch* had published an 'Interview with Famous Statues'. The statues interviewed are the Duke of York, descended from his column, and Victory, who amuses herself by playing hoop-la with her laurel wreaths and her attendant soldiers' bayonets. She later performs a skirt-dance before waltzing with the Duke of York.[2] In 1890, H. Rider Haggard and Andrew Lang published *The World's Desire*, a novel based, according to their Preface, on new discoveries about the connections between 'the Greece of the Achaeans, and the Egypt of the Ramessids' made by Schliemann and Flinders Petrie.[3] The novel is a misogynist fantasy based around the hypothesis that Odysseus' last voyage was into Egypt, where he went in search of the immortal Helen. He was thwarted in this end by Egypt's Queen, Meriamun, who conceived a passion for Odysseus herself, and whose evil sorcery prevents a union between the Wanderer and Helen. The novel is illustrated by Maurice Greiffenhagen RA, a frequent collaborator of Haggard's, who painted in the late Pre-Raphaelite style. In this work images of the classically draped Helen of Troy, the eponymous 'world's desire', abound, a number of which bear a resemblance to Ellen Terry. The theatrical connection is cemented by the illustrations of Meriamun, who resembles Sarah Bernhardt. Arthur Symons's reminiscence of the French actress describes just as aptly Haggard and Lang's villainess:

She had the evil eyes of a Thessalian witch; she could enchant with her slow, subtle and cruel spells men's souls out of their bodies. There was in this tall and thin actress such fire and passion as I have rarely seen in any woman; together with her luxuriousness, languor, indifference, haughtiness and hate. She seemed to me the Incarnation of the Orient.[4]

In comparison, the Greek Helen incorporates a form of peculiarly English beauty, by which the snares of the foreign temptress may be challenged.

The 1890s also saw the final works of Sir Frederic Leighton, arguably the greatest of the Victorian Classical painters. Before his death in January 1896 Leighton completed paintings of *The Return of Persephone* (1890–1), *Perseus and Andromeda* (1891), *The Garden of the Hesperides* (1892), and a classically draped *Flaming June* (1895). He also struggled, as had Watts before him, with the story of Clytie in an energetic canvas which was left unfinished at his death. It is an image of extraordinary and unwonted vigour which shows Clytie (the model for whom was the young actress Dorothy Dene) kneeling with breast uplifted, arms outstretched, and head thrown back as the sun-god passes by overhead. The *Athenaeum* wrote enthusiastically of this last and uncharacteristically passionate manifestation of Leighton's Classicism that,

The greatness of his conception of an ambitious subject is manifest in every element of the design – in the way in which the light shoots upwards to the zenith, to meet there the deep greenish-grey and dun colours of the firmament, defining sharply as it does so the crest of the hill; in the grandeur of the stupendous clouds which drift slowly past the suppliant; and in the raptures of her face and attitude.[5]

In Dene, Leighton had found his own Galatea, a young actress from a working-class background, who in the Academician's canvasses became the heroines of Classical literature, and added a new dramatic interest to the painter's last works. Following Leighton's death in 1896, Dene seems appropriately to have disappeared from the public arena.

On the stage too, the Classical spectacle persisted. Harry Pleon's *A Vision of Venus* was first performed in 1893. It was based on Frederick

Anstey's *The Tinted Venus* (1885), a novel concerning the fortunes of a massive statue of Venus mistakenly brought to life by the hairdresser Leander Tweddle who, following the practice of John Gibson, has to employ his professional skills in colouring the statue so that her marble status goes undetected. The play's humour is based on what a writer in the *Saturday Review* had earlier described as 'the incongruities between modern and mythological habits and ways of thought [which] suggest ready scope for humour and satire'.[6] In the play, the hairdresser, who has become Alphonzo Latherem, bemusedly protests to his goddess, whose costume is described as 'something after the mythological style', 'I'm a respectable hairdresser; and what would people say if they saw me talking to a goddess with only her nightdress on?'[7]

In his review of Sardou's *Fedora*, Shaw lampoons Mrs Campbell's white-washing her arms, a practice which seems designed to heighten the likeness between actress and statue. Mrs Campbell apparently ruined Beerbohm Tree's costume by leaving stripes of white all over his back and trousers. Shaw goes on, 'May I suggest that soap and water is an excellent cosmetic for the arms, and that it does not mark coats? Also that this white-washing malpractice has become an intolerable absurdity.'[8] Alma-Tadema maintained his interest in the stage when he designed the Lyceum *Cymbeline* in 1896, and Beerbohm Tree's *Julius Caesar* in 1898. Gilbert's *Pygmalion and Galatea* was still being played, as is evidenced by an amateur performance at Chelsea Town Hall in April 1894;[9] and, as David Mayer's work has shown, the 'Toga-Play' was a popular theatrical sub-genre at this time, one of the most popular examples of which was Wilson Barrett's early-Christian drama *The Sign of the Cross* (1895).[10]

However, alongside the persistence of the Classical reference, new elements in the theatre and in society in the 1890s were disturbing the terms of theatrical Classicism's success in the previous decade, and, as an inevitable consequence, the signifying capacities of the figure of Galatea. A new self-consciousness about the mechanics of display is perceptible in responses to the classically draped woman. As we have already seen, *Punch's* 'Verses to the Weather Maiden' are unprecedentedly explicit about the function of diaphanous drapery, as are these lines from Gilbert and Sullivan's *The Grand Duke* (1896), a parody of late-Victorian Classicism:

> Mrs Grundy, p'r'aps, may have a word or two to say...
> They wore little underclothing – scarcely anything – or no-thing –

And their dress of Coan silk was quite transparent in design –
Well, in fact, in summer weather, something like 'the altogether'
And it's there, I rather fancy, I shall have to draw the line.[11]

Such self-awareness was facilitated, indeed necessitated, in large part by
what were arguably the most successful theatrical 'statues' of the decade,
the 'Living Sculptures' and 'Living Pictures' which were a highly popular and lucrative feature of the music-hall stage in the early 1890s.

THE LIVING PICTURES

This entertainment provided a spectacle unmarred by the intrusions of
language, and was particularly associated with the Palace Theatre of
Varieties in Shaftesbury Avenue, where it performed the function of
saving the ailing theatre. When the 'Living Pictures' were on display,

Crammed full houses were as much the order of the day at present as empty
benches were of the past. There could be no doubt that in Mr Charles Morton
[the theatre] had a manager who not only gave his personal supervision to all
matters connected with the theatre, but devoted his long experience to every
detail in every department.[12]

The primary result of this long experience was the 'Living Pictures',
carefully staged replicas of well-known paintings and sculptures, which
at their best were held to be able to 'serve more or less those good
purposes which pictorial art is fondly hoped to serve – to refine, to
delight purely, to elevate, and perhaps to teach'.[13] They were described
by the popular London preacher the Reverend H. C. Shuttleworth as
'undeniably exceedingly pretty, and the very great skill and cleverness
with which they are managed is, beyond doubt, an element in their
success' ('The Living Pictures', p. 466). According to its manager,
George Edwardes, the Empire even employed its own sculptor, Mr
Lanterré, to '[superintend] the draping and grouping of the tableaux, so
that a really artistic effect may be attained' (p. 461).

However, alongside such unobjectionable attractions were also displayed more problematic, and more financially lucrative, images. These
were the living pictures which, drawing on the conventions and sometimes even the material of sculpture, 'impersonated the nude'. On the
night when Bernard Shaw went to the Palace, there were sixteen 'Living
Pictures': 'Half a dozen represented naiads, mountain sprites, peris and
Lady Godiva, all practically undraped, and all, except perhaps Lady

Godiva [...] very pretty'.[14] When Frederick Atkins witnessed the 'Living Pictures', it was precisely these images which excited most attention:

At first I was simply delighted. The pictures were surprisingly beautiful, but several enfeebled profligates and bald-headed roués who sat around me were loudly and angrily expressing their disappointment. 'Is that all!' they exclaimed in impatience and despair. Then there was a change. Up went the opera-glasses. The gallery was significantly silent – for somehow indecency has but little attraction for the sons of toil. But the stalls were in raptures. English men in raptures over an exhibition of girls standing in the glare of the electric light with nothing but thin flesh-coloured tights from head to foot. (p. 469)

The question of how the appearance of nudity was achieved occupied a number of critics. Atkins and Shaw believed the women wore body-stockings, while Shuttleworth suggested that 'what looks like flesh is in reality wax; the human figure being encased in a species of framework, excepting the head' (p. 467). In fact as Charles Morton informed readers, the young women were 'wearing little more than fleshings, with, in some cases, plaster moulds over the breasts' (p. 462). The living actress was then physically, rather than simply metaphorically, being immured within a sculptural mould.

There is, of course, something highly paradoxical about this practice: as Arthur Symons notes, 'A picture, for the most part, is an imitation of life, and a living picture is life imitating an imitation of itself, which seems a little roundabout' (p. 464). More pertinently, perhaps, the 'Living Pictures' were staging the conventions of staging which had determined women's presence in the legitimate theatre, and through that act of imitation were revealing the grounds upon which those conventions were based. Nineteenth-century images of Galatea in poetry and paintings, along with their Classical inspiration, are almost invariably naked. The 'Living Pictures' brazenly confronted audiences with this now undeniable fact, if not with actually naked bodies. Just as tableaux vivants are translated into 'living pictures', so the enabling veneer of Classicism in a theatrical reference is crudely translated into the direct appeal of the suggestion of the nude female body. The draperies which implicitly facilitated the accentuation and revelation of the body beneath are largely dispensed with, and the underlying implications of the sculptural metaphor are brought forth. The nakedness of the female body is revealed as that which is at stake at the heart of the theatrical spectacle of the actress. Through the essentially parodic mechanism of this music-hall act, the desire which maintains the theatrical gaze is bluntly conjoined with a frankly sexual desire. For Hawthorne's 'chaste permission' is substituted a bald confrontation with the suggestion of nakedness.

The immediate effect of this music-hall spectacle was to lead theatre critics to insist on an absolute distinction between the legitimate theatre and the music-hall stage in order to minimise the possibility of confusion between these two 'places of public entertainment'. In 1894, the 'Living Pictures' and an objection made that year to the renewal of the licence for the Empire theatre on the grounds that its promenade (an open space at the back of the auditorium) was a place of business for prostitutes,[15] both served to elide the differences between theatres and music-halls. In evidence offered against the promenade, 'theatre' is used as a synonym for 'music-hall' as *The Theatre* angrily noted.[16] The chief ground upon which the two forms of entertainment might be confused at this period was their common reliance upon spectacle: during the County Council hearings John Burns MP refers to an Irving stage-set as 'one of his "living pictures"',[17] within which Ellen Terry was, of course, an important component. The Empire relied upon the notorious women on view in its promenade, just as Irving had long relied upon Terry's charms as an irresistible part of the Lyceum experience.

However, in its attempts to distinguish between the theatre and the music-hall, *The Theatre* is led to articulate an alternative form of theatrical aesthetic, one which was, as we will see, the fruit of the new plays and staging conventions of the early years of the decade, and which had significant implications for the ways in which dramatic actresses could be 'viewed'. In an argument which echoes and reinscribes the terms of George Eliot's distinction between gambling and the imperatives and responsibilities of narrative, *The Theatre* writes, 'At the music hall the play is emphatically not the thing', and continues,

Amusement there is in plenty – song, dance, juggling, feats of strength – All of them capital diversions, but no more allied to the drama than to literature or science. The whole essence of the case for the Empire promenade was that here was a place where you could spend half-an-hour without the trouble of booking a seat – a place to which many people resorted simply because the entertainment demanded no sustained attention, and permitted them to come and go at pleasure. The drama cannot be trifled with in this agreeable way [...It is] an art which is not congenial to the atmosphere of tobacco and the popping of corks. You may find them a solace between the acts, but when the curtain is up you have to concentrate your brain tissue on the intention of the author, the progress of the story, the delicate interpretation of character by the players.

You are, in any intellectual and aesthetic sense, as far removed from the music hall as if it and you were in different planets.[18]

The crucial difference here rests in the nature of the play, and its implications as a literary form. It has an author whose intentions demand concentration, a story whose plot needs close attention, and a cast who delicately interpret character. Attention is shifted away from the isolated spectacle which forestalls narrative, and which *The Theatre* tries to re-write as the sole prerogative of the music-hall. Along with that shift necessarily comes a re-thinking of the actress's role, which was formerly largely if not primarily decorative, and is now ideally interpretative, concerned explicitly with the form of language.

These modifications in the theatrical aesthetic are perceptible in critical responses to Robert Buchanan and Henry Murray's play *A Society Butterfly* (1894), which starred Lillie Langtry. Both as a society figure and as an actress, Langtry had been celebrated for her approximation to the Attic ideal. However, even her powers of attraction were being undermined in the new theatrical context of the 1890s. The tired formulae of *A Society Butterfly* are signalled early in William Archer's review by his comment that the play 'somehow suggested a revue in which all the plays, not only of the season, but of the age, were stirred up together in a monster medley'.[19] *The Theatre* gives a fuller account of the play and of Mrs Langtry's role in it, doing so in such a way as to reveal the profound inconsistency at the heart of the actress's self-display in the 1880s, and of the terms upon which success during that decade had been won; and to demonstrate the new conditions and expectations which shaped her role in the theatre of the 1890s. Mrs Langtry's character, Mrs Dudley, is a 'simple heroine [...] outraged by her silly husband's preference of a creature innocent of beauty or art, wholly ignorant of wile and charm'.[20] Mrs Dudley's response to this slight troubles *The Theatre*'s reviewer: 'She flings away her self-respect, casts her modesty to the winds, and in cold blood, for the cheap applause of a parcel of blasé new-sensation hunters, plays *Lady Godiva* in a London drawing-room' ('A Society Butterfly', p. 333). The review is torn between recognition of the impropriety and inconsistency of this act in one who would 'still preserve her genuine claim to womanhood', and the fact that, as is frankly expressed, 'Mrs Langtry as *Lady Godiva* in a tableau was a happy thought. There are the makings of a "boom" in the idea.' This is not a distinction that could have been made in the 1880s, when self-display and modesty were sufficiently conjoined under the authority of the theatrical audience's gaze, and ultimately within the conventions of display deriving from Galatea. This reviewer is rather uneasily aware of the mechanics of the compromises involved in facilitating that display, and that degree of self-consciousness has proved fatal to the sustaining of the convention. The tableau itself seems to have been a faltering spectacle in a play, 'in which', as Archer notes, 'everything is "taken off" – except Lady Godiva's mantle' ('A Society Butterfly', p. 150). Langtry's Lady Godiva, 'so ill-posed and ill-lighted, so enwrapped and becloaked' (*The Theatre*, 'A Society Butterfly', p. 333), uncomfortably signalled the nakedness not being made available by the actress.

Langtry also fell foul of *The Theatre* reviewer on the grounds of her acting skills. The underlying terms of this criticism reveal a new apprehension of the actress's potential which goes hand-in-hand with the changed dynamics of her spectacular function. As the reviewer clumsily expresses it, 'what [Mrs Langtry] has to be in act, was always truer than what she had to be by tongue' (*The Theatre*, 'A Society Butterfly', p. 333): but her power in being is now both insufficient in itself and unsuitable in a play in which the authors, 'have burdened her with ample views on the inequality of social laws, the right of the deserted woman to tread in the footsteps of the errant man, and so on – views which to sound convincing require an expressive voice, a high-strung nature, the actress temperament – things one must reluctantly say to Mrs Langtry [...] "which you have not"' (*The Theatre*, 'A Society Butterfly', p. 333). Such comments on a once-popular actress reveal a changed relation between language and visual spectacle on stage which impacts directly on the Galatea-aesthetic, qualifying significantly its potency and sufficiency as a means of evaluating the actress on the nineties stage.

The Palace's 'Living Pictures' were untroubled by speech, and it was perhaps only in this absolutely mute form that the attractions of the statuesque spectacle in the theatre of the 1890s could be sustained. Langtry's spectacular potential is fundamentally hampered by what she has to say, in part because, as the brief account which is given of her speech demonstrates, Mrs Dudley is a type of 'New Woman', whose desire for equality, and whose expressions of independence and of self-consciousness, contradict absolutely the tenets of Galatea's position, a situation based on muteness, a relative status, absolute unselfconsciousness, and the sufficiency of the physical. Much of the so-called 'New Drama' of the 1890s, and that of Ibsen in particular, was perceived as providing dangerous new archetypes for women in such figures as Nora Helmer, Hedda Gabler, and Rebecca West. But the New Drama, the so-called 'literary drama', equally opposed the dynamics of Galatea's trope through its formal characteristics and its use of dramatic language. It demanded more from its actresses than their physical looks, rather requiring, as we will see, their critical and intellectual engagement with texts.

THE LITERARY DRAMA

The term 'literary drama' perhaps demands some explanation, for it was itself a source of dispute. The critic H. D. Traill questioned whether it was 'anything more than a pleasing dream of the impossible, a radiant vision of the wedding of two incompatibles'.[21] William Archer, one of the literary drama's most committed champions, countered by re-defining the nature of the language supposed by Traill to constitute the 'literary' on stage, suggesting that in Ibsen for instance, 'a great literary effect is attained by the sedulous dissimulation of literary form', pointing to *Hedda Gabler* as an example of Ibsen's achievement: 'in such a play as *Hedda Gabler* Ibsen has achieved with unexampled completeness the fusion of character, action, and dialogue into an indissoluble whole [...where] the comparative infrequency of mere beauty of phrase is amply compensated by the intensity, or rather the multiplicity, of meaning contained in every line'.[22] The 'literary drama' is scarcely definable, but Archer's description of Ibsen's use of language goes some way to demonstrating both the qualities distinguishing it from the commercial theatre and the extent to which its 'multiplicity' might enable the actress to exceed the simplicity of her spectacular role.

The conflict between the old and the new was part of a broader debate at this time, as Henry Arthur Jones notes, 'between the theatre and the drama',[23] between the attractions and commercial requisites of the spectacle, and the interests of the literary. Henry James later wrote to his brother and sister-in-law of his own theatrical experiences that,

The whole odiousness of the thing lies in the connection between the drama and the theatre. The one is admirable in its interest and difficulty, the other loathsome in its conditions. If the drama could only be theoretically or hypothetically acted, the fascination resident in its all but unconquerable (*circumspice!*) form would be unimpaired, and one would be able to have the exquisite exercise without the horrid sacrifice. (29 December 1893, *Henry James Letters*, vol. III, p. 452)

\ little over a year later, on 9 January 1895, James wrote to William ·ain. The humiliating experience of his play *Guy Domville*'s first night had taken place on 5 January, and James clearly felt that his reception on that evening – during a quarter of an hour when 'all the forces of civilisation in the house waged a battle of the most gallant, prolonged and sustained applause with the hoots and jeers and cat-calls of the roughs' (*Henry James Letters*, vol. III, p. 508) – exemplified the fate of drama in the commercial theatre. At the St James's, under the well-known management of George Alexander, his 'delicate, picturesque, extremely human and extremely artistic little play, was taken profanely by a brutal and ill-disposed gallery which had shown signs of malice prepense from the first' (vol. III, p. 507), and James's career as a playwright was effectively ended despite years spent working over 'the whole stiff mystery of "technique"' (2 February 1895, vol. III, p. 517), seeking out the perfection of form which he had come to relish in Ibsen's acted dramas.[24]

The terms of James's scepticism about the theatre as an art-form are echoed in a series of *Pall Mall Gazette* articles on 'Why I Don't Write Plays' by a number of leading novelists.[25] The series attracted the scorn of Irving, who described as a sorry sight the spectacle of novelists denigrating an art they clearly did not understand ('Some Misconceptions About the Stage', p. 670), but interestingly, the novelists were unanimous about the grounds for their distrust of the stage, and also remarkably oblivious to the innovations of Ibsen, Archer, and J. T. Grein, founder of the new Independent Theatre. They commented rather on the extent to which they believed that contemporary conventions of staging militated against the play's 'getting nearer to the heart and meaning of things' (Hardy, 'Why I Don't Write Plays', p. 1). Likewise, Gissing felt it impossible for the play to convey 'the unuttered life of soul' ('Why I Don't Write Plays', p. 3). The novelists write fearfully of vast theatres, unfamiliar technicalities, and egotistical performers, and are most sceptical of the capacity of audiences to do more than desire simple entertainment. As George Moore wrote: 'Some collaboration on the part of the multitude is necessary to enable the artist to produce art that is vital, and so it seems to me that those who would interpret the life of their time do well to choose the novel, rather than the play, as a means of expression.'[26]

Part of Archer's strategy in championing the 'literary drama' had been to try to collapse the distinction between the play and the novel. In 'The Free Stage and the New Drama' (1891), he writes of the status and public function of the novel as setting the bench-mark for the drama's aspirations to public influence. One of the marks of Ibsen's success is that Nora is as well known as Jane Eyre, Hedda as Becky Sharp.[27] Further, 'Ibsen has proved that the living, actable, acted modern drama is capable of appealing to the artistic intelligence as powerfully as the novel, or any other art-form' ('The Free Stage and the New Drama', p. 667). Indeed, amongst French critics at least, his *Ghosts* was treated as 'a serious piece of literature, to be discussed, analyzed, possibly condemned' (p. 669).[28] Archer envisaged that the literary drama would, by taking advantage of new copyright laws, elevate the ephemerality of the performed play into the durability of the literary text. As a result of her association with the new materiality of the published text, the work of the actress too could acquire both new temporal implications, and demand the kind of close analytical, interpretative attention normally reserved for the writer of fiction.

The advent of 'the new literary movement in the theatre' was intimately bound up with Ibsen's arrival on the English stage ('The Free Stage and the New Drama', p. 671), and the subsequent experimental work of J. T. Grein's Independent Theatre. Productions of Ibsen dominated discussions in the early nineties about English theatre, which as Hamilton Aïdé noted, had never been discussed as much as was currently the case.[29] Due in part, of course, to the subject-matter of Ibsen's plays, which was furiously denounced, the more significant and lasting challenge presented by Ibsen and the playwrights inspired by his example, such as Arthur Wing Pinero and Moore, was to the dominant popular convention of the spectacular stage. The contemporary terms which were used both to promote and to denounce Ibsen's drama make clear the extent to which productions of his plays challenged the principle of pleasure underlying the imperatives of the commercial theatre, and hence the power of the audience; and the ways in which a shift in economic relations and new plays' explicitly recognised literary and intellectual components rendered impossible the sustaining of the Galatea-trope.

IBSEN AND THE ACTRESS

The statuesque actress was from the start a figure of contestation in Ibsen's work. The play which initiated the debate in England was *A Doll's House* (1879). The narrative of *A Doll's House* is, of course, precisely about the emancipation of a living doll, an object of the practice of social Pygmalionism which makes of the wife simply a reflection of her husband's desires, one who is effectively created by those desires in the act of matrimony. Nora is initially complicit in this structure, asking Helmer to choose her costume for a fancy dress ball, but the centrality of this relationship-pattern is made most explicit when Helmer seeks to reinstate himself as Nora's Pygmalion in his relief at their escape from financial disgrace:

You have no idea what a true man's heart is like, Nora. There is something so indescribably sweet and satisfying, to a man, in the knowledge that he has forgiven his wife – forgiven her freely, and with all his heart. It seems as if he has given her a new life, so to speak; and she has in a way become both wife and child to him.[30]

However, as the play shows, it is by rejecting Torvald that Nora achieves true 'animation'. *A Doll's House* was first produced in England in June 1889 by Janet Achurch and her husband Charles Charrington, who thus initiated the Norwegian playwright's unexpurgated introduction to the London stage. This production had far-reaching consequences for the actress, for in a variety of ways it effected a disjunction between spectator and spectacle which was crucial to the dismantling of the foundations of Pygmalion's power.

Contemporary critics were quick to perceive that the drama was 'written partly to show that in a life of civilisation a woman must not be considered as man's creature alone – a ministrant or a toy',[31] but were equally quick to cast doubt on the answer that Ibsen proposed to this problem, and on the independent heroine who resulted. Janet Achurch's Nora was just the first of Ibsen's heroines on the English stage to repel the idealising adjectives usually applied to a play's young female lead. Indeed, in *The Theatre*, Clement Scott explained how she had invented a new 'ideal'. She was: 'not the pattern woman we have admired in our mothers and our sisters, not the model of unselfishness and charity, but a mass of aggregate conceit and self-sufficiency, who leaves her home and deserts her friendless children because she has *herself* to look after'.[32] The personal outrage expressed by Scott is perhaps explained by Archer's analysis of the nature of the critics' disappointment. Writing of the eminent Italian actress Eleanora Duse's 1893 Nora, Archer suggests that

The critics, in fact, sublimely unconscious of the way in which they thereby drive home the poet's irony, fall into the very same misunderstanding of Nora's character which makes Helmer a bye-word for masculine stupidity, and are no less flabbergasted than he when the doll puts off her masquerade dress and turns out to be a woman after all.[33]

What is at stake is clearly the whole theatrical illusion of the actress's doll-like status, an illusion in the sustaining of which critics and audience were alike complicit. This illusion, which is grounded in the Galatea-aesthetic, is challenged not only by the specific nature of this play's sexual politics, and the questionable and troubling desirability of its young heroine, but also by the very possibility of a significant transformation in that character. This attracted derision from many critics who seemed unwilling to forego their expectation of the more usually static nature of female parts in order to embrace the possibility that there actually might be more to an actress than met the eye.[34] The interpretative certainties of the female body are being brought into question. Achurch's attractive physicality should, like that of Galatea, have guaranteed a stable representation and understanding of the part, should have forestalled precisely the metamorphosis that Archer describes. Instead, actress and role are conjoined in a dynamic which can even seem to effect a physical transformation of the actress. Archer wrote of Duse's Nora, 'for each large phase of feeling she has a totally different countenance. Her Nora has four distinct faces' ('*A Doll's House*', p. 160).

The acting of Elizabeth Robins, which spanned the paradigm shift from eighties ingénue to Ibsen heroine, confirmed this possibility. In the same *Theatre* volume in which he excoriates Nora, Clement Scott reviewed Elizabeth Robins's performance as a wronged wife in C. H. R. Dabbs's *Her Own Witness*. Robins played a sleep-walker whose night-time exit from the chamber of a former lover is interpreted by her jealous husband as grounds for separation, despite his wife's adamant denial of infidelity. Three years later, her husband learns of his mistake, and Robins's character willingly allows herself to be 'taken [back] to her husband's heart'.[35] For her representation of such docility, Elizabeth Robins was commended for 'a womanly and tender performance, full of earnestness and strength, one that went straight to the heart of her audience'. Two years later, however, when she was playing Hedda Gabler, Scott suggested that if Robins was attractive in that part, she was only morbidly so.[36]

It is notable that Robins's body, and the physical attractiveness which, in the semantics of conventional drama, should have guaranteed her virtue, is not dwelt on or recreated in reviews of *Hedda Gabler*, which she produced with Marion Lea in 1891. Reference is made, however, to the 'intrinsic prettiness'[37] of Marion Lea's 'gentle, sweet-faced, almost angelic Mrs Elvsted', whose 'mild, wondering face, her pathetic voice

[and] intense trustfulness'[38] are more usual and acceptable aspects of the dramatic heroine. Robins's evident mutability and power to meta-morphose shook a persistent desire to believe in the interpretative stability of women's beauty, as did Janet Achurch's 1896 performance as Rita Allmers in *Little Eyolf.* Bernard Shaw writes of Achurch's perform-ance that, 'A more utter recklessness, not only of fashion, but of beauty, could hardly be imagined: beauty to Miss Achurch is only one effect among others to be produced, not a condition of all effects.'[39] He writes of the way in which Achurch transports her audience through conven-tionalised images of reputable and disreputable femininity finally to have them confront the petrifying figure of the Gorgon Medusa:

She looked at one moment like a young, well-dressed, very pretty woman: at another she was like a desperate creature just fished dripping out of the river by the Thames Police. Yet another moment, and she was the incarnation of impetuous, ungovernable strength. Her face was sometimes winsome, some-times listlessly wretched, sometimes like the head of a statue of Victory, sometimes suffused, horrible, threatening, like Bellona or Medusa. ('*Little Eyolf*', p. 261)

The parts offered to the actress by Ibsen discredited at least temporarily the 'qualifications' which had gained success for her on the English stage of the 1880s,[40] and, as Shaw suggests, by means of the alternative Classical prototype of the Medusa (which we will return to below), the location of power in the mechanism of the gaze is beginning to shift from the audience to the mesmerising, potentially petrifying actress.

Ibsen's principal gift to the actress was to allow her to exceed the possibilities of the spectacular stage, and the constraints, moral, intellec-tual and creative, embodied in the sculptural metaphor previously applied to her. This is iconographically represented in the multiple possibilities of movement embodied by his female characters. His plays may contain actual movements which subvert feminine norms, such as Nora's tarantella, or Rebecca West's throwing herself into the mill-race in *Rosmersholm*, but more often the notion of an anarchic activity is inherent within Ibsen's conception of his characters. The critical terms employed of Robins's Hedda invoke a mercurial movement, both moral and physical, impossible to control. The Examiner of Plays at the time, E. F. S. Pigott, wrote to Robins that 'to my poor perception, all the characters in [*Hedda Gabler*] appear to have escaped from a lunatic asylum!'[41] The critics followed this lead, describing Hedda herself as 'a lunatic of the epileptic class';[42] as passionate, with a 'capricious intensity';[43] and as 'a cunning tigress, wounding and killing without pity'.[44] Robins herself also attracts terms of movement and energy: she is 'all versatility, expressiveness, and distinction' (Egan, *Critical Heritage*, p. 221); her conception of the part is replete with 'rapidity and subtlety of intellect [...] Behind every speech we felt the swift intellectual process that gave it birth.'[45] Mrs Campbell wrote that 'The peculiar quality of Miss Elizabeth Robins' dramatic gift was the swiftness with which she succeeded in sending thought across the footlights' (*My Life*, p. 65). The extent to which Ibsen's women exceed the immurement and stasis of Galatea is demonstrated by an ironic reference to sculpture in Laura Marholm Hansson's essay on Eleanora Duse in *Modern Women* (1894) which undermines traditional invocations of the stillness of ancient marble. Hansson writes that after the rehearsal of the tarantella, when Nora believes her fate can no longer be delayed, Duse 'leaps through the air into [Helmer's] arms with a cry of joy, – to look at her one would think that she was one of those thin, wild, joyless Bacchantes whose bas-reliefs have come down to us from the later period of Grecian art'.[46]

Ibsen was implicated by contemporaries as being largely responsible for having changed perceptions of the actress. Clement Scott, cosseted at the Lyceum during the eighties by Ellen Terry's considerable charms, found it notoriously difficult to reconcile himself to the spectacle of an actress playing Hedda Gabler, and records his perplexities in oxymorons: Hedda is a 'repulsive heroine', a 'sane lunatic [...] a reasoning madwoman' (Egan, *Critical Heritage*, pp. 226, 227). But more importantly perhaps, Ibsen was also a dramatist who changed actresses' perceptions of themselves and of their own work. As Robins wrote in 1928, 'no dramatist has ever meant so much to the women of the stage as Henrik Ibsen. This is no less true although many admirable artists have never played him. They do not know, perhaps, that the parts they have made successes in would not have been written but for Ibsen.'[47] The account Robins gives of her Ibsen years in *Ibsen and the Actress* is imbued with notions of collaboration, both as a form which links her with other women in the theatre, and as a term which denotes the possibility of a new relationship between actress and playwright. She suggests that it was peculiarly Ibsen's property as a playwright that, 'More than anybody who ever wrote for the stage, [he] could, and usually did, collaborate with his actors' (*Ibsen and the Actress*, pp. 52–3), to the extent that he seemed to regard them as 'fellow creator[s]' (p. 53). This, of course, allows the actress to enjoy a status not previously within her remit, and by means of a co-operative, collective dynamic, to exceed the isolation which grounds Galatea's narrative and the terms of her incarnation. Robins conveys her sense of the opportunities offered by Ibsen in an image which rewrites the Pygmalion-metaphor. She writes of the 'unwritten clue' given her by the playwright that it enabled her to come to Hedda, and 'to feel her warm to my touch' (p. 26), a body which the actress may herself animate. Robins ends her essay by invoking Maeterlinck: '"Collaboration." Maeterlinck has said: "*Il y a une plus haute collaboration que celle de la plume – celle de la pensée et du sentiment.*" One of the highest of all is, surely, this collaboration between playwright and player' (p. 56). For Robins, this experience was underwritten by the collaborative work which had the greatest impact on her, that of her literary collaboration with Ibsen. In part the result of her being able to read Ibsen in Norwegian and to translate him, she enjoyed 'a collaboration closer still' (p. 38) than most actresses. It was surely the experience of this creative collaboration, and her later articulation of it, which give the key-note to Robins's Ibsen years.

Having watched Robins's Hedda Gabler in 1891, Henry James had written that Ibsen

is destined to be adored by the 'profession'. Even in his comfortless borrowed habit he will remain intensely dear to the actor and the actress. He cuts them out work to which the artistic nature in them joyously responds – work difficult and interesting, full of stuff and opportunity. The opportunity that he gives them is almost always to do the deep and delicate thing – the sort of chance that in proportion as they are intelligent they are most on the look out for. ('On the Occasion of *Hedda Gabler*', pp. 528–9)

The metaphor of depth here conveys a sense of the opportunities peculiarly afforded the performer by Ibsen, and we encounter it again in Maeterlinck's writing of the modern drama that it went beyond the spectacular restraints of 'exterior action', 'to penetrate ever more deeply into human consciousness, and attribute still greater importance to moral problems'.[48] This spatial metaphor signifies a moving beyond and beneath the externals of spectacle which is effected in part by a new awareness of the 'literariness' of drama. For the actress, the exercise of her interpretative intelligence, her engagement with textuality rather than simply with the immediacy of physical spectacle, meant that she exceeded containment within the visual perspective of the stage. The actress's participation within texts such as Ibsen's which counteract the implications of her physical spectacle necessarily undermines the sufficiency of that spectacle. Pygmalion's Galatea was born into dumbness rather than speech, into a body which served only for child-bearing. Actresses' engagement with the interpretative possibilities of the literary drama forestalled their immurement within a range of purely physical significations.

In practical ways too, Ibsen and the New Drama necessitated new methods of theatrical production which released actresses from the imperatives of the commercial theatres, and the monopoly of the late-Victorian actor-managers.[49] The subscription production was developed as a means both of side-stepping the control of late-Victorian state censorship, and of facilitating performances of good drama such as Ibsen's which was 'far above the very low level represented by the average taste of the huge crowd of playgoers requisite to make a remunerative run for a play' (Shaw, 'Preface', *World of 1894*, p. xx). A new system was surely also necessary when the spectacle of desirable femininity, the stakes upon which the theatre's speculative fortunes rested, was not readily available. Subscribers to productions guaranteed new managements against serious financial loss. The new independent companies were thus able to circumvent the taste of commercial the-atre-goers by self-selecting audiences who would not wish simply to be succoured and entertained. The Independent Theatre was such a ven-ture, as was a series of Ibsen performances mounted by Robins in 1893.

As Shaw notes some of the principal beneficiaries of the new 'sub-scription production' were actresses, particularly the new breed of 'actress-manageress' such as Robins ('Preface', p. xxix). Freed from the imperative to ensure profitability, actresses were able to concentrate on acting rather than simply attracting their audience. Further, the more flexible management structures of the new companies involved actresses on the production side, and thus also challenged the import of their on-stage moments by making them simply one aspect of the actress's 'role': she was no longer constituted simply by her physical incarnation. Within this new system, the possibility of a newly grounded relationship between play, player, and audience was established. Managerial duties, along with the lack of 'speculative' prospects in the new theatre and the nature of actresses' parts, combined to reshape the spectacle of the actress so that it could no longer be so promptly engulfed within the theatre-audience's gaze.

This process is perhaps best demonstrated by the 'Joint Management' scheme of Elizabeth Robins and Marion Lea, the first of whose produc-tions was *Hedda Gabler* which opened at the Vaudeville Theatre in April 1891. Failing to attract an actor-manager to what was perceived as 'a woman's play' with no part for a leading man, the actresses produced and financed the venture themselves. In *Ibsen and the Actress*, Elizabeth Robins recalls: 'Marion had a jewelled bracelet and I had a small treasure that I could throw in the pot. With these "securities" we borrowed from an amiable friend £300, and set to work' (p. 16). Though assisted by William Archer, the two actresses were primarily responsible for the production: they reworked Edmund Gosse's translation to make it more playable; were responsible for casting; for finding a theatre; for the details of production; and for their own parts. In an interview, Lea recounts how she and Robins retreated to a cottage on Richmond Hill to study and 'imbue [themselves] with the spirit and feeling of the whole play – and [their] own parts in particular'.[50] Most appropriately, they unwittingly undid Justin McCarthy's original scheme of planning a production around the eminently commercial, and Classical, figure of Lillie Langtry (Postlewait, *Prophet of the New Drama*, p. 67).

Robins and Lea briefly provided a successful alternative to the spectacular aesthetic of the established companies, one which relied principally on their managerial and creative capacities, but Robins went one step further in escaping from the Galatea-trope when she co-wrote a play with Florence Bell.[51] *Alan's Wife* (1893) was produced by the Independent Theatre, and was based on 'Befriad', a story by the Swedish writer Elin Ameen, which concerned the actions of a recently widowed young mother who decides to kill her crippled baby. She refuses to repent of her action and, in the play, is sentenced to death. The mother's act, based as much on her physical revulsion from the child as on a merciful impulse, is as unpalatable today as most audiences found it at the time. However, the play found acceptance within the Ibsenite school and was championed by William Archer. He wrote an adulatory preface to the printed text, where he likened the play's effect and irreconcilable difficulties to those of Greek tragedy. Grein compared the play's power, sadness, and simplicity to *Ghosts* and described it as 'one of the truest tragedies ever written by a modern Englishman'.[52] The authorship of the play was a closely guarded secret, in part according to Robins because she was anxious to avoid Henry James's interference. He shared in the 'widespread conviction' of the time, 'that no woman can write a good full-length play', and reacted with 'a start, and a look of horror' to Robins's hypothetical suggestion that she might write one.[53] Before she played Hilda Wangel, James had advised Robins, 'Don't be fantastic – be *pretty*, be agreeable, in the right key' (*Theatre and Friendship*, p. 98). For her to write plays would emphatically usurp James's right to instruct her in her self-made theatrical roles.

In starring in her own play, Robins was challenging the Galatea-aesthetic, not only by the nature of the spectacle she presented, but by putting words into her own mouth, and by working with other women both to create a female narrative, and to determine how that narrative should be told. The creative collaboration between the playwrights, the Swedish writer Ameen, and the character of Jean, allows no space for the intervention of male power.[54] The hierarchy of gender made manifest in Pygmalion's legend is thus indisputably dispersed not only in the matter of plays which question gender conventions, but in the staging of theatrical events which are themselves the result of largely female collaborative effort. Crucially too, the vulnerable isolation of Galatea may be countered in female theatrical images known to be the active result of female co-operation, particularly when those who are watching those images are sympathetic to this possibility.

Even outside the new theatres, women were coming together to create a number of sustaining female theatrical alliances. Far from falling into the 'Rival Queens' pattern that was projected for them, the three leading actresses of the decade, Bernhardt, Terry, and Duse, made public their mutual admiration. According to Mrs Comyns Carr, Terry's friend and costumier, 'Sarah Bernhardt and Ellen Terry had a sincere admiration for each other', and when Terry went to see Bernhardt play Marguerite Gautier for the first time, the French star sent a note to Terry saying 'To-night I play for you. – SARAH.'[55] The relationship between Terry and Duse was perhaps even warmer. In Terry's bedroom at Smallhythe, the only non-family portrait displayed is one of Duse, under whose face Terry has written, 'There is none like her – none.' In years which saw the diminishing of Terry's reliance on Irving, and the end of their relationship at the Lyceum, Terry seems to have found a new source of inspiration and identification in her relationships with Bernhardt and Duse, and also herself became at this time a focus of young actresses' aspirations and devotion. While still at the Lyceum, Terry was responsible for allowing many young women to 'walk-on' at the theatre, thus gaining their first professional experience.

As we have seen, Pygmalion's power was grounded in his desiring gaze, so when the nature and power of the audience's gaze becomes fragmented and is disputed, that power is called into question. The thesis of this book is predicated in large part on the belief, attested to by contemporary commentators, that the relation between late-Victorian theatre and its audiences was symbiotic and complex, that the theatre acts on its spectators, and its spectators act on, and inform, the theatre. Susan Bennett writes of the two 'frames' which constitute the theatrical experience, the outer which contains 'all those cultural elements which create and inform the theatrical event' and the inner which 'contains the dramatic production in a particular playing space'. She goes on to suggest that 'It is the interactive relations between audience and stage, spectator and spectator which constitute production and reception, and which cause the inner and outer frames to converge for the creation of a particular experience.'[56] It is, then, only to be expected that out of both new theatrical conventions and dramatic matter, a theatre-going practice might emerge which could challenge the gaze of Pygmalion.

The subscription performances had created a new audience-constituency, but, increasing use of the matinée and new social freedoms also meant that it was easier for women to go to the theatre by themselves, and so, the actual composition of the audience, as well as its female component's disposition, might be changed. In an article on 'Why Women Are Ceasing to Marry' (1899), Ella Hepworth Dixon instances among a list of significant new freedoms women's going to the theatre without a male escort.[57] In addition, the new companies' reliance upon subscription performances offered more women opportunities for financial support of, and greater integration within, the theatrical process than had previously been possible. Mrs J. R. Green, for instance, was 'convenor and first guarantor' of the New Century Theatre with which Elizabeth Robins became involved.[58] A new political awareness might actually be facilitated by theatre-going, as Edith Lees, later Mrs Havelock Ellis, suggests in her account of watching Achurch and Charrington's *A Doll's House*. In viscerally active terms which belie the excitement simply of the moment, she writes of how she and a group of women friends, including Olive Schreiner, Eleanor Marx, and Mrs Holman Hunt, were left at the end of the play,

restive and impetuous and almost savage in our arguments. This was either the end of the world or the beginning of the new world for women. What did it mean? Was there hope or despair in the banging of that door? Was it life or death for women? Was it joy or sorrow for men? Was it revelation or disaster? We almost cantered home.[59]

Edith Lees and her friends responded warmly to the anti-Pygmalion message of the play they had seen, but in their own responses were providing at least as powerful a destructive impulse: the collective sympathy and excitement of their response is clearly disputing

Pygmalion's activating gaze of desire. This play, as even critics such as Scott perceived, required a new viewing practice, not based on conventional desire, and hence not necessarily the prerogative of a male audience. Galatea's isolation, bound by notions of the ideal and the timeless, is dispelled as the female audience participates in an act of identification.

ELEANORA DUSE

The actress could now be seen as functioning within an on-going process of co-operative effort, and of interpretative engagement which disputes the marmoreal finality and completeness of Galatea's outline. As Laura Marholm Hansson writes of Duse,

> in the parts which she did act, she opened to us a new world which had no existence before, because it was her own. It was the world of her own soul, the ever-changing woman's world, which no one before her has ever expressed on the stage, she gave us the secret, inner life of woman, which no poet can wholly fathom, and which only woman herself can reveal, which with more refined nerves and more sensitive and varied feelings has emerged bleeding from the older, coarser, narrower forms of art, to newer, brighter forms, which, though more powerful, are also more wistful and hopeless. (*Modern Women*, p. 97)

Hansson's account is one of confused optimism which disputes the actress's finished spectacle through her concentration instead on the manifestation of 'the secret, inner life'. In Duse's case, this is specifically her secret life as a woman to which a female audience would necessarily make its own gendered response, and which invites a participation grounded in an experience exceeding the moment of theatrical spectacle, calling up instead shared and on-going narratives of women's lives.

The new literary drama necessitated a new dramatic criticism, which responded to the play as a literary as well as theatrical event, and to the actress as primarily an artist rather than simply a desirable image. (William Archer wrote of Ibsen's *The Wild Duck*, first produced in London in June 1894, that the passions it aroused were of 'purely theatrical interest'.[60]) This drama criticism most clearly demonstrates its new terms in Archer and Shaw's championing of Eleanora Duse, who first appeared in London in 1893, and in their concomitant repudiation of Sarah Bernhardt. The terms of both men's responses participate in the negotiation with, and rewriting of, the Galatea legacy for the nineties actress, the poles of possibility for whom are represented in

Shaw's comparison of Duse and Bernhardt. He sets Duse and her work in 'the drama in which emotion exists only to make thought live and move us' against Bernhardt and the 'claptraps' of 'Sardoodledom': 'To me, at least, the whole affair seems antiquated and ridiculous, except when I regard it as a high modern development of the circus and the waxworks' ('Sardoodledom', p. 138). The mental processes invoked by the incarnation of emotion in Duse's drama directly counter the spectacular trappings of Sardou and Bernhardt. Intellectual engagement, with all its narrative potential and implications of artistry, exceeds the lure of the waxworks, a modern commercial travesty of the memorial art of the marble statue. Shaw writes that there are 'years of work, bodily and mental, behind every instant' of Duse's acting, 'work, mind, not mere practice and habit', whereas Bernhardt's lure is that of a 'mere personal fascination [...] which the actress can put off and on like a garment'.[61]

Shaw's most telling comparison of the two women is based on the ways in which each manipulates the effect of her body on stage, and the different processes which give birth to those theatrical bodies. The opportunity very directly to compare the two women arose in June 1895, when both played Magda in Suderman's *Heimat*, re-named '*Magda*' for both French and Italian versions, which premièred in London on 10 and 12 June respectively. The play concerns the fate of a singer who, having been seduced years before, now re-encounters her betrayer. As he is the father of her child, she is ordered by her own father to marry him. She refuses. Bernhardt's impact on Shaw was effected through the artifice of her physical impression: 'Those charming roseate effects which French painters produce by giving flesh the pretty color of strawberries and cream, and painting the shadows pink and crimson, are cunningly reproduced by Madame Bernhardt in the living picture.'[62] Archer had previously spoken of Bernhardt as 'no longer a real woman, but an exquisitely-contrived automaton, the most wonderful *article de Paris* ever invented, perfect in all its mechanical airs and graces, but devoid alike of genuine feeling and artistic conscience'.[63] The artifice of Bernhardt's attractions militates against the possibility of art, and signals for Shaw the extent to which she remains trapped within her own person: 'The dress, the title of the play, the order of the words may vary; but the woman is always the same. She does not enter into the leading character: she substitutes herself for it' ('Duse and Bernhardt', p. 150). The measure of the actress's achievement in the 1880s, of her synonymity with her role, is now thus turned against her.

For Bernhardt's 'stock of attitudes and facial effects', Shaw suggests that 'Duse produces the illusion of being infinite' in part because behind every stroke of her acting there is a 'distinctively human idea', but also because her use of her body is one based on suppleness and variety ('Duse and Bernhardt', p. 151). The supreme achievement of this conjunction of body and idea, which of course substantially re-sites the body within processes of imaginative and intellectual application rather than spectacular appeal, occurs in *Magda*, at the moment when Duse meets her lover again. Shaw's account is worth quoting at length:

He paid his compliments and offered his flowers; they sat down; and she evidently felt that she had got it safely over and might allow herself to think at her ease, and to look at him to see how much he had altered. Then a terrible thing happened to her. She began to blush; and in another moment she was conscious of it, and the blush was slowly spreading and deepening until, after a few vain efforts to avert her face or to obstruct his view of it without seeming to do so, she gave up and hid the blush in her hands. After that feat of acting I did not need to be told why Duse does not paint an inch thick. I could detect no trick in it: it seemed to be a perfectly genuine effect of the dramatic imagination. In the third act of La Dame aux Camélias, where she produces a touching effect by throwing herself down, and presently rises with her face changed and flushed with weeping, the flush is secured by the preliminary plunge to a stooping attitude, imagination or no imagination; but Magda's blush did not admit of that explanation; and I must confess to an intense professional curiosity as to whether it always comes spontaneously.

I shall make no attempt to describe the rest of that unforgettable act [...] there really was something to roar at this time. There was a real play, and an actress who understood the author and was a greater artist than he. And for me, at least, there was a confirmation of my sometimes flagging faith that a dramatic critic is really the servant of a high art, and not a mere advertiser of entertainments of questionable respectability of motive. ('Duse and Bernhardt', pp. 153–4)

Cosmetic effects are replaced by those of the imagination, as Shaw accords to the actress a recognition of her artistry and imaginative autonomy.

This moment of process achieves its full significance when set alongside the moment of blushing self-awareness experienced by awakening Victorian Galateas. The difference here is that Duse is crucially able to stage-manage her own effect. Her blush, like Galatea's the recognition of a form of sexual knowledge, is the result of Duse's own, rather than a Pygmalion's, manipulation of her physical effects, and is evidence of an achieved self-consciousness so profound that it actively determines

Duse's physical incarnation. This moment, replete for Shaw with its implications of years of theatrical training, incontestably exceeds Galatea's moment of coming into being, and the properties and qualities which are ever after bound by the implications of that moment. Shaw went on in the following year to elucidate the dramatic and ethical implications of actresses' access to the new drama, as opposed to a 'dramatic work that aims at sensuous and romantic beauty alone',[64] in which the actress becomes revelatory, rather than simply attractive, a mirror or reflection of the deepest profundity rather than a thin spectacle.

According to Archer, Duse achieves this status through the conjunction in herself, to which he pays repeated tribute, of intelligence and executive power, 'of an astonishing breadth of intellectual sympathy and versatility of executive power' (*World for 1893*, p. 150). Her imagination becomes a 'creative' function, capable of shaping and reshaping her physicality.[65] Archer sets up this quality as a mark of Duse's 'genius', a term he uses frequently of her:

She does not act merely with a set of surface nerves which long habit has dissociated, or, so to speak, insulated, from the real centres of sensation. She throws her very being into her task, and while her intelligence keeps vigilant control of every gesture and accent, her whole physical organism responds with sensitive alertness to the touch of her imagination.[66]

By contrast, Bernhardt is 'marvellous [but] monotonous', incapable of 'bending her genius' to the interpretation of the drama (p. 205), and expecting rather that tame playwrights like Sardou would bend themselves, and sometimes enable Shakespeare to bend, to her. As Archer notes, 'It is the playwright's business to interpret her – to provide her with a new name and new costumes in which to go through the old round of poses and paroxysms' (*World for 1895*, pp. 205–6). The measure of Duse's art is the extent to which she achieves within herself a creative transformation, which enables her 'absolutely [to] differentiate and individualise different parts' (*World for 1893*, p. 150), and indeed to transfigure through 'the heat of her creative imagination and the light of her incomparable executive power' the parts given to her to play (*World for 1895*, p. 201).[67] She thus not only exerts a metamorphic capacity over her own body, but over the previously determining words of the playwright too. No longer 'restricted by her sympathies' (*World for 1895*, p. 207), as was the exemplary actress of the 1880s, Duse is free to metamorphose at will on the international stage.

FROM GALATEA TO GORGON

Not all commentators, however, were as generously excited by the 'new' actresses as Shaw and Archer. Indeed, the emergence of plays by Ibsen and Pinero, such as the latter's infamous *The Second Mrs Tanqueray* (1893), had placed the actress in a double bind. By the reasoning of the mid-eighties which saw the actress as ideally an exemplification of her persona off-stage, either she was an inherently disturbing if not evil presence; or she was acting, being creative, and hence potentially dissimulating. One solution was to suggest, as William Ferrero did in 1893, that the 'imitatory arts' were extensions of sinister faculties inherent in women: the 'simulating [of] emotions not actually felt, and the powerful psychological intuition which is instinct in all women', albeit 'specially developed and strengthened in great actresses by more than average intellectual power'.[68] Female creativity is further constrained by the argument's Darwinian premise that women's art is a 'feeble trace' compared to the 'potent stamp' imprinted by men on their works ('Woman's Sphere in Art', p. 554). Also, acting exemplified women's transitory status: 'Woman is destined to live in the present, and to pass away leaving her stamp only among her contemporaries, perhaps only among those who have seen her in the heyday of her beauty' ('Woman's Sphere in Art', p. 559). In the same year George Moore wrote that 'the best in woman's art is done within the limits' of 'themes invented by men – amiable transpositions suitable to boudoirs and fans', and in the art of being womanly, for which the stage gives the greatest scope: 'In their own costume they have succeeded as queens, courtesans, and actresses.'[69] He adds that 'all art that lives is full of sex' (p. 221), but clearly if women's art is in question, it has to be confined to parameters defined by male desire.

The implications for the Galatea-aesthetic of the actress's new conditions and position are also, at times uneasily, explored in three works of fiction which variously acknowledge the changes brought about as a result of the 'literary drama'. Crucially, all invoke the figure of the Gorgon Medusa as part of their concern to articulate a new position for the actress. In 1922, Freud described 'The terror of Medusa' as 'a terror of Castration that is linked to the sight of something'.[70] Clearly the new actress challenged the sexual prerogatives of a male audience's gaze, and was also perceived as having undergone something of the same metamorphosis as Medusa, who had once been beautiful, but who had been turned into a hideous monster by Athena as punishment for

Medusa's being raped by Poseidon in Athena's temple. It is highly appropriate that the new actress's challenge should be articulated in terms of a Classical figure who threatens to take upon herself the reifying powers of a Pygmalion, and to use her gaze to petrify.

Henry James is content to allow Medusa's powers to erupt onto the late-Victorian stage, and resists the temptation to make of himself a Perseus-figure. His theatrical novel, *The Tragic Muse*, was written mainly during 1889 at a time when James was contemplating a career as a playwright and when he and London theatre audiences were responding to the first visit of André Antoine's pioneering Théâtre Libre. His incisive review of the company's visit to London, 'After the Play' (1889), itself written in dramatic form, pre-empts the later calls of reformers such as Archer for the publication of plays, and crucially recognises the Théâtre Libre's attempts to unite theatre and drama. As 'Dorriforth', the voice combining elements of Jamesian sensitivity and Gabriel Nash's insouciance declares, 'They are the two blades of a pair of scissors.'[71] Gabriel Nash is the elusive dandy and aesthete who intermittently troubles the pages of *The Tragic Muse*, a novel which sets the parameters of James's vision of the theatre and prefigures his own downfall within it, a downfall he came to attribute to the unexpected vulgarity of his audience. Given James's dissection of English audiences' inadequacies in his dramatic criticism, and his exposure of what he perceived as the cowardly Philistinism at the heart of English society in *The Tragic Muse*, his disappointment should not have been so unexpected.

In his novel the success of his actress, Miriam Rooth, is achieved almost in spite of her audience. Miriam inspires them with her integrity, even though they can fall back only on a jaded, abstract terminology to express their appreciation: 'She was beauty, she was music, she was truth; she was passion and persuasion and tenderness.'[72] The real measure, however, of Miriam's success lies in her overcoming the very explicitly conjured conditions of the commercial stage, in her transmuting 'the mess of preparation' into 'the finished thing, the dish perfectly seasoned and served' (vol. i, p. 211); and in disturbing through entrancing the most fastidious and knowledgeable of English spectators, the diplomat Peter Sherringham. Sherringham is precisely the type of committed spectator of the eighties who has to be radically re-educated before the theatre can be rejuvenated. Although not crudely concerned primarily with female spectacle, Sherringham contains the theatre in a framework of nocturnal pleasures which relieve from, rather than inform, daily life: the theatre is his 'night-work' (vol. i, p. 204), 'a passion exercised on the easiest terms' (vol. II, p. 48). Only when Miriam's talent emerges and he falls in love with her is his confident control shaken, and his sense aroused of drama's capacity to move him beyond the limits he imposes. She is the novel's embodiment of the drama, which comes to set the terms of its own influence over Peter. Appropriately enough, this occurs after Peter has seen Miriam's revelatory performance of Juliet. Here, Sherringham's vision is one of the genius and purity of the stage as a vehicle of art, rather than simply a medium of pleasure:

Peter Sherringham, though he saw but a fragment of the performance, read clear at the last, in the intense light of genius that this fragment shed, that even so, after all, he had been rewarded for his formidable journey. The great trouble of his infatuation subsided, leaving behind it something tolerably deep and pure [...] he felt somehow recalled to reality by the very perfection of the representation. He began to come back to it from a period of miserable madness. He had been baffled, he had got his answer; it must last him. (vol. III, p. 255)

Doubly removed from him by her artistry, and by a theatrical marriage which will keep her on stage, Miriam resists Miss Bretherton's assimilation into a socially stabilising domesticity, as the drama too is conceded its credentials as an autonomous art-form.

James wrote to Henry Adams on 21 March 1914 of the 'inexhaustible sensibility' which he supposed he possessed by virtue of being 'that queer monster the artist' (*Henry James Letters*, vol. v, p. 706). Sherringham's concession to Miriam's artistry entitles her to inhabit the realm of the monstrous, which, in the context of James's novel, is ineluctably linked with the artistic. For instance, when the painter Nick Dormer explains his reluctance to follow in his family's political tradition, he describes himself as 'a wanton variation, an unaccountable monster' (vol. I, p. 171). Sherringham's final vision of female theatrical genius fulfils the terms of his initial premonition of its monstrosity:

a woman whose only being was to 'make believe', to make believe that she had any and every being that you liked, that would serve a purpose, produce a certain effect, and whose identity resided in the continuity of her personations, so that she had no moral privacy, as [Sherringham] phrased it to himself, but lived in a high wind of exhibition, of figuration – such a woman was a kind of monster, in whom of necessity there would be nothing to like, because there would be nothing to take hold of. (vol. I, p. 179)

In Peter Sherringham's eyes Miriam brings on her monstrousness, her departure from the appropriate form, in being 'the odd animal the artist who happened to have been born a woman' (vol. I, p. 219). The word is advisedly chosen. The possibility of his own 'monstrous' behaviour dogs Peter's relations with Miriam: Caliban-like, he 'dumbly and helplessly raged' when confronted with her 'histrionic hardness' (vol. III, p. 179). In their final meeting, the actress describes her suggestion that Peter throw up diplomacy for the stage as a 'monstrous step' (vol. III, p. 183).

His proposal is prompted by the 'strangeness' engendered by Miriam's acting, and his desire to prevent its producing 'something monstrously definite', for 'Miriam was a beautiful, actual, fictive, impossible young woman, of a past age and undiscoverable country, who spoke in blank verse and overflowed with metaphor' (vol. III, pp. 153–4), who was beginning to transcend the linear narrative of the 'theatre', and to achieve the figurative multiplicity of the 'drama'. Miriam's artistry releases her from the embeddedness of her social context, and enables her to enter a realm where, rather than being subject to romantic or theatrical Pygmalions, she can confound her male spectators. In so doing, she appropriately invokes the Classical reference which supplants that of Pygmalion and Galatea. Miriam turns on her audience what Nick Dormer describes as her petrifying Medusa-like powers: 'I'd rather see you as Medusa crowned with serpents. That's what you look like when you look best' (vol. III, p. 53).

This metaphor also emerges in Bram Stoker's *Dracula* (1897), in initially unlikely conjunction with the figure of Ellen Terry. In his *Reminiscences of Henry Irving*, Stoker, the Lyceum's theatre-manager, professes to have revered and loved Terry's 'enchanting personality' and according to him, this was the view generally taken of Terry by all who worked with her.[73] But in *Dracula*, Lucy Westenra makes of Terry's charm a diabolical enchantment, and a mask for a voracious sexuality.[74] Following Lucy's death, a report of children going missing in Hampstead, to be found later with throat-wounds, appears in the 'Westminster Gazette'. The children all reported going for a walk with a 'bloofer' lady whom they impersonate in their games. The report goes on,

It is only in accordance with general principles of human nature that the 'bloofer lady' should be the popular rôle at these *al fresco* performances. Our correspondent naïvely says that even Ellen Terry could not be so winningly attractive as some of these grubby-faced little children pretend – and even imagine themselves – to be.[75]

This strange compliment, and the ambivalence of the phrase 'pretend – and even imagine', ominously link the dreadful charms of the 'Un-Dead' Lucy with the spell of Terry's stage beauty.

During her lifetime Lucy epitomised the pure attractions of the young Englishwoman, just as Terry had advertised such virtues on stage.[76] But after her apparent death, Lucy's voice takes on a diabolical sweetness (p. 253); the same eyes that were once pure and gentle are now 'unclean and full of hell-fire'; the sweet features are turned to 'adamantine, heartless cruelty, and [their] purity to voluptuous wantonness' (pp. 252–3). Her brow has become 'wrinkled as though the folds of flesh were the coils of Medusa's snakes' (p. 254). The danger lies in Lucy's persistent attraction despite her horrific transformation. One is reminded of the similarly shocking transformation of Terry in *Macbeth* a few years earlier, an identification cemented by Lucy's throwing a child from her when confronted by her enemies, as Lady Macbeth suggests she could have done: 'I would, while it was smiling in my face, / Have pluck'd my nipple from his boneless gums, / And dash'd the brains out' (*Macbeth*, 1.7.56–58). Lest Lucy's desirability destroy her adorers, she must herself be destroyed, and in an extraordinarily gruesome scene, effectively a rape of Lucy which forces submission upon her, her danger is eradicated, and 'unequalled sweetness and purity' (p. 259) of aspect return to her. Masculine potency is restored by a wooden stake, and Lucy's Medusa-powers removed when Dr Seward and Professor van Helsing follow Perseus' example in severing her head. In this novel, and in George du Maurier's *Trilby* (1894), which also invokes Ellen Terry, the figures of Medusa and Galatea represent the dichotomies of femininity which are being contested.

A desire to immobilise the potential mutations of the female performer structures du Maurier's *Trilby*, a novel of Bohemian life set in Paris's Latin Quarter. Its ostensible villain is the musician Svengali, who, like Dracula, is of mysterious Eastern European origin, and has also entered into popular awareness as an archetypal villain. However, as we will see, this villain not only shares certain fundamental characteristics with the novel's British heroes, but is also a late-Victorian reworking of Pygmalion, with Trilby his hapless Galatea. *Trilby*'s heroes are a band of intrepid Britons, Little Billee, Taffy Wynne, and the Laird, who study art, as did their author, in the Paris of the 1840s. The trio of painters fall in love with Trilby, initially a comic figure who works as a milkmaid and nude model in the Latin Quarter, until the refinements (or squeamishness) of her British friends make her ashamed of her work, and she becomes instead a respectable *blanchisseuse de fin*. Thus the heroes initiate the practice of moulding Trilby to their desires in which Svengali also participates when he later hypnotises the tone-deaf Trilby and makes her into La Svengali, the century's greatest singer. He uses his powers of mesmerism as the Laird of Cockpen, Little Billee and Taffy Wynne use their affections to instil in Trilby a reverence for British notions of femininity.

As his illustrations of Trilby demonstrate, du Maurier also participates in this Pygmalion-process. In his drawings she goes through a number of physiological mutations which show how she is in thrall to du Maurier's narratorial control. The bizarrely dressed milkmaid wearing the petticoats of a grisette and a military over-coat and slippers moves into a bourgeois phase when both clothes and features become much finer. It is also then that her height is diminished. She had towered over Little Billee, her most-favoured suitor, but in the illustration of his proposal to her, "Answer me, Trilby!", her eye-level is scarcely above his.[77] As a singer on stage her height is restored to her, and she towers monumentally over Svengali. But rather than representing the irrepressibility of Trilby's sheer bulk,[78] this figuration seems rather to confirm Trilby's immurement within the hypnotic powers of Svengali, and the female performer's re-inscription within a sculptural form on stage. There is, however, no indication here of the oxymoronic 'living marble' image, rather Trilby's statuesque appearance is one of absolute immobility. In *Trilby*, then, the Pygmalion–Galatea relationship forcefully re-emerges, but here, rather than the controlled animation of a statue, we see the disturbing moulding of a living woman into a marmoreal, and finally a dead, form.

The novel is imbued with references to sculpture which, for a late-Victorian audience, might amply have foretold its heroine's plight. It opens with a lengthy description of the artistic clutter of a studio. Amongst the 'foils, masks, and boxing-gloves' are 'plaster casts of arms and legs and hands and feet', and a 'Lapith from the Elgin Marbles' (*Trilby*, p. 1). Du Maurier continues:

Along the walls, at a great height, ran a broad shelf, on which were other casts in plaster, terra-cotta, imitation bronze: a little Theseus, a little Venus of Milo, a little discobolus; a little flayed man threatening high heaven (an act that seemed almost pardonable under the circumstances!); a lion and a boar by Barye; an anatomical figure of a horse, with only one leg left and no ears; a horse's head from the pediment of the Parthenon, earless also; and the bust of Clytie, with her beautiful low brow, her sweet wan gaze, and the ineffable forward shrug of her dear shoulders that makes her bosom as a nest, a rest, a pillow, a refuge – the likeness of a thing to be loved and desired for ever, and sought for and wrought for and fought for by generation after generation of the sons of men. (p. 2)

Plate 13   George du Maurier, 'Twin Gray Stars', *Trilby* (1895)

Although anachronistic, as the novel is set in the 1840s, and Watts did
not begin his bust until the 1860s, it would seem from the similarities
between du Maurier's description and Swinburne's, that it is Watts's
bust that du Maurier has in mind here. In this moment, du Maurier
denies the autonomy of Clytie's desire, rewriting her suffering as an

image of placid availability. The dimensions of Clytie's fate are echoed in the body of the novel, where they poignantly prefigure the shape of Trilby's life.

The bust of Clytie is also arguably the first of the novel's references to Ellen Terry who, as du Maurier's illustrations demonstrate, is clearly an inspiration behind Trilby. Both are of ample build, and Trilby's eyes in particular seem modelled on Terry's limpid, beseeching gaze, as du Maurier's 'Twin gray stars' (p. 129) demonstrates (plate 13). Terry is specifically mentioned by du Maurier, when he tells the reader that Trilby 'was about as tall as Miss Ellen Terry – and that is a charming height, *I* think' (p. 129). The links are, however, made most explicit when Trilby goes on stage as La Svengali. She towers monumentally on stage as did Terry in Sargent's painting of her as Lady Macbeth, a part which is also invoked by du Maurier's description of Trilby's stage-costume: 'a tall female figure appeared, clad in what seemed like a classical dress of cloth of gold, embroidered with garnets and beetles' wings [...] her thick light brown hair tied behind and flowing all down her back to nearly her knees' (p. 304). Further, in describing the effect of La Svengali's appearance, du Maurier invokes another of Terry's parts, significantly that of Camma: 'No such magnificent or seductive appar-ition has ever been seen before or since on any stage or platform – not even Miss Ellen Terry as the priestess of Artemis in the late laureate's play *The Cup*' (p. 304). Du Maurier goes on to note that 'Our three friends were almost turned to stone in the immensity of their surprise' (p. 305) at discovering La Svengali to be their Trilby. Although mesmerised herself, clearly La Svengali's spectacle threatens, Medusa-like, to petrify her distinguished British admirers and, like Terry's Lady Macbeth, to confuse the relationship between morality and desirability. Her poten-tial for disruption has to be controlled, and once Svengali has died of a sudden heart-attack, Trilby dies too, bereft of the man who made her and gave her life.

Late in the novel, Trilby is said to resemble the Venus de Milo, with arms (p. 355), a reference which, as we have already seen, would have been recognisable to the readers of *Punch* for whom du Maurier did most of his work as a cartoonist. However, a more appropriate Classical derivation is suggested in the illustration of the moment when Trilby is recognised as 'La Svengali' by the British painters (p. 305). The drawing, 'It was Trilby' (plate 14), has a representative status in also acting as a frontispiece to the novel. Here, Trilby most strongly resembles classical statues of Athena, the virgin goddess of war and patron of the arts and

Plate 14   George du Maurier, 'It was Trilby!', *Trilby* (1895)

crafts, and in particular the Vellétri Athena in the Louvre which du Maurier may have seen while an art-student in Paris.[79] This Athena's blank aspect is particularly marked, even given the Classical tradition of non-realistic representation, and peculiarly resembles Trilby's mesmerised gaze. Also, the sheer mass of the Athena and the heaviness of her limbs make her more closely resemble Trilby than does any other Classical figure.

One of Athena's acts was to sponsor Perseus' destruction of Medusa, in token of which her statues bear the aegis of the Gorgon. But du Maurier's Trilby–Athena does not bear this token. The artist has removed this sign of forbidding unavailability from the chaste goddess, thus forestalling her power, whilst also signalling a cultural desire to control the petrifying power of the female performer to ensnare all who look on her. The 'unconscious Trilby of marble' (p. 441) relies for her determination on the gaze and desire of the artists who made her. She is formed by them, just as surely as Athena sprang ready-formed from Zeus's forehead, the child of one male parent, and as Galatea likewise emerged parthenogenetically from the hands of Pygmalion. Hence Trilby's performances reconstitute female public appearances under a new generation of would-be Pygmalions. Taken together, the effect of *Dracula* and *Trilby* is to suggest that even Terry's charms might inspire disquiet in an audience grown wary of the power of the performing woman whose beauty, like that of Robins and Achurch, might mask dangers redolent of the emasculating Medusa's horrors.

As reviews of the play based on the novel demonstrate, Trilby offered a way out of such a dilemma, and a way of reinstating the male audience's privileges. The stage-version of *Trilby* was produced by Beerbohm Tree in 1895, first in Manchester and then at the Haymarket. Trilby was played by Dorothea Baird, a relatively unknown young actress, whose apprenticeship had included her performances as Galatea with the Oxford University Dramatic Society, and as Hermione in Mr Greet's Stratford Memorial performances.[80] Baird not only plays those parts most famously associated with Mary Anderson, but also revives the arguments that Anderson had provoked. As Wedmore notes in the *Academy*, for most of her audience Baird's 'loveable' qualities, her full, rich voice, and her appearance, more than compensated for what she lacked in experience and artistry:[81] she was, in the words of *The Theatre* reviewer, 'all that could be wished for'.[82] Bernard Shaw in the *Saturday Review* invokes Mary Anderson by name in his review of the play, and suggests in a return to the idealising rhetorical mode associated with the statuesque, that as Trilby Baird becomes 'the incarnation of womanly sympathy'.[83] Such a phrase also reinstates the actress as one made, rather than in the position of maker; and Shaw's comment that 'there never was any such person as Trilby [...] she is a man's dream' ('Trilby', p. 617) follows du Maurier's lead in seeming to rejuvenate the powers of Pygmalion for the male audience.

It is tempting to speculate that *Trilby* may have prompted Shaw's later use of the Pygmalion and Galatea story as the basis of his own *Pygmalion*. Although not written until 1912, the idea for the play seems to have occurred to Shaw in late 1897.[84] Beerbohm Tree played both Svengali and Shaw's first Professor Higgins, opposite Mrs Patrick Campbell. Svengali's Pygmalion-like powers are more insisted upon in reviews of the play than of the novel, largely because the role of Svengali is more prominent in the adaptation. *The Theatre* epitomises the general opinion that Tree had never done anything more powerful and convincing, and describes his character as one 'desiring to sway the actions of another through his mind' ('In the Provinces', p. 233). Tree/Svengali simply replaces the sculptor's manipulation of marble with the hypnotist's mesmeric power. The power and popularity of the resulting spectacle is attested to in the two parodies it promptly spawned ('A Trilby Triflet' and 'A Model Trilby') and in the fact that on the proceeds of this play Tree was able to begin building His Majesty's Theatre.[85]

ESCAPING 'THE HANDS OF THE POTTER'

Ellen Terry was touring in America when *Trilby* was playing in London in late 1895. Earlier that year she had played a mature Guinevere in Comyns Carr's *King Arthur*, and had drawn the comment from William Archer that 'Miss Ellen Terry is an ideal Guinevere to the eye; it is impossible to conceive a statelier or more gracious figure; and her performance is altogether charming.'[86] Archer's words confirm how, in the final years at the Lyceum, Terry was, in spite of Lady Macbeth, still attracting the restrictive critical formulations that had accompanied her for most of her career, the more malevolent implications of which are played out in *Dracula* and *Trilby*. Terry was at this period very conscious of the limitations of the Lyceum stage for her own career. She complains bitterly to Shaw of the poor parts on offer at the now financially stricken theatre. Irving's commercial strategy at this time was to insist on Terry's presence, but not to safeguard the quality of her part. Of a new play proposed for the Lyceum, she writes, 'My part in it is just drivel. In the nineteenth century only a child of fourteen could express herself as I have to. If I'm not in a play at the Lyceum it does a good deal to harm that play. If I play this part it will "harm" me, in as much as I shall be simply ridiculous!' (31 January 1898, *Terry–Shaw Correspondence*, p. 272). Whereas Irving and his authors seem simply to have been intent on ensuring Terry's physical presence, she is concerned about the quality of her part, her words.

Shaw was a questionable ally in this dissension, for though denying that he regarded Terry as only a 'living picture', as 'a person needing to be arranged with sphinxes and limelights to be relished by a luxurious public' (8 August 1899, *Terry–Shaw Correspondence*, p. 313), he is nonetheless concerned in his letters to liberate Terry from the Lyceum so that she may be more readily available to be moulded by Shaw himself. Whilst using his *Saturday Review* drama column publicly to enjoin Terry to leave behind 'what she learnt in the studio', 'the art of the picture gallery',[87] Galatea's full liberation is not achievable through him, because Shaw privately insisted on his right as a dramatist to control her language, thus denying for the actress the final essential condition of autonomy. One of the sustaining narratives of the published Shaw–Terry correspondence is the couple's battle over the author's right to put words into the mouth of the actress. He continually presses Terry to play Lady Cicely in *Captain Brassbound's Conversion*. According to Shaw, Lady Cicely was Ellen Terry, but her first reaction was 'it's not the sort of play for me in the least' (3 August 1899, *Terry–Shaw Correspondence*, p. 307), a view never essentially shaken even after she had played the part in 1906. Shaw was equally firm in his belief that Lady Cicely should fit Terry 'like a glove' (4 August 1899, *Terry–Shaw Correspondence*, p. 309) so closely was it moulded around her personality. The metaphor and presumptions of the adoring sculptor infuse the whole correspondence. Shaw's 'Preface' begins by '[conceding] a pedestal' to the 'goddess-like' Ellen Terry, without '[pausing] to consider whether this attitude would have earned the approval of Ibsen or Strindberg' (*Terry–Shaw Correspondence*, p. xii). It concludes with his claim (subsequently disputed by Gordon Craig) that Shaw 'destroyed [Terry's] belief in [Irving] and gave shape and consciousness to her sense of having her possibilities sterilized by him' (p. xxxi).

Terry was not the only actress to attract such attentions from Shaw. He had tried to interview Elizabeth Robins on 4 February 1893, prior to her production of *The Master Builder*, but records in his diary that, 'Miss Robins got rather alarmed about the interview and swore she would shoot me if I said anything she did not approve of.'[88] In the event, Robins's prickliness, which recalled one of Hedda Gabler's most notorious moments, meant that Shaw was unable to publish their interview. He responded the next day with a letter which shows how successful Robins was in avoiding being manipulated by him. But Shaw seeks to turn the matter around, suggesting that Robins was only responding predictably to his ploys: 'Never in my life have I had such a professional success. You were clay in the hands of the potter. I have interviewed beautiful women before; but none of them were ever so noble as to threaten to shoot me.'[89] The guarded threat of the potter's image confirms Robins's actually having escaped on this occasion, whilst signifying the persistent terms of male–female theatrical collaboration which had constantly to be resisted.

In the light of such a comment, it is of course ironic that it should be Shaw who took up the Pygmalion and Galatea story in his play *Pygmalion*, which shows how a humble flower-girl can be newly created by being trained to use the correct accent. The play itself is largely a comedy about class, but in his sequel, Shaw discusses the extent to which it is also intended to confound the expectations of a theatre-audience that Higgins should marry Eliza, that her Pygmalion should marry Galatea. The sequel is an elaborate fiction which explains in great detail just why this cannot be, namely because Higgins is too devoted to his mother, and because Eliza could never tolerate a marriage to someone for whom she would not come first, and whose 'dominating superiority' would not be palatable.[90] Shaw goes on to construct a position of educated financial independence for Eliza, as she and Freddy Eynsford Hill run a florist's shop together, in which partnership she is clearly in charge. However, Shaw teasingly concludes by suggesting that from time to time Eliza has, 'secret mischievous moments in which she wishes she could get [Higgins] alone, on a desert island, away from all ties and with nobody else in the world to consider, and just drag him off his pedestal and see him making love like any other man' ('Sequel to *Pygmalion*', p. 757). But in the end, he suggests, she simply does not like Higgins: 'Galatea never does quite like Pygmalion: his relation to her is too godlike to be altogether agreeable' (p. 757). In this final assessment, Shaw implicitly and humorously recognises the nature and shortcomings of Pygmalion's position, and the on-going challenge being made by actresses in the early twentieth century to the powers of the Victorian Pygmalion.

Conclusion. Writing actresses

In 1899, Vernon Lee wrote a story whose content and title may have been inspired by Ibsen's *A Doll's House*. 'The Doll' was recounted to Lee by an old Italian friend, Pier Desiderio Pasolini. She professes not to know the origin of the story: 'this story is not by me at all, nor do I know whether it is by anybody, or, so to speak, a natural product'.[1] However, she adds to the story her own 'invented *finale*', which entails the burning of the doll of the title. It is this final detail which constitutes its departure from the restrictions of the Pygmalion legend, and which demonstrates how far women had moved in the 1890s towards the destruction of the Galatea-role.

The narrator of the tale is a well-to-do collector of bric-à-brac who travels widely in pursuit of her hobby. At the time she writes of, she is spending a few days in the Umbrian town of Foligno. There, in a house where she is inspecting a set of Chinese plates, she comes across the doll of the title, an exact copy of the first wife of the grandfather of the current owner of the house, made after the wife's early death in child-birth. Dressed in an original gown, and with a wig made of the deceased woman's hair, the doll has gradually been relegated from her own chamber, to one of her closets, to a cupboard in the servants' quarters, where her once-pristine clothing is now black with dust. A bond grows between the narrator and the doll, and the former 'somehow knew everything about [the doll] and the first items of information' which she gained from her guide 'did not enlighten [her] in the least, but merely confirmed what [she] was aware of' ('The Doll', pp. 216–17).

The 'doll' had been married very early, straight out of convent school to a man of 'easy, overflowing, garrulous, demonstrative affection' (p. 217), who kept her secluded from the world, and thus trapped in her shyness and inexperience. The narrator continues,

I became aware that in a deep, inarticulate way she had really cared for him more than he cared for her [...] he could not be silent about his love for two minutes, and she could never find a word to express hers, painfully though she longed to do so. Not that he wanted it; he was a brilliant, will-less, lyrical sort of person, who knew nothing of the feelings of others and cared only to welter and dissolve in his own. In those two years of ecstatic, talkative, all-absorbing love for her he not only forswore all society and utterly neglected his affairs, but he never made an attempt to train this raw young creature into a companion, or showed any curiosity as to whether his idol might have a mind or a character of her own. (pp. 217–18)

And so things continued, until, 'At last the spell seemed broken: the words and the power of saying them came; but it was on her death-bed. The poor young creature died in child-birth' (p. 218). The parallels with the Pygmalion story are clear, the silence and purity of the 'statue', her function as an object of admiration and inspiration, and as a mother, and they are heightened by the nature of the punishment which comes when those parallels are transgressed, when the doll speaks. Lee's confirmation of the relevance of Ovid's legend to her story comes after the young wife's death, when her husband's treatment of her, in the shape of the doll, is unchanged. She was only, and always, this inanimate object to him, her value residing in her power to inspire her husband, rather than in her subject-status. He eventually tires of the doll as he would have tired of the living woman.

    While the doll exists, the un-named dead woman remains trapped within her place in the legend. Only by the doll's destruction can she escape the constant reminder of her doll-like status; when the female narrator buys the doll and burns it (Lee's invented ending), she frees the dead woman to rest in her own named identity beneath her tomb-stone. Thus, through one woman's destruction of a mute, impotent image, another woman is born into identity. That identity is conferred through the act of writing, which at this time was being harnessed to very particular political ends by the so-called New Woman writers of the 1890s, such as Sarah Grand, Mona Caird, George Egerton, and Lee, who were attempting to show up the iniquities of those contemporary practices, most notably marriage, which seemed part of a concern to constrain women. They hoped thereby also, in the words of Sarah Grand, 'to raise the race a step higher in the scale of being'.[2] Lee's story epitomises the efforts of the actresses and New Women who were variously engaged in disputing acts of Pygmalionism, in trying to create, to name, and to 'author' new theatrical and social identities for women.

It thus acts also to position the work of the new actresses in a broader contemporary context.

During the nineties, the actress and the New Woman had been mischievously and misleadingly linked, via the figure of Ibsen, by detractors whose strategy was simply to deem all 'new' cultural elements 'decadent'. In 1894, Hubert Crackanthorpe wrote, 'Decadence, decadence, you are all decadent nowadays. Ibsen, Degas, and the New English Art Club; Zola, Oscar Wilde, and the Second Mrs Tanqueray',[3] thus neatly exposing the coverage of the term, and the extent to which conservative criticism created an homogenised target which misrepresented the multiplicity of the 'New' movement it sought to vilify. However, the link between the actress and the New Woman at this time was substantial and revealing, most particularly in terms of their relationship to 'words', and in their opportunities for the public manipulation of language. This link is cemented iconographically in *Punch*'s satire on the New Woman as 'Donna Quixote', and in the poster for Sydney Grundy's 1894 play *The New Woman*, actually an anti-New Woman play (plates 15 and 16). The women in both images are framed and defined by the multiplicity of the words spilling around them, fuelling their errant desires. For the cleanness and simplicity of Galatea's classically-robed outline are substituted fragmentary, mutating borders, for her discrete narrative a plethora of scattered pages offering her a choice of new narratives, with such titles as 'Revolt of Daughters', 'Man the Betrayer', and 'Naked but not Ashamed'. It is perhaps little wonder then that Janet Hogarth perceived that in women's writing, 'A want of balance, a deficient sense of proportion with a resulting lack of humour, and a total absence of any sort of reticence in the expression of emotion, are its most characteristic notes. Nothing could be farther from the well-balanced serenity of the classical spirit, with its instinct for proportion and its love of restraint.'[4] Arthur Waugh also condemned the New Woman, in terms implicitly derived from a popularised form of Classical aesthetic, for her immoderation and a lack of both self-respect and stoicism. He concludes:

Without dignity, without self-restraint, without the morality of art, literature has never survived; they are the few who rose superior to the baser levels of their time, who stand impugned among the immortals now. And that mortal who would put on immortality must first assume that habit of reticence, that garb of humility by which true greatness is best known. To endure restraint – that is to be strong.[5]

DONNA QUIXOTE.

[" A world of disorderly notions *picked out of books*, crowded into his (her) imagination."—*Don Quixote*.

Plate 15   'Donna Quixote', *Punch*, 106 (1894)

Plate 16   Poster for Sydney Grundy, *The New Woman* (1894)

In the face of the New Woman's challenge to conventions of literature and society, and the New Drama's challenge to theatrical conventions of writing, staging, and management, critics such as these responded by articulating a reactionary Classical agenda which sought to trap the arts within an aesthetic based upon the criterion that a work, like a statue, should 'weather well'.

The New Woman writer was content to risk the prize of long regard for the immediate gain of a political voice with which to participate in contemporary politics, and as she threw off her 'garb of humility', so her contemporary, the 'new' actress, was able to throw off her increasingly restrictive, marmoreal habit. In the 1890s a range of new identities had become available to women, not all of which were compatible with the sustaining of the Pygmalion-dynamic. The New Women writers of the 1890s contested Pygmalion's powers of determination in specific demands for reform, for the suffrage for instance, and for sexual autonomy, but also in their effort to draw women together, to make the act of reading an act of collaborative self-creation and affirmation, as the Ibsen actresses had tried to do in drawing female audiences to their productions. A female audience might be able to experience the actress as telling that audience's own story, giving voice to a previously silent narrative in a reciprocal act of narrativisation and collective empathy. In *Theatre and Friendship*, Robins recounts how 'One lady of our acquaintance, married and not noticeably unhappy, said laughing, "Hedda is all of us"' (p. 18). Shaw writes of Achurch and Duse that, 'Every woman who sees Duse play Magda feels that Duse is acting and speaking for her and for all women as they are hardly ever able to speak and act for themselves. The same may be said of Miss Achurch as Nora.'[6] Similarly, Archer notes of Duse that 'women should hail her with enthusiasm, for she seems to consummate and ennoble all the nobler possibilities of her sex';[7] for which ability, Helen Zimmern suggests, Duse 'has won the unswerving love of those who know her best, the love and friendship of her own sex'.[8]

Duse was telling her audience's actual and potential stories, acting in some measure autobiographically, and I would like to suggest that it is through the form of autobiography that the greatest challenge to the rights of Pygmalion is made. The form was, in the late-nineteenth and early-twentieth centuries neccessarily both an individual and a potentially collective act, and as we will see, the actress's access to the autobiographical mode took a variety of forms. She might write her own autobiography; she might be perceived as telling the story of herself, her audience, or both; or her acting might seem to derive from an aesthetic based on an autobiographical principle. However, no matter how she participates in it, the actress's autobiographical 'act' at this period is a mark of her radicalism.

ACTRESSES AND AUTOBIOGRAPHY

Commentators at the end of the century found an autobiographical principle in the acting of Duse in particular. The extent to which, as Helen Zimmern puts it, Duse 'sinks her part in herself rather than herself in her part' became a critical commonplace, and along with her intellect was seen by many commentators as the source of her uniqueness, of what Zimmern, with a backward glance at J. S. Mill, calls Duse's 'originality' ('Eleanora Duse', pp. 987, 988). Her art was 'a part of herself' (Zimmern, 'Eleanora Duse', p. 990), an assessment similar to that made earlier by William Archer who writes that Duse's 'most marvellous' creations are 'facets of her natural self' ('Eleanora Duse', p. 305). Indeed Arthur Symons writes that it is even by being 'more and more profoundly herself' that she is most 'profoundly true to the character she is representing'.[9] Duse's art, he continues, is 'wrought outwards from within, not from without inwards' ('Eleanora Duse', p. 202). Duse's acting is thus 'profoundly' autobiographical, telling not of her own experiences, but of her cumulative sympathetic and emotional capacities. Hansson is eager to claim that this autobiographical source lies in Duse's womanliness, thus making of that art a collective female 'autobiographical' expression:

> There can be no doubt that there is a kind of genius peculiar to women, and it is when a woman is a genius that she is most unlike man, and most womanly; it is then that she creates through the instrumentality of her womanly nature and refined senses. This is the kind of productive faculty which Eleanora Duse possesses to such a high degree. (*Modern Women*, p. 123)[10]

That the responsibility or authorship of this impression is Duse's rather than that of the playwrights she works with is suggested by these critics' perceptions that, without changing the words of the characters she acts, Duse nonetheless changes so radically the conception of her parts that they are scarcely recognisable to the playwright. Of her Marguerite Gautier, critics wrote that 'The picture of manners which Dumas intended disappears in the drama of pure emotion' (Archer, 'Eleanora Duse', p. 302), and that 'she had revealed in [the role] possibilities unknown even to [Dumas]' (Zimmern, 'Eleanora Duse', p. 992). Hansson notes the same of Duse's Nora, 'a being who has no place in the written words, and whom the author never thought of' (*Modern Women*, p. 110). As Zimmern continues, 'Duse collaborates with her authors, and creates their characters anew and afresh' ('Eleanora Duse', p. 992–3). Duse is thus thoroughly self-created, emphatically not the result of others' manipulation, neither that of the playwright nor that of the audience, to whom she is rather a 'riddle' (Archer, 'Eleanora Duse', p. 300) than a gratification.

The extent of her self-making is perhaps best acknowledged in Archer's and Symons's adoption of the metaphor of sculpting to describe Duse's artistry. Archer writes of her Magda that she is 'a figure, designed and modelled beforehand, proportioned, poised, and polished to the finger-tips with a sculptor's patient assiduity' ('Eleanora Duse', p. 304); while Symons uses the metaphorical likeness between actor and sculptor to assert that through her art Duse even controls 'Nature into the forms of her desire, as the sculptor controls the clay under his fingers' (p. 196). Thus her art is seen as explicitly challenging the prerogatives of Pygmalion. Symons goes on to elaborate on this function of the actress, and by invoking Rodin, equates the art of his fingers with that of the actress's soul, in which equation of course Duse becomes self-determining, and her body simply her instrument rather than her end:

The face of Duse is a mask for the tragic passions, a mask which changes from moment to moment, as the soul models the clay of the body after its own changing image. Imagine Rodin at work on a lump of clay. The shapeless thing awakens under his fingers, a vague life creeps into it, hesitating among the forms of life; it is desire, waiting to be born, and it may be born as pity or anguish, love or pride; so fluid is it to the touch, so humbly does it await the accident of choice. The face of Duse is like the clay under the fingers of Rodin. (Symons, 'Eleanora Duse', p. 199)

Duse's theatrical body then is made not given, and her maker is herself. Symons is thus perhaps the most telling witness of the implications of the autobiographical impulse for the actress. In that impulse there is no space for the moulding hands and gaze of a Pygmalion, for his role has been filled by the actress's self-conscious self-manipulation, and out of that substitution a new critical language, capable of recognising and of appreciating female 'genius', 'intellect', and 'originality' is born.

Other actresses chose to function autobiographically through writing, thereby not only choosing their own words, but constructing their whole role through their manipulation of narrative, thus making a claim for both 'cultural and literary authority'.[11] The autobiographical 'act' of the actress differs significantly from other women's accession to that form. In her professional life, she can already 'command an audience',[12] has already a place in 'the public arena' (Smith, *Poetics of Women's Autobiography*, p. 52), and is perpetually engaged on stage in negotiating the acts of 'cultural ventriloquism' which Smith suggests are most characteristic of women's struggle with the autobiographical form, and their decision as to the voice in which their story is to be told (p. 57). In some respects then, autobiographical writing coincides with the actress's usual practice, but it does so in such a way as to free that practice from its constraints within the Pygmalion-metaphor. The autobiographical subject is both the material of which art is made, and the creator of that art. If the actress can be so acknowledged as both creator and created too, then the analogy between the two art-forms enables the possibility that the authority of the playwright may be displaced and the real power of creativity be seen to reside with the actress, as was clearly the case with Duse. This leads to a form of cultural or artistic parthenogenesis which may seem to parallel, but actually displaces, that of Pygmalion. In self-contemplation, the female autobiographer creates a literary entity out of the self, claiming Pygmalion's right to determine, through authoring, moulding, her own life. The actress's access to the autobiographical impulse, and her newly acknowledged creativity, afford her a similar privilege.

In Helena Faucit Martin's case, this privilege was carefully camouflaged. First collected in 1885, her autobiographical writings are hidden behind the title *On Some of Shakespeare's Female Characters*, a displacement which perhaps recognises the implicit claims to authority and self-creation in the act of swapping the stage for the page. In her account of how she became an actress, Faucit Martin invokes a narrative of self-effacement appropriate to the 1880s as she stumbles unselfconsciously into the part of Juliet in the Richmond theatre. She writes of how, on a day when it was too hot to walk by the river, she and her sister stole into the cool, dark theatre whose doors were usually open. Believing themselves to be alone in the place, they acted the balcony-scene from *Romeo and Juliet*, with Faucit playing Juliet. Later, they found that they had had a listener:

When our friends arrived some days later, the lessee told them that, having occasion to go from the dwelling-house to his private box, he had heard voices,

listened, and remained during the time of our merry rehearsal. He spoke in
such warm terms of the Juliet's voice, its adaptability to the character, her
figure, – I was tall for my age, – and so forth, that in the end he prevailed upon
my friends to let me make a trial on his stage [...] Thus did a little frolic prove to
be the turning-point of my life.[13]

And thus Faucit Martin's career began. Her writing herself into that
unselfconscious moment, however, necessarily disrupts the third-party
ascription of the unselfconsciousness which was a crucial part of theatrical fictions of the 1880s, of that decade's performances of Juliet, and of
Galatea's role. Later, as we have already seen, Faucit Martin chose to
disrupt her sculptural reification still further by seeming to speak from
inside the statue as she recounted her experience of playing Hermione
to Macready's Leontes.

The most prolific of the actress–autobiographers of the period was
Elizabeth Robins, whose autobiographical writings take a variety of
forms and practices. *Both Sides of the Curtain* is a partial autobiography
which submerges the young Robins's attempts to find a place in the
London theatre within a history of that theatre in the 1880s. Her own
story uneasily infiltrates the more conventional theatre-history, just as
she herself tried to move onto the London stage, and ends just before she
became an Ibsen-actress. *Raymond and I* (published posthumously in
1956) is an adventure-narrative which takes up Robins's life after her
work in the new theatre had finished, and is an account of her journey to
Alaska to find and nurse her brother Raymond. The Ibsen years are
covered in the essay *Ibsen and the Actress*, and in *Theatre and Friendship*, an
edition of Henry James's letters about the theatre to her and to Florence
Bell. Robins's story is told in the commentary which links and contex-
tualises the letters, and in her strategy of selection which, as Angela V.
John notes, demonstrates as great an interest in the story of Robins's
collaboration with the recently dead Bell, as in James. The personae in
each version are intriguingly varied, from the young ingénue, to the
pioneer of theatre, the responsible but adventurous traveller and sister,
to the writer who ambivalently posed as one in awe of James, 'the
Master', whilst paying greater tribute to her friend Florence Bell, and
taking great delight in evading James's admonitory attentions. In these
public texts, Robins self-consciously interrogates the range of roles
which were open to her as a woman at that time; and creates and
re-creates herself in a variety of images which necessarily exceed
Galatea's public stasis and consistency. As a novelist, she even adopted a
male pseudonym (C. E. Raimond) for her satirical portrait of the

opposition to contemporary women writers in *George Mandeville's Husband* (1894).

Ironically, in order to achieve this freedom of personation Robins had to leave the stage. Despite her efforts in the theatre, opportunities for the actress still seemed restrictive. In *Theatre and Friendship*, she writes that: 'My brief experiences of having a theatre, and a company of my own, had taught me a number of things. In "leading lady" leading-strings I found the long fascination of the Theatre wearing thin' (p. 151). Indeed, by the end of the century, she professes to have come to feel that even Ibsen had let her down. She records of *When We Dead Awaken* that

His new play (his last) was a disappointment to some of those who cared most for him. 'When We Dead Awaken' was not, as each of the previous plays had been, a fresh attack; it was full of echoes for the mind and the ear that had much of the older plays by heart. To me the new play was matter almost for tears – no, I would not produce it, even if I were not making ready to go away. The Master hand had weakened, the Master voice was failing.[14]

It is in this play, and in the story of the sculptor's model Irene that a final comment on Ibsen's relationship with the Victorian actress is provided, for her story is to some extent that of the actress too. Irene's history is imbued with motifs of the theatre in the nineties, and initially exemplifies that of the actress whose independence and creativity are contained within roles determined by her physicality. Irene's first appearance in the play is appropriately as a walking statue, dressed in a costume of classically inspired robes. We learn that she has existed for Rubek professionally and only through the body, and her course after his desertion is to fulfil his vision by turning herself more completely into a statue. We even learn that she has 'posed in music-halls, naked on a turn-table, as a living statue'.[15] The course of the play shows Irene achieving her liberation from the deadened sculptural form which Rubek had imposed upon her. This is managed through the complementary means of a recourse to a palpably 'symbolic' language which flirts with the anarchy of madness, and through the final vertical movement of the play, which characterises Ibsen's last works.[16] Irene is liberated finally, of course, into death, but here it acts also as a retrospective entrance into the complexity of a fully realised life which exceeds the death-in-life of the idealised marmoreal statue-form. Robins's leaving the theatre that she had done so much to try to reform, in order to take up writing, might seem a similarly complex and paradoxical movement.

A final intriguing twist to Robins's story is given in a previously unpublished letter which confirms the self-making and remaking potential of language and writing, particularly when divorced from the constraints of the stage, whilst upsetting the accepted version of her disillusionment with the legitimate theatre given in *Theatre and Friendship*. Before we concur in this construction, we need to note the evidence of a letter written by Robins in June 1899 which demonstrates the redundancy she perceived in the new theatres at that time. While claiming that 'up to the end of 1899 [...] there was no slackening on the part of the New Century Theatre Committee in the keen look out for the work of sound quality. We seemed to be always reading plays' (*Theatre and Friendship*, p. 215), Robins was simultaneously wooing Sir Henry Irving in the hope of becoming his leading lady after the departure of Ellen Terry from the Lyceum. Robins writes (in a letter emphatically marked 'Private') in terms which implicitly repudiate her part in the Ibsen revolution:

My Dear Sir Henry,
    It just occurs to me: since the opportunity hitherto of doing any Shakespeare in London has been barred to me, & since I cannot hope you will realize that such parts are what I do best – would it simplify matters at all if I got up ... say Portia, & came & rehearsed her for you on approval? I've never done such a thing but why not try to <u>show</u> you?
    I am conscious that I must seem to you like the hundreds of cocksure young women who haunt your door – but think! ever since I came to England it has been my dream to work with you. And I have waited, waited – hoping you would ask me. And now at the eleventh hour, I am putting a pressure upon myself very foreign to my nature in striving to show you that what I want would not be ill-bestowed.
    I am
        Yours very sincerely;
        Elizabeth Robins
I was telling the Lewises last night of having seen you; Sir George very kindly offered the enclosed.[17]

This letter of course counters Robins's published texts, but it is surely possible to read these conflicting narratives not as simple contradictions, but as evidence of how far the actress has managed to exceed the definition implied and confined within the moment of on-stage reification. Galatea is neither contradictory nor various, but Robins is able to construct herself as both of these things, albeit having left the stage behind.

Plate 17   'Miss Ellen Terry as "Hermione"', *Tatler*, 12 September 1906

LITERARY MONUMENTS AND LAUGHING STATUES

I end by returning to Ellen Terry. Shortly before Terry's *The Story of My Life* was published, the actress made her last professional performance with Beerbohm Tree at the Drury Lane Theatre in 1906, when she played Hermione to Tree's Leontes (plate 17). Terry's career was bounded by *The Winter's Tale*. In 1856, at the age of eight, she had played Mamilius for 102 nights in Charles Kean's production, and barring some benefit performances, her professional career ended with the same play. Intriguingly it was Shaw who had suggested the play to her eleven years earlier: 'by the way, if you will let Shakespeare steal you to decorate his plays with, why not play Hermione?' (1 November 1895, *Terry–Shaw Correspondence*, p. 17). When she did come to take on the part, however, the actress was far from an exemplary statue. Describing her performance to Graham Robertson, Terry wrote,

> A dreadful thing – I laughed last night!! as the statue! and I'm laughing now!
> Who could help it! With Leontes shouting and Paulina shouting they just
> roared so I could not help it! oh, Graham I was rather glad – for I've not been
> able to laugh at all lately (and that's downright wicked) but I'm so afraid I may
> do it again if they will shout!! – You see (as a statue) I don't *look* at 'em – I only
> hear them – and it's excruciatingly funny = I'm mad at myself.[18]

Terry's characteristic style and notation struggle to exceed the syntax of her letter, just as her notorious and irrepressible sense of the ridiculous out-ran the rigours of the statue's limitations.[19] In some measure, the moment exemplifies the tensions of Terry's career: the conflict between the actress whose beauty was considered her primary theatrical qualification, and the woman whose energy and independence had sustained her in a professional career for fifty years. This incident is particularly interesting, however, in demonstrating the means by which an actress's engagement with writing may elucidate, complicate, elaborate, and finally dispute, her identification with the spectacular statue. Her written account defies the statue's simplicity, its iconic availability, and assumptions about its creator. As the overlapping narratives of her professional and private lives have demonstrated, there was a frequent insistence upon the appropriateness of the sculptural metaphor for one who was commonly held to be the most popular, most 'charming', actress of her generation. However, Terry's autobiographical writings, along with her annotations, and letters, all forms of self-writing, retrospectively disrupt her spectacular appeal, and dispute Galatea's form and function on the late-Victorian stage.

Though Ellen Terry's *The Story of My Life* was not published until 1908, her first autobiographical writings appeared in the *New Review*, under the disarming title, 'Stray Memories', in 1891.[20] Just as she achieved supremacy on the stage by being charming, so did Terry adopt a similar practice in these writings, which are a pleasurable, loosely chronological string of anecdotes. However, the crucial factor here is that we are undeniably aware of Terry's decision as an author to be, rather than to be found, 'damned Charming'. The act of writing, previously the privilege of her critics, enables her to position her audience, characterising them in the role of the beloved, to be charmed and wooed by her text, and subsequently, to have their reactions influenced, if not determined, by the decisions that she as a writer is making. Terry's rhetoric of charm functions skilfully to camouflage the substance of her text; it acts as a substitute for the romantic interest which is entirely lacking in her writing, and detracts attention from, or at least mollifies apprehensions of, the almost entirely professional narrative she writes.

These early memoirs analyse Terry's career in such a way as scarcely to mention Irving, or the other men with whom she was associated. She omits any mention at all of G. F. Watts and Edward Godwin, her relationships with whom were well known, and the two men are engulfed anonymously in the textual gaps of her absences from the stage. The articles are shrewdly constructed accounts of the actress's training, leavened with the kind of personal reminiscence associated with theatrical memoirs. But even the latter contain appreciations of particular skills, such as Mr Kean's voice projection ('Stray Memories', p. 337), or lead to reflection on theatrical practices. Terry is effectively outlining how she had moulded her own career, acknowledging as a mentor only her early teacher, Mrs Kean (p. 333). These are professional rather than personal memoirs, and in their autobiographical matter, as well as their form, publicly constitute Terry's claim to professional autonomy. For Terry, writing autobiographically is not simply a matter of describing 'how the author acquired or came to do without a room of her own; how she came to command an audience rhetorically, ideologically and socio-economically' (Broughton, 'Women's Autobiography', p. 79). Rather the act constitutes her claim to order, and to have ordered both her narrative and the life she describes. Such a strategy, later more fully played out in *The Story of My Life*, is not the act of a submissive or reflexive Galatea, whose identity is constituted by another.[21] For the actress to enter into the world of authorship is to enter upon new possibilities of self-constitution, and specifically to envisage new temporal possibilities for the persistence of the evidence of that self. Reliance upon the body and its impact is surpassed in the act of writing. This disturbing effect is aided by the articles' lack of illustrations, which further isolates and protects her words from the connotations of Terry's body, and also by their being published alongside Henry James's ground-breaking essay on *Hedda Gabler* in the *New Review*.

In the same year as 'Stray Memories' were published Terry took on another project which helped to re-write her role in the Lyceum. She appeared with her son Gordon Craig in an adaptation of Charles Reade's curtain-raiser, *Nance Oldfield*, based on the life of the famous eighteenth-century actress, Ann Oldfield. When it was originally offered to the Lyceum, Irving turned the play down, and it was bought instead by Terry. The actress was a key participant in this theatrical event which gave a new lease of life to one of her professional ancestors, and in the course of which Terry asserted her awareness of her own place within a historical community of actresses. She also tasted the power of the playwright and producer in collaborating with Bram Stoker in the adaptation of the play. Stoker's account of his work with the actress, and of her part in specifying the alterations desired is worth quoting at length for the ambivalence of its attitude to Terry:

she was not herself an experienced dramatist. She knew in a general way what it was that was wanting and what she aimed at, but she could not always give it words. During rehearsal or during the play she would in a pause of her own stage work come dancing into my office to ask for help. Ellen Terry's movements, when she was not playing a sad part, always gave one the idea of a graceful dance. Looking back now to twenty-seven years of artistic companionship and eternal community of ideas, I cannot realise that she did not always actually dance. She would point to some mark which she made in the altered script and say:

'I want two lines there, please!'

'What kind of lines? What about?' I would ask. She would laugh as she answered:

'I don't know. I haven't the least idea. You must write them!' When she would dance back again I would read her the lines. She would laugh again and say:

'All wrong, absolutely wrong. They are too serious', or 'they are too light, I should like to convey the idea of—' and she would in some subtle way – just as Irving did – convey the sentiment, or purpose, or emotion which she had wished conveyed. She would know without my saying it when I had got hold of the idea and would rush off to her work quite satisfied. (Stoker, *Personal Reminiscences*, vol. I, pp. 194–5)

Whilst conceding to the actress an instinct for 'stage art' and the status of a 'conscious artist', Stoker seems unwilling to complement these gifts with a full command of language, and seeks to return Terry to the role of a flighty nymph or Muse figure, rather than recognising her as the professional actress he professes to admire. His comments seem to mask frustration through the process of infantilising their object.

Nance Oldfield opened on 12 May and became a stock part of Terry's repertoire, but is disparagingly referred to by Shaw in his letters as 'wicked frivolity' (28 August 1896, *Terry–Shaw Correspondence*, p. 40), and as a play that does not give Terry any trouble (9 April 1897, *Terry–Shaw Correspondence*, p. 160). What Shaw fails to recognise is that the play is far from being a simple vehicle for displaying Ellen Terry, for in her version, it may be read both as an act of communication with the long-dead actress; and as Terry's comment on her role and place as a contemporary actress. Through its treatment of the working life of a historical figure, the play signals a degree of self-consciousness on Terry's part which militates against the easy assumption that she is created simply through the desires of her spectators. Nance Oldfield's reflections on acting necessitate the recognition of Terry's own adoption of a professional role, as, for instance, when Nance reveals what she feels when acting on-stage:'I ride on the whirl-wind of a poet's words; I wave my mimic sceptre with more power than the kings of Europe – they govern millions of bodies, but I sway a thousand hearts – and the next day I sink to woman!'[22] The character goes on to pillory the control supposed to rest with playwrights when she says to the irate father of her young suitor: 'You are aware, sir, that we play actors have not an idea of our own in our skulls, our art is to execute beautifully the ideas of those who think' (p. 13). In the attempt to disabuse her young admirer, played by Terry's son, we even have Terry's own comment on the Diderot debate: 'Now, my good soul, if I was really to vex my self <u>night after night</u> [Terry's manuscript emphasis] for Clytemnestra and Co. I shouldn't hold together long. No, thank you. I have Nancy Oldfield to take care of, and what's Hecuba to her?' (p. 17). Further, in most self-conscious mode, Terry parodies her own roles in the plays of 'Willy Shakespeare', with brief renditions of Lady Macbeth and Juliet. Her acting edition of the play is full of such amendments to her part. In this play, Terry challenges the parameters of her role as the Lyceum's leading-lady, for in many of her activities, and especially as adaptor and owner of the play, she was usurping Irving's more usual responsibilities. It was perhaps this which encouraged Stoker's hostile reference to Terry in *Dracula*. But Terry also uses the role to tell her own professional story, to narrate her own understanding of her part in the theatre, and thus to write another form of autobiography.

In the concluding paragraph to *Ellen Terry's Memoirs*, we find the actress's final posthumous engagement with the sculptural metaphor and the Galatea-narrative by which she, more persistently perhaps than any other Victorian actress, had been defined. Here, Edy Craig and Christopher St John echo, in a more particular form, George Eliot's assertion that writing may recuperate, or compensate for, the transitoriness of physical representations. Much of these women's lives after Terry's death was dedicated to propagating Terry's memory, in the interest of which they describe Terry's printed works as her monuments, and write of the *Memoirs* that, 'We have in this monument, and in those other literary monuments, Ellen Terry's autobiography, and her lectures on Shakespeare, as well as in her shrine at Smallhythe, something to inspire those who come after us with the same devotion to her memory' (*Memoirs*, p. 354). As they had noted earlier, 'Iliads are more enduring that Parthenons' (p. 350), and a written record would allow Terry's fame to endure beyond 'the memory of a diminishing band of elderly people' (p. 348). However, the history of Terry's writings, and indeed her text itself, has little of the stability that St John and Craig's analogy suggests.

The Story of My Life, in the writing of which Terry was helped by St John, is an idiosyncratic autobiography in its principles of organisation, its omissions, and its style, an overtly conversational mode, the apparent inconsequentialities of which in fact determine both the work's tone and much of its appeal. Of Disraeli, for instance, she writes 'I love Disraeli's novels – like his tie, brighter in colour than anyone else's' (*Story of My Life*, p. 54). Her recollection of great men generally is tinged with a freshness and self-effacement which has the effect of revivifying her subjects sympathetically, if not very exaltedly: 'my want of education may be partly responsible for the unsatisfactory blankness of my early impressions. As it takes two to make a good talker, so it takes two to make a good hero – in print, at any rate. I was meeting distinguished people at every turn, and taking no notice of them' (p. 56). This reflection, however, prompts a string of recollections of Tennyson, of Terry's youthful preference for games with his children rather than for the Laureate's own doings, and of her later enjoyment of his company and his work. Terry's apparent irreverence throughout in fact enables her story's affectionate and fresh tone.

In the Preface to Terry's *Memoirs* St John and Edith Craig write of their work as editors that 'We felt that if we began tinkering with Ellen Terry's work we might deprive it of its spontaneity, and decided to let well alone' (*Memoirs*, p. v). They elaborate on their editorial practice thus: 'very few alterations have been made in the original text, beyond some cuts necessitated by the addition of the biographical chapters which complete the narrative. Corrections of slips, and other revisions calculated to increase the value of the book as an authoritative record, have been included in the editorial notes' (*Memoirs*, p. v). The editors are, however, disingenuous, for not only does the addition of weighty footnotes and of highly partisan chapters on the last years of Terry's life irredeemably alter the nature of Terry's reminiscences, but their interference with Terry's own words is extensive and not a little distorting. Neither of the two extracts quoted above, for instance, survive, and also removed are some of Terry's admittedly inconsequential generalisations about the theatre, for instance, 'I don't think that any drama which is vital and *essential* can ever be old-fashioned' (*Story of My Life*, p. 72). Missing too are some of Terry's reflections on how 'fated' her life seemed to her, on some of the things she did not do, and on some of the revelations hindsight gave her. Perhaps the saddest omissions are many of the humorous passages which give the autobiography its charm, and which woo the reader into a sense of intimacy through the actress's rueful confessions. She writes of playing Iolanthe in 1880 that twice,

I forgot that I was blind! The first time was when I saw old Tom Mead and Henry Irving groping for the amulet, which they had to put on my breast to heal me of my infirmity. It had slipped to the floor, and both of them were too short-sighted to see it! Here was a predicament! I had to stoop to pick it up for them.

The second time I put out my hand and cried: 'Look out for my lilies,' when Henry nearly stepped on the bunch with which a little girl friend of mine supplied me every night I played the part. (*Story of My Life*, p. 188)

St John and Craig also distort Terry's record of her relations with her male partners, notably increasing Godwin's share in Terry's narrative, and almost eradicating her affectionate account of her second husband, Charles Kelly. Terry wrote of her version of Kelly's life that it 'was absurdly faint praise' (*Story of My Life*, p. 137). This is omitted in the *Memoirs*.

Terry heavily annotated one copy of her autobiography which is marked on the inside cover 'For revision – by E. C. [Ellen Carew]', but the editors seem not to have used these annotations as a basis for their revisions.[23] In her annotations she expresses regret for quoting an unfavourable account of Mrs Kean's Portia (*Story of My Life*, p. 186), scribbling in the margin, 'Nasty in me to quote this letter: E. T. <u>Sorry</u> ='. But the letter is kept in the *Memoirs*. St John and Craig also use their editorial material in footnotes to contest Terry's own words and self-understanding for their own ends, most pertinently perhaps when they challenge her statement that she was more woman than artist. They write, somewhat uneasily, 'Ellen Terry honestly thought this was true …[but] It is impossible to identify this theoretical Ellen Terry, in whom Ellen Terry herself believed, with the Ellen Terry of fact' (*Memoirs*, p. 150 n. 3).

The alterations have gone largely unnoticed, as recent readers have tended to take the *Memoirs* as simply a new and expanded version of *The Story of My Life*. However, I would argue that, small though the alterations made to the 1908 text may seem individually, the number of them is so great that their cumulative effect, along with the editors' adherence to a more strictly chronological narrative, represents a substantial re-writing of Terry's story, and as such implicitly offers a new interpretation, a re-building of the 'monument' Terry left behind.

The 1933 edition of the *Memoirs* is itself the result of a process of wrangling over the 'ownership' of Terry's memory, and the shape of her legacy, which began when, with Christopher St John's encouragement, the correspondence between Bernard Shaw and Terry was published in 1931. This volume, and in particular its preface, an extended and affectionate essay by Shaw on how Terry's talents had been wasted at the Lyceum, offended Gordon Craig to the extent that he was moved to publish his own account of Ellen Terry, *Ellen Terry and Her Secret Self*, in the next year. Craig's reasons for writing are given in a clumsily argued Annex to the work, which is entitled 'A Plea for G. B. S.'. In it Craig enumerates a catalogue of complaints, ranging from his sense of Shaw's lack of chivalry in allowing a lady's private correspondence to be published; through his accusations of Shaw's self-interestedness in publishing, and the self-aggrandisement resulting; to the most poignant complaint of all, which consists of Craig's sense of Shaw as a rival for Terry's maternal affections:

to such wonderful women […] we are all of us just children – and the naughty ones are often preferable to the good. All we have to do is to pout, and they love us.

G. B. S. pouted ever so pretty, and so E. T. 'loved' him. That she was really a little fond of him is clear but then she was fond of 'twenty such' – and twenty more.[24]

Craig was also concerned to defend Irving against what he saw as another assault on the actor-manager's reputation, perhaps fearing that Terry would be retrospectively implicated in that attack. His response took the form of an extended insistence on the fact that the correspondence is flawed because it is inadequate, not a whole representation of a woman whom he represents as fundamentally fractured, living a dual existence as both 'that little Nelly who was my mother – her secret self – [...and] that redoubtable adversary, her other self ... Ellen Terry' ('Preface', *Terry and Her Secret Self*, pp. vii–viii). Statuesque monuments are not however, at least purposely, fractured and divided against themselves, but this is what her children make of Terry, a flawed masterpiece, exceeding a simple reading, and not to be encompassed by a single gaze.

Thus it would seem that the most important and liberating aspect of self-writing for the actress is not the promise of endurance offered in St John and Craig's allusions to the *Iliad* and the Parthenon, but rather, as the number of works about Terry now demonstrate, of an entry into the realm of interpretation and consequent mutability and variety, a realm foreign to Pygmalion's statue, and of which Terry had her first experience when she acted Lady Macbeth to such controversial effect. The too-solicitous St John misses the point of Terry's writing, which, rather than substituting one lapidary form for another, instead inserts Terry into the variety and complexity of the textual witness which is profoundly at odds with the dimensions of a commemorative monument. It is thus through access to her own language that the actress may most assuredly surpass Galatea's aesthetic.

In her 1941 essay on Terry, Virginia Woolf suggests that with her pen Terry has 'painted a self-portrait', but that this is 'not an Academy portrait, glazed, framed, complete'.[25] She goes on in terms which appropriately both dismember the actress's remembered and much-adored body, and reconstitute that body as a self-constructed literary artefact:

It is rather a bundle of loose leaves upon each of which she has dashed off a sketch for a portrait – here a nose, here an arm, here a foot, and there a mere scribble in the margin. The sketches done in different moods, from different angles, sometimes contradict each other. The nose cannot belong to the eyes; the arm is out of all proportion to the foot. It is difficult to assemble them. (p. 68)

Difficult that is to make them cohere in a stable, sculptural form. Writing herself has enabled Terry to elude her Pygmalions by forcing them to engage with her in the medium of language which was so disablingly denied to Galatea at her 'birth', and which has enabled this actress to survive beyond the moments at which, Galatea-like, she was brought into being by the attentions of her audience.

Notes

INTRODUCTION

1 Mrs Jameson, *Characteristics of Women, Moral, Poetical, and Historical*, 2 vols. (London: Saunders and Otley, 1832), vol. II, p. 22.

2 Mrs Jameson, *A Handbook to the Courts of Modern Sculpture*, Crystal Palace Library (London: Bradbury & Evans, 1854), p. 7.

3 Henry Siddons, *Practical Illustrations of Rhetorical Gesture and Action* (London: Sherwood, Neely, and Jones, 1822), pp. 181–2. Since Classical times, dramatic representations of Niobe have been associated with a statue-like image. In *The Frogs*, Aristophanes criticises a play, now lost, by Aeschylus in which the tragedian has Niobe sit mute on stage whilst action proceeds around her:

> EURIPIDES: He'd bring some single mourner on, seated and veiled, 'twould be
> Achilles, say, or Niobe – the face you could not see –
> An empty show of tragic woe, who uttered not one thing.
> DIONYSUS: 'Tis true.
> EURIPIDES: Then in the Chorus came, and rattled off a string
> Of four continuous lyric odes: the mourner never stirred.

Aristophanes, *The Frogs*, trans. by Benjamin Bickley Rogers (London: Heinemann; Cambridge, MA: Harvard University Press, 1968), lines 911–15.

4 In his account of *The Winter's Tale*'s nineteenth-century performance history, Dennis Bartholomeusz notes that when Charles Kean was rehearsing the play at the Princess's Theatre in 1856, it was rumoured that he was producing a Greek play, so established had become the play's Classical trappings and the presence of the classicised statue (Dennis Bartholomeusz, *The Winter's Tale in Performance in England and America, 1611–1976* (Cambridge University Press, 1982), p. 86). The programme of this production advertised that amongst the production's attractions would be 'A Classical Allegory, Representing the Course of Time, Luna in Her Car', an 'Ascent of Phoebus in the Chariot of the Sun', and a 'Festival of Dionysus (or Bacchus)'.

5 Valerie Traub, *Desire and Anxiety: Circulations of Sexuality in Shakespearean Drama*

(London and New York: Routledge, 1992), p. 26.

6 The term is borrowed from Abbé Blum, ' "Strike All that Look upon Her with Mar[b]le": Monumentalizing Women in Shakespeare's Plays', in *The Renaissance Englishwoman in Print: Counterbalancing the Canon* (Amherst: University of Massachusetts Press, 1990), pp. 99–118.

7 Quoted in Richard Jenkyns, *The Victorians and Ancient Greece* (Oxford: Blackwell, 1980), pp. 87–8.

8 Michael R. Booth, *Victorian Spectacular Theatre, 1850–1910* (London: Routledge and Kegan Paul, 1981), p. 8.

9 See Martin Meisel, *Realizations: Narrative, Pictorial and Theatrical Arts in Nineteenth-century England* (Princeton University Press, 1983).

10 I use the term 'legitimate' advisedly to signal two usually complementary functions of a particular kind of theatre: first, the term is intended to distinguish the dramatic stage from that of the burlesque or music-hall; and second, to signal, during the latter part of the century, the ascription of a form of social and cultural authority to the theatre. The complementarity of these two attributes was at its peak in the 1880s at the Lyceum theatre, then under the management of Henry Irving. However, the relationship between them is essentially fluid, and often mediated by the intervention of other forms of theatre. My work seeks both to be sensitive to that fluidity, and to offer insights into the particular forms it takes in the later-nineteenth century. As will become clear, theatrical 'legitimacy' is intimately bound up with the 'Galatea-aesthetic'.

11 Johann Wolfgang von Goethe, *Italian Journey*, trans. by W. H. Auden and Elizabeth Mayer (Harmondsworth: Penguin, 1962), p. 129.

I VICTORIAN PYGMALIONS

1 Francis Haskell and Nicholas Penny, *Taste and the Antique: The Lure of Classical Sculpture, 1500–1900* (New Haven and London: Yale University Press, 1981), p. 118.

2 'The mystery and wonder of the gallery, however – the Venus di Medici – I could nowhere see, and indeed was almost afraid to see it; for I somewhat apprehended the extinction of another of those lights that shine along a man's pathway, and go out in a snuff the instant he comes within eyeshot of the fulfilment of his hope' (*Passages from the French and Italian Note-books of Nathaniel Hawthorne*, 2 vols. (London: Strahan, 1871), vol. II, p. 5; quoted in Haskell and Penny, *Taste and the Antique*, p. 118). Hawthorne goes on to say that the Venus is 'very beautiful, very satisfactory, and has a fresh and new charm about her unreached by any cast or copy' (vol. II, pp. 7–8).

3 Samuel Phillips, *Guide to the Crystal Palace* (London, 1862); quoted in Haskell and Penny, *Taste and the Antique*, p. 330.

4 Cornelia Carr (ed.), *Harriet Hosmer: Letters and Memories* (London: Lane, Bodley Head, 1913), p. 23.

5 Quoted in Ian Jenkins, *Archaeologists and Aesthetes in the Sculpture Galleries of the*

British Museum, 1800–1939 (London: British Museum Press, 1992), p. 39. Jenkins also gives details of the number of visits made by art students to the Museum's sculpture and cast galleries. These rose from 2,981 in 1870, to 3,911 in 1871, to 4,769 in 1872, 6,281 in 1873, 7,185 in 1874, and 15,626 in 1879 (p. 39).

6 The term is Christopher Wood's, and is taken from his *Olympian Dreamers: Victorian Classical Painters, 1860–1914* (London: Constable, 1983).

7 Quoted in Richard D. Altick, *The Shows of London* (Cambridge, MA, and London: Harvard University Press, 1978), p. 339.

8 Thus was recuperated the notorious Classical practice of using statues for sexual stimulation. In the *Amores* of pseudo-Lucian, a long account is given of a young man who was so smitten by Praxiteles' Aphrodite of Cnidus that he allowed himself to be locked into her temple at night, when 'In the end the violent tension of his desires turned to desperation and he found in audacity a procurer for his lusts' (*Works of Lucian*, trans. by M. D. Macleod, 8 vols. (London: Heinemann; Cambridge, MA: Harvard University Press, 1967), vol. VIII, p. 175). The statue was marked by a blemish on its thigh to show its sexual violation, and the young man is said to have vanished, supposedly throwing himself 'over a cliff or down into the waves of the sea'. The story is also referred to in Lucian's *Essays in Portraiture* where it initiates a discussion about the works of Praxiteles, and the way in which the participants in the dialogue might combine the best features of each statue to make the perfect female image. For other instances of statue-violation, see Hans Licht, *Sexual Life in Ancient Greece*, trans. by J. H. Freese (London: Panther, 1969; first published in 1932).

9 E. T. Cook and Alexander Wedderburn (eds.), *The Works of John Ruskin*, 39 vols. (London: Allen, 1903–12), vol. I, p. 433. As his editors note, Ruskin later repudiated this version of events, when he wrote in *Praeterita* that he 'at once pronounced [...] the Venus de' Medici, an uninteresting little person' (*Works*, vol. XXXV, p. 269). This is perhaps due to his feeling that the beauty of the 'Venus de' Medici, is perfectly palpable to any shallow fine lady or fine gentleman', and that to discern its attractions is the sign of an 'eager self-complacency' (vol. V, p. 98).

10 Haskell and Penny record that for the traveller Henry Matthews, who visited Europe between 1817 and 1819, the charms of the Venus de' Medici were like those of the angels 'who are of no sex' (quoted in *Taste and the Antique*, p. 328).

11 W. Graham Robertson, *Time Was* (London: Hamish Hamilton, 1931), pp. 68–9.

12 Lori Anne Loeb includes in her *Consuming Angels: Advertising and Victorian Women* (Oxford University Press, 1994) an advertisement for Pear's Soap which features five classically draped women issuing from a temple of health. The women are all named as contemporary actresses, and include Lillie Langtry, Adelina Patti, and Mary Anderson. Loeb suggests that their Grecian drapery 'defines the actresses' sexuality (or at least disguises it in

elevating garb' (p. 96). Richard Jenkyns also features an advertisement for
Beecham's Pills in his *Dignity and Decadence: Victorian Art and the Classical
Inheritance* (London: HarperCollins, 1991), where a sculpturally draped figure of Health is crowning a similarly dressed 'Beauty'. Jenkyns suggests that
the fashion for Classical references in adverts demonstrates both 'vulgarity
and some small pretension to culture' (p. 309).

13 The poem was first published in 1879, and appeared in Wilde's *Poems* of
1881. Wilde's Classical compliments were not just for public consumption,
as this letter to Langtry shows. It sets up an interesting sculptural comparison between Langtry and Constance Lloyd:

> And so I write to tell you how glad I am at your triumphs – you, Venus Victrix of our
> age – and the other half to tell you that I am going to be married to a beautiful girl
> called Constance Lloyd, a grave, slight, violet-eyed little Artemis, with great coils of
> heavy brown hair which make her flower-like head droop like a blossom, and
> wonderful ivory hands which draw music from the piano so sweet that the birds stop
> singing to listen to her. (Oscar Wilde to Lillie Langtry, 16 December 1883, in
> Rupert Hart-Davis (ed.), *The Letters of Oscar Wilde* (London: Hart-Davis, 1962), p. 74)

14 Stephen Jones, Christopher Newall, et al., *Frederic Leighton* (London: Royal
Academy of Arts and Abrams, 1996), p. 196.

15 Walter Pater, *The Renaissance: Studies in Art and Poetry* (Oxford University
Press, 1986; first published in 1873), p. 44. Pater goes on to suggest that
Michelangelo achieves a similar 'vivacity' in his sculpture by 'leaving nearly
all his sculpture in a puzzling sort of incompleteness, which suggests rather
than realises actual form' (p. 44).

16 William Hazlitt, *Liber Amoris, or The New Pygmalion* (Oxford and New York:
Woodstock, 1992), pp. 118, 119.

17 Vernon Lee, *Miss Brown*, 3 vols. (Edinburgh and London: Blackwood, 1884),
vol. I, pp. 24, 25. Anne Brown is a dark, heavy beauty of the Jane Morris
type painted by D. G. Rossetti in his work of the 1860s and 1870s, but one of
Lee's most precise and scathing references to the Pre-Raphaelites is made in
a description of a portrait of Anne, entitled 'Venus Victrix', and unmistak-
ably inspired by Rossetti's 'Beata Beatrix', the portrait of Lizzie Siddal
which he began shortly after her early death in 1862:

> Hamlin made a sketch of a lady in a dress of sad-coloured green and gold brocade,
> seated in a melancholy landscape of distant barren peaks, suffused with the grey and
> yellow tints of a late sunset; behind her was a bower of sear-coloured palms, knotting
> their boughs into a kind of canopy for her head, and in her hand she held, dragged
> despondingly on the ground, a broken palm-branch. The expression of the goddess
> of Love, since such she was, was one of intense melancholy. It was one of those
> pictures which go to the head with a perfectly unintelligible mystery, and which
> absolutely preclude all possibility of inquiring into their exact meaning. (vol. I, pp.
> 128–9)

18 Henry James, *The Portrait of a Lady*, New York edition, 2 vols. (London:
Macmillan, 1908), vol. II, p. 11. This phrase replaces 'she would have been as
bright and soft as an April cloud' in the first edition of the novel (*The Portrait
of a Lady*, 3 vols. (London: Macmillan, 1881), vol. II, p. 126). The latter phrase

brings out more explicitly the overtones of Pygmalion latent in Osmond, which characterise his relations with both Isabel and his daughter Pansy.

19 George Meredith, *The Egoist* (Harmondsworth: Penguin, 1968; first published in 1879), p. 80.

20 Thomas Hardy, *The Well-Beloved: A Sketch of a Temperament* (London: Macmillan, 1986), pp. 13, 62.

21 George Eliot, *The Mill on the Floss*, Cabinet edition, 2 vols. (Edinburgh and London: Blackwood, [n.d.]), vol. II, pp. 274–5.

22 Unsigned review, *Saturday Review* (1860); quoted in David Carroll (ed.), *George Eliot: The Critical Heritage* (London: Routledge & Kegan Paul, 1971), pp. 114–19 (pp. 118, 119).

23 Heinrich Heine, 'Florentine Nights', in Havelock Ellis (ed.), *The Prose Writings of Heinrich Heine* (London: Scott, 1887), pp. 179–242 (p. 182).

24 Havelock Ellis, *Studies in the Psychology of Sex*, 4 vols. (New York: Random House, 1936), vol. II, p. 188.

25 Benjamin Tarnowsky, *The Sexual Instinct and its Morbid Manifestations, from the Double Standpoint of Jurisprudence and Psychiatry*, trans. by W. C. Costello and Alfred Allinson (Paris: Carrington, 1898), pp. 84–5.

26 It is perhaps to this practice, associated with the Ancient Greeks and Romans, that Joyce refers in an otherwise puzzling reference to statuary in *A Portrait of the Artist as a Young Man*: 'The past is consumed in the present and the present is living only because it brings forth the future. Statues of women, if Lynch be right, should always be fully draped, one hand of the woman feeling regretfully her own hinder parts' (James Joyce, *A Portrait of the Artist as a Young Man* (London: Cape, 1964; first published in 1916), p. 255).

27 Judging by the evidence of Jane Davidson Reid (ed.), *The Oxford Guide to Classical Mythology in the Arts, 1300–1990s*, 2 vols. (Oxford University Press, 1993), the figures of Pygmalion and his statue were frequently invoked in European drama, ballet, poetry, and painting from the early-sixteenth century, but seem not to have achieved a prominent *nachleben* in English culture until the Victorian period. Thus, it may be contended that Pygmalion could be part of a specifically Victorian heritage for Ellis.

28 Ovid, *Metamorphoses*, trans. by A. D. Melville (Oxford University Press, 1986), p. 233.

29 For an account of how 'Galatea' came to get her name, see Helen H. Law, 'The Name Galatea in the Pygmalion Myth', *The Classical Journal* 27 (1931–2), 337–42.

30 J. Hillis Miller, *Versions of Pygmalion* (Cambridge, MA, and London: Harvard University Press, 1990), p. 5.

31 Lady Eastlake (ed.), *Life of John Gibson, R. A. Sculptor* (London: Longmans, Green, 1870), p. 209.

32 Thomas Hardy's short story, 'Barbara of the House of Grebe' (1891), seems to contradict Ellis's observations. It centres around a young woman's infatuation with a beautiful, but otherwise apparently unsuitable, young man with whom she elopes. On their return home, the husband is per-

suaded to undertake a European tour under the guidance of a tutor, after which he will be more appropriately trained for the station of husband to his noble wife. He thus undergoes a form of 'moulding'. Whilst travelling, he has his statue made, shortly before being horribly disfigured in a fire. On his return his wife rejects him, and never sees him again. However, she later falls in love with his statue which is subsequently disfigured by her jealous second husband. The story is essentially one of dark sexual torment and sadism, but its use of the Pygmalion-motif merits consideration. Rather than being a gender-reversal of the legend, however, the story seems to dispute the wisdom of the practice of Pygmalionism, for we are told in the story's last words that

there is no doubt that an infatuation for the person of young Willowes was the chief feeling that induced her to marry him; which was the more deplorable in that his beauty, by all tradition, was the least of his recommendations, every report bearing out the inference that he must have been a man of steadfast nature, bright intelligence, and promising life. (Thomas Hardy, 'Barbara of the House of Grebe', in *Outside the Gates of the World: Selected Short Stories* (London: Dent, 1996), pp. 267–96 (p. 296))

33 In the second edition of his work on prostitution, William Acton makes of the Pygmalion-impulse an intrinsic part of a man's relationship with the prostitute. Acton claims that the client is moved 'to make, if possible, of every woman the thing that he desires – a toy, a plaything, an animated doll' (William Acton, *Prostitution, Considered in its Moral, Social and Sanitary Aspects*, second edition (London: Cass, 1972; first published in 1870), p. 167).

34 See Buchanan's article, written under the pseudonym Thomas Maitland, 'The Fleshly School of Poetry: Mr D. G. Rossetti', *Contemporary Review* 18 (1871), 334–50.

35 *The Poetical Works of Robert Buchanan*, 3 vols. (London: King, 1874), vol. II, p. 256.

36 *The Writings of Arthur Hallam* (New York: MLA; London: Oxford University Press, 1943), p. 112.

37 Dr Elizabeth Blackwell, *The Human Element in Sex: Being a Medical Enquiry into the Relation of Sexual Physiology to Christian Morality* (London: Churchill, 1884), p. 48.

38 The term is Erich Gombrich's, and is taken from *Art and Illusion: A Study in the Psychology of Pictorial Representation* (London: Phaidon, 1960), p. 80.

39 *The Works of Thomas Lovell Beddoes* (London: Oxford University Press, 1935), p. 81. The poem was written between 1821 and 1825.

40 'Pygmalion', in W. C. Bennett, *Queen Eleanor's Vengeance, and Other Poems* (London: Chapman and Hall, 1857), p. 23.

41 Ernest Dowson, *Verses* (London: Smithers, 1896), p. 54.

42 Marina Warner, *Monuments and Maidens: The Allegory of the Female Form* (London: Picador, 1987), pp. 228, 240.

43 Gillian Beer, *Darwin's Plots* (London: Ark, 1983), p. 64.

44 The *OED*'s first reference to the practice of putting someone on a pedestal

occurs in 1857, confirming this as a peculiarly Victorian practice. The reference is, however, to Tennyson's 'Merlin and Vivien', and the metaphor is used by Vivien to flatter Merlin into trusting her:

> O, I, that flattering my true passion, saw
> The knights, the court, the King, dark in your light,
> Who loved to make men darker than they are,
> Because of that high pleasure which I had
> To seat you sole upon my pedestal
> Of worship. (lines 872–7)

The constraining implications of putting someone onto a pedestal are revealed perhaps even more strongly through Tennyson's reversal of the practice's more usual gender-positions.

45 Other Victorian renderings of the Pygmalion story include Ernest Hartley Coleridge, 'Pygmalion's Bride', in *Poems* (London and New York: Lane, Bodley Head, 1898), George Eric Lancaster, 'Pygmalion in Cyprus', in *Pygmalion in Cyprus and Other Poems* (London: Clowes, 1880), 'From Pygmalion by Edward Burne-Jones', in *The Poems of T. Sturge Moore* (London: Macmillan, 1931), William Morris, 'Pygmalion and the Image', in *The Earthly Paradise* (London: Ellis, 1868), Frederick Tennyson, 'Pygmalion', in *Daphne, and Other Poems* (London: Macmillan, 1891), and Thomas Woolner, *Pygmalion* (London: Macmillan, 1881). A useful account of the Pygmalion-legend in the nineteenth century is given in Jane M. Miller, 'Some Versions of Pygmalion', in Charles Martindale (ed.), *Ovid Renewed: Ovidian Influences on Literature and Art from the Middle Ages to the Twentieth Century* (Cambridge University Press, 1988), pp. 205–14.

46 Merle Bevington, *The Saturday Review, 1855–1868* (New York: Columbia University Press, 1941), p. 110.

47 [Eliza Lynn Linton], 'The Girl of the Period', *Saturday Review* 25 (1868), 339–40 (p. 340). The article was first published under Lynn Linton's name in a two-volume collection of her essays, *The Girl of the Period, and Other Social Essays* (London: Bentley, 1883).

48 For further details of the extent of the article's popular renown, see 'Eliza Lynn Linton and "The Girl of the Period"', in Elizabeth K. Helsinger, et al. (eds.), *The Woman Question: Society and Literature in Britain and America, 1837–1883, Volume 1: Defining Voices* (University of Chicago Press, 1983), pp. 103–25 (pp. 114–17).

49 See for instance, 'Modern Women', *Atlantic Monthly* 22 (1868), 639–40; and J. B. Mayor, 'The Cry of the Women', *Contemporary Review* 11 (1869), 196–215.

50 Anthony Trollope, *He Knew He Was Right* (Harmondsworth: Penguin, 1994), p. 673.

51 See '"The Girl of the Period"', *Tomahawk*, 4 April 1868, p. 136.

52 This situation, whereby Lynn Linton effectively subverts her conservative position through her espousal of it as a woman, was to beset, even to determine, Lynn Linton's career as a conservative, professional, female

journalist and novelist whose most vilified target was the independent working woman.

53 'Modern Views about Women', *Tinsleys' Magazine* 5 (1869–70), 660–4 (p. 663).

54 M. E. Braddon, 'Whose Fault Is It?', *Belgravia* 9 (1869), 214–16 (p. 214).

55 Henry James, 'Modern Women', *Nation* 7 (1868), 332–4 (p. 334).

56 Christina Rossetti, 'In an Artist's Studio', in William M. Rossetti (ed.), *Poems of Christina Rossetti* (London: Macmillan, 1904), p. 280. For details of the visit to D. G. Rossetti's studio on Christmas Eve 1856 which inspired the poem, see Jan Marsh, *Christina Rossetti: A Literary Biography* (London: Cape, 1994), p. 186.

57 W. M. Tirebuck, *Dante Gabriel Rossetti: His Work and Influence* (London, 1882), and Thomas Hall Caine, *Recollections of Dante Gabriel Rossetti* (London, 1882); quoted in Jan Marsh, *The Legend of Elizabeth Siddal* (London: Quartet, 1989), pp. 19 and 22.

58 William Bell Scott, *Autobiographical Notes*, 2 vols. (London, 1892); quoted in Marsh, *Legend*, p. 39; Arthur Hughes, quoted in G. B. Hill (ed.), *Letters of Rossetti and William Allingham* (New York, 1897); quoted in Marsh, *Legend*, p. 53; and W. M. Ross, 'Dante Gabriel Rossetti and Elizabeth Siddal', *Burlington Magazine* (1903); quoted in Marsh, *Legend*, p. 59.

59 George J. Romanes, 'Mental Differences Between Men and Women', *Nineteenth Century* 21 (1887), 654–72 (p. 655).

60 Alfred Austin, 'Woman's Proper Place in Society', *Temple Bar* 33 (1871), 168–78 (p. 173). One possible exception to women's lack of imaginative capacity was Elizabeth Barrett Browning, but according to the *Edinburgh Review*, her work was marred by this unusual acquisition: 'Her reading seems to have been too exclusively imaginative to the destruction of the reasoning faculties, and thus her mind lacked both health and tone. A poet [...] needs the discipline of fact and reason to dull his intellectual energies and sensibilities into something like hardness and consistency' ([William Stigand], 'The Works of Elizabeth Barrett Browning', *Edinburgh Review* 114 (1861), 513–34 (p. 533)).

61 John Stuart Mill, 'The Subjection of Women', in Stefan Collini (ed.), *On Liberty, and Other Writings* (Cambridge University Press, 1989), p. 186.

62 Watts was the first of the many artists with whom Terry collaborated in her professional life. Graham Robertson describes her as 'the Painter's Actress' (*Time Was*, p. 54), partly because of her obvious beauty, but also because Terry herself had a strong sense of the stage's pictorial effect, believing that 'drama is for the eye as well as for the ear and the mind' (Ellen Terry, *The Story of My Life* (London: Hutchinson, 1908), p. 307).

63 Hugh Macmillan, *The Life-Work of George Frederick Watts, RA* (London: Dent, 1903), p. 30.

64 Algernon Charles Swinburne, 'Notes on Some Pictures of 1868', in *Essays and Studies* (London: Chatto and Windus, 1875), pp. 358–80 (pp. 359–60). Watts's painting, which was one of two which were 'impressed on [Swin-

burne's] memory more deeply and distinctly than the rest' (p. 359), also attracted the attention of Gladstone, who wanted to buy it.

65 M. S. Watts, *G. F. Watts*, 3 vols. (London: Macmillan, 1912), vol. i, p. 238.

66 Quoted in Joy Melville, *Ellen and Edy: A Biography of Ellen Terry and her Daughter Edith Craig, 1847–1947* (London: Pandora, 1987), p. 26.

67 Graham Robertson to Kerrison Preston, 9 January 1939; quoted in David F. Cheshire, *Portrait of Ellen Terry* (Charlbury: Amber Lane, 1989), p. 26.

68 David Loshak, 'G. F. Watts and Ellen Terry', *Burlington Magazine* 105 (1963), 476–85 (p. 480). The petition was drawn up just over twelve years after his ten-month-long marriage ended.

69 *Ellen Terry's Memoirs*, with Preface, Notes and Additional Biographical Chapters by Edith Craig and Christopher St John (London: Gollancz, 1933), n. 6, p. 52. The *Memoirs* are a heavily annotated and edited version of Terry's *The Story of My Life*, and will be discussed in more detail in my conclusion.

70 Ronald Chapman, *The Laurel and the Thorn: A Study of George Frederick Watts* (London: Faber and Faber, 1945), p. 66.

71 Nina Auerbach, *Ellen Terry: Player in Her Time* (London: Dent, 1987), p. 100.

72 Mrs Russell Barrington, *George Frederick Watts: Reminiscences* (London: Allen, 1905), p. 36. Mrs Barrington, also a friend of Terry's, was herself an aspiring artist who, under Watts's influence, had lined the walls of her studio with casts of the Parthenon Frieze and figures from the Nike Athena temple on the Acropolis. She records that Watts believed these works to be 'full of truth to nature' (p. 63).

73 Quoted in Benedict Read, *Victorian Sculpture* (New Haven and London: Yale University Press, 1982), pp. 278–9.

74 R. E. D. Sketchley, *Watts* (London: Methuen, 1904), p. 167.

75 A. M. W. Stirling, *Life's Little Day* (London, 1924); quoted in Melville, *Ellen and Edy*, pp. 32–3.

2 ACTING GALATEA, 'THE IDEAL STATUESQUE'

1 Mayhew does not, however, seek to establish a simple continuity, writing for instance that 'in the English, as distinct from the Classical drama, plot or fable is not of the first importance' (Edward Mayhew, *Stage Effect: or, the Principles which Command Dramatic Success in the Theatre* (London: Mitchell, 1840), pp. 71–2). The point is rather the readiness of Mayhew's reference to a Classical register for comparison.

2 [George Grant] 'A Veteran Stage', *An Essay on the Science of Acting* (London: Cowie and Strange, 1828), p. 22.

3 John Styles, DD, *The Stage: Its Character and Influence* (London: Ward, 1838).

4 *The Elements of Dramatic Criticism. Containing an Analysis of the Stage under the following Heads, Tragedy, Tragi-Comedy, Comedy, Pantomime, and Farce. With a sketch of the Education of the Greek and Roman Actors; Concluding with Some General Instructions for Succeeding in the Art of Acting by William Cooke, Esq. of the Middle*

Temple (London: Kearsly, Robinson, 1775), p. 183.

5 For example, the editor collects 'oh the sculptor might have studied her features to improve the Medician Venus. Her eyes, complexion, form', from *Morton's Town and Country*; and quotes 'Handsome! Venus de Medicis was a sibyl to her' from Sheridan's *Duenna*, first performed in 1775 (*Beauties of the Modern Dramatists* (London: Mann, 1829), pp. 12, 13).

6 C. Willett Cunnington, *English Women's Clothing in the Nineteenth Century* (London: Faber and Faber, 1937), p. 28.

7 Dr Oskar Fischel and Max von Boehn, *Modes and Manners of the Nineteenth Century*, trans. by M. Edwardes, intro. by Grace Rhys, 4 vols. (London: Dent; New York: Dutton, 1927), vol. I, p. 123.

8 F. Mocchetti, (ed.), *Opere del Cavaliere Carlo Gastone, Conte della Torre Rezzonico, VII: Giornale del Viaggio di Napoli negli Anni 1789 e 1790* (Como, 1819); quoted in Ian Jenkins and Kim Sloan, *Vases and Volcanoes: Sir William Hamilton and His Collection* (London: British Museum Press, 1996), p. 260.

9 Kirsten Gram Holmström, *Monodrama, Attitudes, tableaux vivants: Studies in Some Trends of Theatrical Fashion, 1770–1815* (Stockholm: Almqvist & Wiksell, 1967), p. 135.

10 Quoted in Hugh Tours, *The Life and Letters of Emma Hamilton* (London: Gollancz, 1963), p. 94.

11 Comte J. T. d'Espinchal, *Journal d'Emigration*, ed. by Ernest D'Hauterie (Paris, 1912); quoted in Flora Fraser, *Beloved Emma: The Life of Emma Lady Hamilton* (London: Weidenfeld and Nicolson, 1986), p. 150.

12 The objectification of Emma is made more complete through an incident recollected by Goethe during a second visit to Sir William. He writes of
a chest which was standing upright. Its front had been taken off, the interior painted black and the whole set inside a splendid gilt frame. It was large enough to hold a standing human figure, and that, we were told, was exactly what it was meant for. Not content with seeing his image of beauty as a moving statue, this friend of art and girlhood wished also to enjoy her as an inimitable painting, and so, standing against this black background in dresses of various colours, she had sometimes imitated the antique paintings of Pompeii or even more recent masterpieces. (pp. 315–16)

Sir William's predilection prefigures the central device of Vernon Lee's 'The Doll' (written in 1899), which will be referred to in my conclusion.

13 M. Charles Nicoullaud (ed.), *Mémoires de la Comtesse de Boigne* (Paris, 1907); quoted in Holmström, *Monodrama, Attitudes*, p. 114.

14 Altick suggests (*Shows of London*, p. 333) that Madame Tussaud may have been inspired to put on this exhibit because of the popularity of the wax-replica made of the 21-year-old Princess Charlotte after she had died in child-birth, and exhibited at Savile House in 1818.

15 *Illustrated London News*, 17 October 1846; quoted in Altick, *Shows of London*, p. 346.

16 These entertainments also enjoyed great fame, and even greater notoriety, in America. See Jack W. McCullough's detailed account of *Living Pictures on the New York Stage* (Epping: Bowker, 1981).

17 John Coleman, *Players and Playwrights I Have Known*, 2 vols. (London: Chatto and Windus, 1888), vol. I, p. 255.

18 For an account of Planché's desire to reform English theatre with his burlesques, to give it a strong indigenous, and largely moral, tradition, see Dougald Macmillan's articles, 'Some Burlesques With a Purpose, 1830–1870', *Philological Quarterly* 8 (1929), 255–63; and 'Planché's Early Classical Burlesques', *Studies in Philology* 25 (1928), 340–5.

19 J. R. Planché, *History of British Costume*, 3rd edition (London: Bell, 1893), p. xvi.

20 J. L. Carr, 'Pygmalion and the *Philosophes*: the Animated Statue in Eighteenth-century France', *Journal of the Warburg and Courtauld Institutes* 23 (1960), 239–55 (p. 242).

21 'Pygmalion. Scène lyrique', in *Œuvres Complètes de J. J. Rousseau*, 13 vols. (Paris: Hachette, 1873), vol. V, pp. 232–6 (p. 233).

22 See Holmström, *Monodrama, Attitudes*, pp. 40–6. Holmström also points out here that the Pygmalion story had inspired two French ballets in the eighteenth century, those of Mlle Sallé (first produced in 1734) and Rameau (1748).

23 Carr notes that between 1771 and 1813 there were six German translations of Rousseau's play. He suggests that this version of 'Pygmalion' proved so interesting in Germany because it invested the Classical prototype with Faustian overtones ('Pygmalion and the *Philosophes*', p. 243).

24 Johann Wolfgang von Goethe, *Elective Affinities*, trans. by Judith Ryan (Princeton University Press, 1995), p. 196.

25 Rachel M. Brownstein, *Tragic Muse: Rachel of the Comédie Française* (New York: Knopf, 1993), p. 172. See further pp. 172–83 which provide a range of mainly French examples of statue-imagery in reviews of Rachel's work.

26 Vicomte de Calonne, 'The Stage in France', *Macmillan's Magazine* 34 (1876), 176–81 (p. 180).

27 Charlotte Brontë, *Villette* (Harmondsworth: Penguin, 1979), p. 339.

28 G. H. Lewes, 'Rachel', in *On Actors and the Art of Acting* (London: Smith, Elder, 1875), pp. 23–31 (p. 25).

29 See the second and third of Arnold's three 'Rachel' poems in Kenneth Allott (ed.), *The Poems of Matthew Arnold*, 2nd edition ed. by Miriam Allott (London and New York: Longman, 1979), pp. 523, 524. The poems were written in 1868, and were apparently inspired by Arnold's reading 'Madame de B's' two-volume *Memoirs of Rachel* (London: Hurst and Blackett, 1858).

30 Matthew Arnold, 'The French Play in London', *The Nineteenth Century* 6 (1879), 228–43 (p. 230).

31 The critic, Hamilton, was commenting on Rachel's 1855 Phèdre at the Metropolitan Theatre in New York. His review is quoted in George C. D. Odell, *Annals of the New York Stage* (1931), and is reproduced from that source in Brownstein's book, p. 177.

32 [Theodore Martin], 'Rachel', *Blackwood's* 132 (1882), 271–95 (pp. 294–5).

33 Further mention will be made of Faucit's own account of playing Hermione in chapter 3. Faucit was variously know as Helen and Helena during her life-time, with the latter being her most usual stage-name, and the name which appears on her writings. For these reasons, I have chosen to use 'Helena' when writing of her, but retain 'Helen' when that name is given in a quotation.

34 Faucit's articles appeared under the name Helena Faucit Martin and the generic title 'On Some of Shakespeare's Female Characters, by One who has Personated Them' in *Blackwood's*. Her articles were on 'Ophelia', *Blackwood's* 129 (1881), 66–77, 'Portia', 198–210, 'Desdemona', 324–45; 'Juliet', 131 (1882), 31–43, 'Juliet, Part 2', 141–69; 'Imogen, Princess of Britain', 133 (1883), 1–41; 'Rosalind', 136 (1884), 399–437; 'Beatrice', 137 (1885), 203–31; and 'Hermione', 149 (1891), 1–37.

35 Sir Theodore Martin, *Helena Faucit (Lady Martin)* (Edinburgh and London: Blackwood, 1900), pp. 74–5, 75.

36 [Margaret Stokes and Georgina Colmache], 'Helen Faucit', *Blackwood's* 138 (1885), 741–60 (p. 741).

37 In 1885, however, Nina Kennard struck a contradictory note in publishing a revisionist biography of Rachel, which sought to assess her as an artist, and not simply as a dangerously immoral French woman: Nina Kennard, *Rachel* (London: Allen, 1885).

38 Juliet Pollock, 'The "*Théâtre Français*"', *Quarterly Review* 139 (1875), 138–69 (p. 166).

39 Lester Wallack, *Memories of Fifty Years* (New York, 1889), and Robert D. Lowe, in Brander Matthews and Laurence Hutton (eds.), *Actors and Actresses of Great Britain and the United States*, 4 vols. (New York, 1886); quoted in Donald Mullin (ed.), *Victorian Actors and Actresses in Review: A Dictionary of Contemporary Views of Representative British and American Actors and Actresses, 1837–1901* (Westport, CT, and London: Greenwood, 1983), p. 185.

40 Thomas de Quincey, 'The Antigone of Sophocles', *Tait's Edinburgh Magazine* 13 (1846), 111–16, 157–62 (p. 160).

41 These were some of the grounds upon which the *Glasgow Courier* compared the two actresses in 1861. Rachel was found lacking; quoted in Martin, *Helena Faucit*, p. 262.

42 *The Letters of Elizabeth Barrett Browning*, 2 vols. (London: Smith, Elder, 1897), vol. II, p. 148.

43 Gilbert wrote to Steer, 'If you do not comply with my wishes [...] I give you notice that on Monday I shall apply for an injunction to prevent your playing the piece, or otherwise as I may be advised' (quoted in Hesketh Pearson, *Gilbert: His Life and Strife* (London: Methuen, 1957), p. 41).

44 This visit will be discussed in more detail in chapter 3.

45 William Brough, *Pygmalion; or, The Statue Fair*, Lacy's Acting Edition (London: Lacy, 1867), n. p.

46 This scene continues with Pygmalion bidding 'my peerless statue move and live'. Venus responds, 'A living statue! Such a thing's ne'er thought on, / At least not since the days of Madame Wharton' (p. 20).

47 W. S. Gilbert, *Pygmalion and Galatea: An Original Mythological Comedy*, in *Original Plays* (London: Chatto and Windus, 1876), p. 71.

48 See Sidney Dark and Rowland Grey, *W. S. Gilbert: His Life and Letters* (London: Methuen, 1923), p. 52.

49 'Haymarket Theatre', *Athenaeum*, 16 December 1871, pp. 802–3 (p. 803).

50 *Dame Madge Kendal, by Herself* (London: Murray, 1933), p. 169. She also notes intriguingly that Ruskin was an enthusiastic admirer of the play. Unfortunately, no mention of *Pygmalion and Galatea* is made in Ruskin's published diaries or letters, but he did, albeit often with little enjoyment, go to the Haymarket to watch the Kendals. His highest praise is given to their production of 'Queen Mab' in March 1874, which 'gave [him] an entirely satisfactory evening' (*The Diaries of John Ruskin*, ed. by Joan Evans and John Howard Whitehouse, 3 vols. (Oxford: Clarendon Press, 1957–9), vol. III, p. 782).

51 'The Week', *Athenaeum*, 27 January 1877, p. 127.

52 Details of the Bancrofts' work, their relationship with Robertson, and an assessment of their influence are given in George Rowell, 'The Return of Respectability', in *The Victorian Theatre, 1792–1914: A Survey*, second edition (Cambridge University Press, 1978), pp. 75–102, especially pp. 75–84; and Michael R. Booth, *Theatre in the Victorian Age* (Cambridge University Press, 1991), pp. 52–3. On Robertson's 'drawing-room style', Booth quotes *The Times*'s 1870 review of the play *MP*: the actors are 'almost at arm's length of an audience who sit, as in a drawing-room, to hear drawing-room pleasantries, interchanged by drawing-room personages' (*The Times*, 25 April 1870; quoted in Booth, p. 53).

The popularity of plays such as *Society* (1865), *Ours* (1866), and *Caste* (1867), described by Henry James as 'among the most diminutive experiments ever attempted in the drama', persisted long after their author's death in 1871. James derisorily described measures such as those taken by the Bancrofts as '[testifying] to the theater's being the fashion among a certain class, and the last luxury of a few, rather than taking its place in the common habits of the people, as it does in France'. James's comments are taken from 'The London Theaters', *Scribner's Monthly* 21 (1880–1), 354–69 (pp. 363, 357). James cites such theatrical 'reforms' as concerned principally to promote the comfort of the audience rather than the health of the theatre, and as tending to make the state and status of the audience one with the condition of the theatre. This was precisely what the Kendals, Bancrofts, and other popular managements intended.

3 GEORGE ELIOT, 'DANIEL DERONDA', AND THE SCULPTURAL AESTHETIC

1 Eliot's Journal for 4 August records, 'To-day, under much depression, I began a little dramatic poem, the subject of which engaged my interest at Harrogate' (J. W. Cross (ed.), *George Eliot's Life, as Related in Her Letters and Journals*, Cabinet edition, 3 vols. (Edinburgh and London: Blackwood, [1885]), vol. III, p. 100).

2 George Eliot, 'Armgart', in *The Works of Jubal, and Other Poems, Old and New*, Cabinet edition (Edinburgh and London: Blackwood, (n. d.)), pp. 75, 98.

3 The statue-image is used in an interesting way as a threat when Graf prophesies that Armgart's thirst for excellence will render her,

> an ivory statuette,
> Wrought to perfection through long lonely years,
> Huddled in the mart of mediocrities.   (p. 91)

Armgart challenges Graf with the thought that what he offers in exchange is pregnancy, a peculiarly female form of excellence, and one which functions here, like the sculptural metaphor, as another form of physical restriction. This treatment of pregnancy both looks forward to Alcharisi's story, and back to Galatea's fate.

4 George Eliot, *Middlemarch*, Cabinet edition, 3 vols. (Edinburgh and London: Blackwood, (n. d.)), vol. III, p. 465.

5 'Liszt, Wagner, and Weimar', in Thomas Pinney (ed.), *Essays of George Eliot* (London: Routledge and Kegan Paul, 1963), pp. 96–122 (p. 99); first published in *Fraser's Magazine* (1855).

6 Eliot also visited Harriet Hosmer's studio, whose work pleased her more: 'Miss Hosmer's Beatrice Cenci is a pleasing and new conception; and her little Puck, a bit of humour that one would like to have if one were a grand seigneur' (Cross, *George Eliot's Life*, vol. II, p. 158).

7 In his review of Cross, James notes that '[Eliot] enumerates diligently all the pictures and statues she sees, and the way she does so is a proof of her active, earnest intellectual habits, but it is rarely apparent that they have, as the phrase is, said much to her, or that what they have said is one of their deeper secrets' (Henry James, 'George Eliot's Life', *Atlantic Monthly* 55 (1885), 668–78 (p. 674)).

8 George Eliot, *Daniel Deronda*, Cabinet edition, 3 vols. (Edinburgh and London: Blackwood, (n.d.)), vol. I, p. 360. The same image is also used in *Middlemarch* in relation to Lydgate's first medical studies.

9 Critics who have tried to get a purchase on what Leavis called the 'good' and 'bad' halves of the novel (F. R. Leavis, *The Great Tradition* (London: Chatto & Windus, 1948), p. 80), have variously located the definition of parts in the distinctions between continental Judaism and the indigenous English; between good and bad music (Shirley Frank Levenson, 'The Use of Music in *Daniel Deronda*', *Nineteenth-Century Fiction* 24 (1969–70) 317–34); 'good' and 'bad' acting (see Brian Swann, 'George Eliot and the Play: Symbol and Metaphor of the Drama in *Daniel Deronda*', *Dalhousie Review* 52 (1972–3), 191–202); and between Italianate and English styles of portraiture (see Hugh Witemeyer, *George Eliot and the Visual Arts* (New Haven and London: Yale University Press, 1979), pp. 96–100).

10 Irving's 'Shakespearean notes' for the *Nineteenth Century* were on 'The Third Murderer in *Macbeth*', 1 (1877), 327–30; 'Hamlet and Ophelia, Act III, Scene 1', 1 (1877), 524–30; and ' "Look Here, upon This Picture, and on This" ', 5 (1879), 260–3. He also wrote later in the same periodical on Coquelin (21

(1887), 800–3); on actor-managers (27 (1890), 1052–3); and 'Some Misconceptions About the Stage', (32 (1892), 670–6).

11 This neo-Classical drama will be discussed more fully in the next chapter.

12 H. Hamilton Fyfe, 'Organising the Theatre', *Fortnightly Review* (1902); quoted in James Woodfield, *English Theatre in Transition, 1881–1914* (London and Sydney: Croom Helm, 1984), p. 8.

13 Inspired by the French example, the mid-seventies saw the beginnings of the agitation for an English national theatre, protected by subsidy from the perils of the commercial system.

14 Juliet Pollock, 'The *Comédie Française*', *Contemporary Review* 18 (1871), 43–55 (p. 55).

15 J. P. [Juliet Pollock], 'The French Stage', *Macmillan's Magazine* 21 (1869–70), 400–4 (p. 402).

16 [Alfred Austin], 'The Present State of the English Stage', *Temple Bar* 33 (1871), 456–68 (p. 461).

17 Juliet Pollock, 'Art in its Dramatic Aspects', *Contemporary Review* 23 (1873–4), 363–79 (p. 374).

18 George Bernard Shaw, 'Preface' to William Archer, *The Theatrical 'World' of 1894* (London: Scott, 1895), pp. xi–xxx (pp. xiii–xiv).

19 Thornton Hunt, 'The Game of Speculation', *Leader* (1851); quoted in Rosemary Ashton, *G. H. Lewes: A Life* (Oxford: Clarendon Press, 1991), p. 123. The French play, itself based on Balzac's *Le Faiseur* was speedily translated for an English production by Lewes, at that time the stock author for the Lyceum, which was then under the management of Charles James Mathews and Eliza Vestris. For an account of the play and Lewes's part in its production, see Ashton, pp. 123–5.

20 Charles Dickens, *Bleak House* (Harmondsworth: Penguin, 1996), p. 278.

21 Gillian Beer, 'The Reader's Wager: Lots, Sorts and Futures', *Essays in Criticism* 40 (1990), 99–123 (p. 109).

22 [H. B. Baker], 'The Theatres', *Temple Bar* 39 (1873), 547–52 (p. 547).

23 Gordon S. Haight (ed.), *The George Eliot Letters*, 9 vols. (New Haven and London: Yale University Press, 1954–78), vol.ix, p. 275. Eliot responded in similar fashion to Sydney M. Samuel, who wrote proposing an adaptation of *Daniel Deronda*:

> With all obligation to you for your deference to my wishes, I must repeat that I can have nothing whatever to do with the adaptation of my work to the stage, and I must decline to have my name connected with such adaptation.
>
>   It is unnecessary for me to enter into my reasons which are too many and various to be overcome. (1 February 1880, *Letters of George Eliot*, vol. ix, pp. 288–9)

24 G. H. Lewes wrote of Rachel at this period that although she had fallen from her greatest heights, she was still greater than any of the actors sharing the stage with her ('Rachel', in John Forster and George Henry Lewes, *Dramatic Essays*, ed. by William Archer and Robert W. Lowe (London: Scott, 1896), pp. 243–5 (p. 245)).

25 It is perhaps worth noting that, consistent with the practice of their middle-

class contemporaries, the Leweses at least once tried to put on a charade. The event was not entirely successful, as Eliot irritably tells Mrs Congreve:

The party was a 'mull'. The weather was bad. Some of the invited were ill and sent regrets, others were not ardent enough to brave the damp evening – in fine, only twelve came. We had a charade, which, like our neighbours, was no better than it should have been [...] However, Mr Pigott made a woman's part in the charade so irresistibly comic that I tittered at it at intervals in my sleepless hours. (19 February 1865, *Letters of George Eliot*, vol. IV, p. 178)

26 As we have seen, Faucit was one of the most popular mid-Victorian actresses, but Eliot and Lewes enjoyed a rather uneasy relationship with her. Between 1853 and 1865 the relationship was warm and admiring, if a little formal. At one stage, Eliot even seems to have been thinking of writing a play for Faucit. But following Lewes's unfavourable review of Faucit's Rosalind in the *Pall Mall Gazette*, 10 March 1865, their relationship cooled temporarily: 'The Martins, as I feared, are disgusted with my notice of Rosalind. She is so accustomed to be smeared with fulsome undiscriminating praise that criticism is an offence' (G. H. Lewes to Mr and Mrs Charles Lee Lewes, 25 March 1865, *Letters of George Eliot*, vol. IV, p. 186).

27 In 'Rachel's "Terrible Beauty"', John Stokes presents Rachel as one mediating between the rival French and English schools of tragedy, between Racine and Shakespeare. What made Rachel unique was 'her regeneration of the ancient classics of the French stage':

So profound was the impact of Rachel that she obliged even the English to revise the time-honoured antithesis and allow for the possibility of Shakespeare in Racine, or occasionally, Racine despite Shakespeare: the unsuspected presence of 'sympathy' and 'nature' within a supposedly didactic and moribund form. (John Stokes, 'Rachel's 'Terrible Beauty': an Actress Among the Novelists', *ELH* 51 (1984), 771–93 (pp. 771–2, 772–4)).

28 The essay, 'Rachel and Racine – Mrs Glover', is reprinted in *Dramatic Essays*, 94–9. Rachel was apparently rather feeble and in ill-health for this performance, but still showed her greatness.

29 *Andromaque*, in *Œuvres de Racine* (Paris: Compagnie des libraires, 1713), IV. 2. 1130, 1139.

30 Gwendolen's most intimate suffering is figured in images of wounding and wrenching physical pain, because her sense of self is initially constituted by her physical body. Thus, 'The belief that to present herself in public on the stage must produce an effect such as she had been used to feel certain of in private life, was like a bit of her flesh – it was not to be peeled off readily, but must come with blood and pain' (vol. I, p. 383). Klesmer's doubting words bite 'into her self-confidence and [turn] it into the pain of a bleeding wound' (vol. I, p. 392). Only by escaping physical definition, can she defend herself against such appalling vulnerability.

31 Adrian Poole, '"Hidden Affinities" in *Daniel Deronda*', *Essays in Criticism* 33 (1983), 294–311 (p. 297).

32 Thomas P. Wolfe, 'The Inward Vocation: an Essay on George Eliot's *Daniel Deronda*', *Literary Monographs* 8 (1976), 1–46 (pp. 43–4).

33 The details of her garments, and of Alcharisi's internal wasting, recall Brontë's Vashti, who is similarly 'hollow, half-consumed: an orb perished or perishing – half lava, half glow' and 'wasted like wax in flame' (*Villette*, p. 339).

Alcharisi also owes considerable debts to Lewes's description of Rachel's performances in Racine's *Phèdre* (1677), a play appropriately concerned with the warring of incestuous desire and the conscience. Lewes was collecting some of his theatrical criticism for re-publication in *On Actors and the Art of Acting* while *Daniel Deronda* was being written, and it is from that collection that this extract comes:

The finest of her performances was of Phèdre. Nothing I have ever seen surpassed this picture of a soul torn by the conflicts of incestuous passion and struggling conscience; the unutterable mournfulness of her look and tone as she recognised the guilt of her desires, yet felt herself so possessed by them that escape was impossible, are things never to be forgotten. What a picture she was as she entered! You felt that she was wasting away under the fire within, that she was standing on the verge of the grave with pallid face, hot eyes, emaciated frame – an awful ghastly apparition. (p. 25)

34 George Eliot's Journal, April 1858; quoted in Cross, *George Eliot's Life*, vol. II, p. 19.

35 'The Natural History of German Life', *Westminster Review* n. s. 10 (1856), 51–79 (p. 54).

36 Nina Auerbach, 'Secret Performances: George Eliot and the Art of Acting', in *Romantic Imprisonment: Women and Other Glorified Outcasts* (New York: Columbia University Press, 1985), pp. 253–67 (pp. 255, 254).

37 'One Who Knew Her' [Julia Wedgwood], 'The Moral Influence of George Eliot', *Contemporary Review* 39 (1881), 173–85 (p. 177).

38 Edith Simcox, 'George Eliot', *Nineteenth Century* 9 (1881), 778–801 (p. 800).

39 The ideologies underlying critics' reception of Eliot are discussed in Deirdre David, *Intellectual Women and Victorian Patriarchy: Harriet Martineau, Elizabeth Barrett Browning, George Eliot* (London: Macmillan, 1987), pp. 161–76; and Elaine Showalter, 'Queen George', in *Sexual Anarchy: Gender and Culture at the Fin de Siècle* (London: Bloomsbury, 1991), pp. 59–75.

40 'The Antigone and its Moral', in Pinney (ed.), *Essays of George Eliot*, pp. 261–6 (p. 262); first published in *The Leader*, 1856.

41 'Notes on Form in Art', in Pinney (ed.), *Essays of George Eliot*, pp. 431–6 (p. 433); written c. 1868, and first published in Pinney.

42 Elizabeth Robins, *Both Sides of the Curtain* (London: Heinemann, 1940), p. 283.

4 VERY LOVELY GREEK STATUES: THE LONDON STAGE IN THE 1880S

1 Alexander Allardyce, 'George Eliot', *Blackwood's* 129 (1881), 255–68 (p. 255).

2 Leslie Stephen, 'George Eliot', *Cornhill* 43 (1881), 152–68 (p. 152).

3 The *Dublin Review* speaks of 'the multitude of wire-hung puppets that romance-writers are perpetually dancing up and down before us', and goes

on to suggest that Eliot occasionally mistook 'an artificial creature for a creation of art', for instance, in Daniel Deronda, 'a thing of leather and prunella, a "wax-doll"' (Wm. Francis Barry, 'The Genius of George Eliot', *Dublin Review* 5 (1881), 371–94 (p. 373)).

4 Methods of birth-control had been practised before then, and were discussed in avant-garde circles (for example, the Bray coterie in Coventry: see Ina Taylor, *George Eliot: Woman of Contradictions* (London: Weidenfeld and Nicolson, 1989), p. 56), but it was only after the trials of Charles Bradlaugh and Annie Besant in 1877 and 1878 for publishing cheap birth-control literature that the subject became common currency, and then that fears of it could be voiced. On the boost which the trials gave to birth-control publicity see Carol Dyhouse, *Feminism and the Family in England 1880–1939* (Oxford: Blackwell, 1989), pp. 158–9.

5 These key events are referred to by Jeffrey Weeks in his description of 1885 as 'an *annus mirabilis* of sexual politics' (*Sex, Politics and Society: The Regulation of Sexuality since 1800* (London: Longman, 1981), p. 87).

6 Eleanor Marx Aveling and Edward Aveling, 'The Woman Question: from a Socialist Point of View', *Westminster Review* n. s. 69 (1886), 207–22 (p. 218). Other social ills included lunacy and suicide, which is sadly ironic in the light of Marx's own suicide in 1898, possibly occasioned by hearing of Aveling's marriage to a young actress (see Ruth Brandon, *The New Women and the Old Men: Love, Sex and the Woman Question* (London: Secker & Warburg, 1990), pp. 153–9).

7 See Blackwell, *The Human Element*, pp. 18–19, 43–5.

8 Hamilton Aïdé, 'The Actor's Calling', *Nineteenth Century* 17 (1885), 521–6 (p. 522).

9 E. Lynn Linton, 'The Stage as a Profession for Women', *National Review* 5 (1885), 8–19 (p. 12).

10 Lynn Linton's views may have been shaped by her own theatrical sympathies. In a letter to Henry Irving, dated 17 October 1886, she reveals how her affectionate response to Ellen Terry as 'that delightful bit of deliciousness' (letter in the Bram Stoker archive, Brotherton Collection, Leeds University Library) is unsullied by any apprehension of the latter's unconventional personal life.

11 Margaret Lonsdale, 'Platform Women', *Nineteenth Century* 15 (1884), 409–15 (pp. 412, 410). Lonsdale argues that platform women imperil the grounds of all women's intangible influence by their public appearances, and suggests that their influence will detrimentally affect the younger generation who 'shall have rid themselves of all latent feelings of retirement, and quietness, and dislike of being stared at bodily and spiritually by the multitude' (p. 414).

12 Kathleen Fitzpatrick, *Lady Henry Somerset* (London: Cape, 1923), p. 173.

13 Benjamin Ward Richardson, 'Woman's Work in Creation', *Longman's Magazine* 8 (1886), 604–19 (p. 614); 'Female Poaching on Male Preserves', *Westminster Review* 129 (1888), 290–7 (p. 294).

14 Frederick Wedmore, 'The Theatrical Revival', *Nineteenth Century* 13 (1883), 217–28 (p. 218).

15 [Theodore Martin], 'The English Stage', *Quarterly Review* 155 (1883), 354–88 (p. 388).

16 D. M. Craik, 'Merely Players', *Nineteenth Century* 20 (1886), 416–22 (p. 416).

17 'A Foreign Resident' [T. H. S. Escott], *Society in London* (London: Chatto & Windus, 1885), pp. 295–6.

18 The term 'inversion' was both the precursor of 'homosexuality', which achieved currency in the 1890s, but also signified a broader range of deviations from gender norms. As David M. Halperin writes, 'deviant object-choice was viewed as merely one of a number of pathological symptoms by those who reversed, or "inverted", their proper sex-roles by adopting a masculine or feminine style at variance with what was deemed natural and appropriate to their anatomical sex' (David M. Halperin, *One Hundred Years of Homosexuality, and Other Essays on Greek Love* (New York and London: Routledge, 1990), pp. 15–16).

19 Tracy C. Davis, *Actresses as Working Women: Their Social Identity in Victorian Culture* (London and New York: Routledge, 1991), p. 161.

20 Frederick Wedmore, 'The Stage', *Academy* 24 (1883), 404. In this article he reviews Wilson Barrett's production of W. G. Wills's *Claudian*.

21 Louise Jopling, *Twenty Years of My Life, 1867–1887* (London: Lane, 1925), p. 290.

22 Cassandra was played in this production by Dorothy Dene, who was later to become the model for Lord Leighton's last paintings.

23 *The Graphic*, 12 May 1886, 547.

24 *Ibid*, 29 May 1886, 588.

25 John Stokes, *Resistible Theatres: Enterprise and Experience in the Late-nineteenth Century* (London: Elek, 1972), p. 63.

26 'Drama', *Athenaeum*, 15 December 1883, 785–6 (p. 785). In the same review Mary Anderson's first Galatea is described as 'inanimate' compared with Mrs Kendal's.

27 'The New Drama of the Laureate', *Pall Mall Gazette*, 5 January 1881, 10–11 (p. 10).

28 Mowbray Morris, *Essays in Theatrical Criticism* (London, 1882); quoted in Mullin, *Actors and Actresses in Review*, p. 442.

29 'Drama. The Week', *Athenaeum*, 8 January 1881, 65.

30 'The Cup', *Theatre* n. s. 3 (1881), 86–90 (p. 90). In *Ellen Terry* (London: Lane, 1907), Christopher St John writes of assurances given her that *The Cup* had not been surpassed as a beautiful spectacle in twenty-five years (p. 52).

31 Alfred, Lord Tennyson, *The Cup*, in *Poetical Works*, ed. by Geoffrey Cumberlege (London: Oxford University Press, 1953), Act I, scene 1.

32 An account of the couple's relationship is given in Dudley Harbron, *The Conscious Stone: The Life of Edward William Godwin* (London: Latimer House, 1949). Appropriately, the epigraph to Harbron's book is a couplet from

Emerson's 'The Problem': 'He builded better than he knew;- / The conscious stone to beauty grew' (lines 23–4).

33 Mrs Oliphant, *Dress* (London: Macmillan, 1878), p. 68.

34 St John and Craig refer to a note written by Godwin to Terry during a performance of *The Cup*, advising her as to which attitudes were justified in a representation of a Greek Priestess of that period (*Memoirs*, n. 3, p. 97). The note has been lost.

35 Quoted in Stokes, *Resistible Theatres*, p. 36.

36 'Cup and Ball at the Lyceum', *Punch* 80 (1881), 13.

37 Clement Scott, '*The Cup*', in *From 'The Bells' to 'King Arthur'* (London: Macqueen, 1896), pp. 190–204 (p. 201).

38 Frederick Wedmore, 'The Stage: Mr Tennyson's New Play', *Academy* 22 (1881), 34–6 (p. 35).

39 Terry's claims give some indication of the possibilities for self-legitimation offered by the genre of autobiography which will be examined in more detail in the conclusion.

40 Virginia Woolf, *Freshwater: A Comedy* (London: Hogarth Press, 1976), p. 24. The play is based on the artistic circle, including Watts, Terry, and Tennyson, who converged on Freshwater, the Isle of Wight home of Woolf's aunt, the photographer Julia Margaret Cameron.

41 Mary Anderson (Mme de Navarro), *A Few Memories* (London: Osgood, McIlvaine, 1896), p. 149.

42 'Pygmalion and Galatea', *Theatre* 3 (1884), 48–50 (p. 49).

43 'Drama. The Week', *Athenaeum*, 15 December 1883, 785–6 (p. 786).

44 Frederick Wedmore, 'The Stage: "Pygmalion and Galatea" at the Lyceum', *Academy* 24 (1883), 440–1 (p. 441).

45 'Mr L. Alma-Tadema on "Galatea"', *Pall Mall Gazette*, 10 December 1883, p. 3. All subsequent references to Alma-Tadema's participation in this production are taken from this article.

46 Anderson was later to become a very similar sort of statue when she represented 'America' during a First World War pageant. In *A Few More Memories* (London: Hutchinson, 1936), Anderson records her participation in benefit performances in London during the war. The parts she played most frequently were Hermione, Juliet, and Galatea (pp. 148–59).

47 'Punch's Fancy Portraits – No. 168', *Punch* 85 (1883), 310.

48 'Dramatic Gossip', *Athenaeum*, 13 September 1884, 346.

49 'Occasional Notes', *Pall Mall Gazette*, 8 September 1884, 3. This review was followed a few days later by an interview with Anderson ('A Short Chat with Miss Anderson', 16 September, p. 6) which publicised her forthcoming tour and the rest of the Lyceum season.

50 'Our Omnibus-Box', *Theatre* 4 (1884), 310–20 (p. 311).

51 Clement Scott, 'Romeo and Juliet', *Theatre* n. s. 5 (1882), 231–42 (p. 235).

52 George Rowell, 'Mercutio as Romeo: William Terriss in *Romeo and Juliet*', in Richard Foulkes (ed.), *Shakespeare and the Victorian Stage* (Cambridge Univer-

sity Press, 1986), pp. 87–96 (pp. 87–8). The quotation from Irving is taken from *Memoirs of Ellen Terry*, p. 162.

53 *Memories and Impressions of Helena Modjeska* (New York and London: Blom, 1969; first published in 1910), p. 138.

54 'Court Cards', *Punch* 80 (1881), 165.

55 Laurence Irving records that, although not as great a critical success as the previous year's acclaimed *Merchant of Venice*, the Lyceum *Romeo and Juliet* nonetheless attracted equally large audiences (Laurence Irving, *Henry Irving: The Actor and His World* (London: Faber and Faber, 1951), p. 390).

56 [Henry James], 'London Pictures and London Plays', *Atlantic Monthly* 50 (1882), 253–63 (p. 262).

57 Frederick Wedmore, 'The Stage: "Romeo and Juliet" at the Lyceum Theatre', *The Academy* 21 (1882), 200–1 (p. 201).

58 Wilde to Mary Anderson, 23 March 1883, *Oscar Wilde Letters*, p. 137.

59 'The Stage', *The Academy* 26 (1884), 420.

60 'Nibbs', 'Letters to Some People', *Punch* 87 (1884), 232–3 (p. 232); Frederick Wedmore, 'The Stage. "Romeo and Juliet" and the Comedy at the Vaudeville', *The Academy* 26 (1884), 330–2 (p. 331).

61 This moment aptly prefigures the end of Anderson's professional career, a career which was framed by early appearances in America as Galatea, and by her final professional performance as Shakespeare's Hermione, in this instance a statue who is unable fully to come to life. Beset by nervous exhaustion, Anderson poignantly retreated back into the silence of the statue at her professional career's conclusion:
> There was only one more act to go through. Donning the statue-like draperies of Hermione, I mounted the pedestal [...] Every moment there was an hour of torture to me, for I felt myself growing fainter and fainter. All my remaining strength was put into that last effort. I descended from the pedestal, and was able to speak all but the final line. This remained unuttered, and the curtain rang down on my last appearance on the stage. (*A Few Memories*, p. 259)

62 William Archer, 'The Myths of Romeo and Juliet', *National Review* 4 (1884–5), 441–50 (p. 449).

63 'The Flame Once Kendal'd', *Punch* 87 (1884), 193. The column is written in response to Mrs Kendal's publication of her address to the Congress of the National Association for the Promotion of Social Science. The talk was published as *The Drama* (London: Bogue, 1884). *Punch* seems to have objected to Mrs Kendal's criticism of a theatre degraded by a new emphasis on forceful publicity, in a publication whose frontispiece was a full-length photograph of the actress.

64 George Moore, 'Our Dramatists and Their Literature', in *Impressions and Opinions* (London: Nutt, 1891), pp. 181–214 (p. 209); originally published in the *Fortnightly Review* (1889). This is a theme which Moore touches on in *A Mummer's Wife* (1885).

65 Harriett Jay, *Through the Stage Door*, 3 vols. (London: White, 1883), vol. i, p. 115.

66 Florence Marryat, *My Sister the Actress*, 3 vols. (London: White, 1881), vol. i,

p. 7. Marryat's later theatre-fiction, *Peeress and Player* (1883) presents a similar heroine.

67 See Laura Mulvey, 'Visual Pleasure and Narrative Cinema', in *Visual and other Pleasures* (London: Macmillan, 1989), pp. 14–26; and E. Ann Kaplan, 'Is the Gaze Male?', in Ann Snitow, Christine Stansell, and Sharon Thompson (eds.), *Powers of Desire: The Politics of Sexuality* (New York: Monthly Review Press, 1983), pp. 309–27.

68 Lisa Moore, 'Sexual Agency in Manet's *Olympia*', *Textual Practice* 3 (1989), 222–33 (p. 226). Moore holds that the *Olympia* disrupts the usual descent of sexualising power through its unconventional play of female gazes.

69 John Coleman, 'The Social Status of the Actor', *National Review* 5 (1885), 20–8 (p. 24).

70 George Moore, *A Mummer's Wife* (London: Vizetelly, 1885), p. 252.

71 George Bernard Shaw, *The Irrational Knot* (London: Constable, 1905), p. 263. The novel was actually written in 1880 – 'Everybody wrote novels then' – but not published until 1885–7, when it appeared in Annie Besant's *Our Corner*, 'a little propagandist magazine of hers'. Comments are taken from Shaw's preface to the 1905 edition of the novel, pp. vii–xxvi (p. vii). Shaw also contributed fine arts and theatre reviews to the 'Art Corner' of the magazine.

72 See Elaine Aston, *Sarah Bernhardt: A French Actress on the English Stage* (Oxford: Berg, 1989).

73 'Mdlle Sarah Bernhardt's Works', *Art Journal* n. s. 18 (1879), 223. The funds raised by the sale of works from this exhibition aided the birth of one of the best-known of Bernhardt's escapades, for she used the money to purchase a cheetah, a wolf-hound, and six chameleons, which created havoc in her London house. For further details, see Arthur Gold and Robert Fizdale, *The Divine Sarah: A Life of Sarah Bernhardt* (London: HarperCollins, 1992), pp. 152–3.

74 *My Double Life: Memoirs of Sarah Bernhardt* (London: Heinemann, 1907), p. 256.

75 The description of Bernhardt's costume is taken from the *Daily Telegraph* (1884), which describes the attention excited by advance publicity photographs of Bernhardt; quoted in Aston, *Sarah Bernhardt*, p. 75. The references to Delilah and the sirens are taken from the *Pall Mall Gazette* (1884); quoted in Aston, p. 76.

76 In line with his comparatively radical vision of the female performer, Zola's dramatic criticism was an important stimulus to reform in the French theatre. For an account of his influence on the founder of the Théâtre Libre, André Antoine, see Jean Chothia, *André Antoine* (Cambridge University Press, 1991), pp. 3–6.

77 Emile Zola, *Nana* (Harmondsworth: Penguin, 1972), p. 223. This was one of the three Zola novels for publishing translations of which Henry Vizetelly was prosecuted in 1888. The other novels were *La Terre* and *Pot-Bouille*. For details of the trial, see Ernest Alfred Vizetelly, *Emile Zola, Novelist and*

Reformer: An Account of His Life and Work (London: Lane, Bodley Head, 1904), pp. 268–85.

78 Despite both being about Parisian courtesans, we should note that *La Dame aux camélias* and *Nana* were perceived as substantially different in England during the eighties. Notably, Marguerite Gautier is free from the absolute ruthlessness in her greed which distinguishes Nana. In 1885, W. S. Lilly wrote of Marguerite that she had an ethical element in her, and that, unlike Nana, her trade had not killed her soul ('The New Naturalism', *Fortnightly Review* 38 (1885), 240–56 (p. 256)).

79 William Archer, 'A Well-Graced Actress', *National Review* 7 (1886), 770–80 (p. 773).

80 'XX' [Henry James], 'The Comédie-Française in London', *Nation*, 31 July 1879, 72–3 (p. 73).

81 Mrs Humphry Ward, *Miss Bretherton* (London: Macmillan, 1884), p. 41.

82 Henry James to Mary Ward, 9 December 1884, in Leon Edel (ed.), *Henry James Letters*, 4 vols. (London: Macmillan, 1974–84), vol. III, pp. 59–60.

83 See John Sutherland, *Mrs Humphry Ward: Eminent Victorian, Pre-eminent Edwardian* (Oxford University Press, 1990), p. 101.

84 G. Barnett Smith, 'New Novels', *Academy* 26 (1884), 407–8 (p. 408).

85 Denis Diderot, *The Paradox of Acting*, trans. by Walter Herries Pollock (London: Chatto & Windus, 1883), p. 7.

86 The precise contemporary meaning of 'sensibility' is difficult to recover, but light may be shed on Irving and the 1880s' understanding of the term by Talma's *On the Actor's Art* (first published in France in 1825), a translation of which had appeared in *The Theatre* in 1877, and which was published as a pamphlet with a preface by Irving in 1884. There, Talma describes sensibility as not only a faculty which the actor possesses of being moved himself, and of physically conveying his emotions, but also,

> that faculty of exaltation which agitates an actor, takes possession of his senses, shakes even his very soul, and enables him to enter into the most tragic situations, and the most terrible of passions, as if they were his own. The intelligence which accompanies sensibility judges the impressions which the latter has made us feel; it selects, arranges them, and subjects them to calculation. (Talma, *On the Actor's Art* (London: Bickers, 1884), p. 14.)

This differs little from the understanding of 'sensibility' which may be extrapolated from Diderot's writing, but Irving, wooed by the greater dignity ascribed the actor in Talma, lauds Talma where he only disparages Diderot. He writes in his preface to *On the Actor's Art* that it is 'a permanent embodiment of the principles of our art; a kind of *vade mecum* of the actor's calling' (p. 3).

87 William Archer, 'The Anatomy of Acting', *Longman's Magazine* 11 (1888), 266–81 (p. 268). A more extended version of Archer's findings is given in his *Masks or Faces? A Study in the Psychology of Acting* (London: Longmans, Green, 1888).

88 These annotations appear in Ellen Terry's acting edition of the play, which

was amended for production by Henry Irving. The edition is kept at the Ellen Terry Memorial Museum, Smallhythe, Kent.

5 LIVING STATUES AND THE LITERARY DRAMA

1 From 'Verses to the Weather Maiden', *Punch* 107 (1894), 93; reprinted in *The Daily Graphic*, 24 August 1894, 5. The previous stanza describes the Weather Maiden as

> Serenely contemplating the Atlantic
> In raiment which, if fashionable here,
> Would greatly shock the properly pedantic,
> Make Glasgow green with rage, and Mrs Grundy frantic.

2 'Interviews with Famous Statues: IV. – The Duke of York's Column and Victory', *The Sketch*, 3 January 1894, 545–6.
3 H. Rider Haggard and Andrew Lang, *The World's Desire* (London: Longmans, Green, 1894), p. ix. Flinders Petrie also organised a popular exhibition in London's Egyptian Hall in 1888 of Egyptian mummy-portraits. The exhibition ran alongside the Hall's usual displays of telepathy and occult events, a conjunction which shapes Haggard and Lang's novel of sorcery and mystery.
4 Arthur Symons, 'Impressions of Sarah Bernhardt', *London Mercury* (1923); quoted in Karl Beckson (ed.), *The Memoirs of Arthur Symons: Life and Art in the 1890s* (University Park and London: Pennsylvania State University Press, 1977), p. 191.
5 *Athenaeum* (1896); quoted in Leonée Ormond and Richard Ormond, *Lord Leighton* (New Haven and London: Yale University Press, 1975), pp. 127–8.
6 'The Strand Burlesque', *Saturday Review*, 24 November 1888, 614–15 (p. 614).
7 Harry Pleon, *A Vision of Venus* (London: Dicks, [n. d.]), p. 6.
8 Bernard Shaw, 'Sardoodledom', in *Our Theatre in the Nineties*, 3 vols. (London: Constable, 1932), vol. I, pp. 133–40 (p. 139). This review, like the others in Shaw's collection of his drama criticism, was originally published in the *Saturday Review*. It appeared on 1 June 1895.
9 For a review of this production, see *The Theatre* 23 (1894), 287, where it is recorded that finally an actress had emerged who did not play Cynisca as a jealous virago.
10 See David Mayer, *Playing Out the Empire: Ben Hur and other Toga Plays and Films, 1883–1908. A Critical Anthology* (Oxford: Clarendon Press, 1994).
11 Quoted in Jenkyns, *Dignity and Decadence*, p. 307.
12 'The Palace Theatre Company Limited', *Daily Graphic*, 24 August 1894, 11.
13 Marcus Stone RA, who was part of a *New Review* symposium on 'The Living Pictures', *New Review* 11 (1894), 461–70 (p. 463). The other contributors were George Edwardes of the Empire Theatre, Charles Morton of the Palace, A. W. Pinero, W. A. Coote, Secretary of the National Vigilance Association, Arthur Symons, the Reverend H. C. Shuttleworth, and Frederick A. Atkins, editor of *The Young Man*.

14 Bernard Shaw, 'The Living Pictures', in *Our Theatre*, vol. i, pp. 79–86 (p. 80); 16 April 1895.

15 An account of this issue, ' "Prudes on the Prowl": the View from the Empire Promenade', is given in John Stokes, *In the Nineties* (University of Chicago Press, 1989), pp. 53–93. In a hearing before the Theatre and Music-Halls Committee of the London County Council in October 1894, objections were made to the renewal of the Palace's licence because of its 'Living Pictures'. The licence was renewed, although the Committee urged the Palace management to exercise greater caution over its show (Stokes, p. 56). Objections to the Empire promenade, led by Mrs Ormiston Chant of the Britishwoman's Temperance Association, generated a much more protracted battle which resulted in the promenade being temporarily cordoned off from the rest of the theatre, before the partition was destroyed by a party of young men (Stokes, pp. 58–9).

It is worth noting that William Archer was fairly relaxed about the presence of the 'Living Pictures', which he seems to have regarded as part of the rich capacity of theatricality in which he believed. He writes that the London stage should not only show plays like *The Second Mrs Tanqueray*, asserting that 'I have not outgrown my taste for lollipops if only they be delicately flavoured, and not too heavily "loaded" with Plaster of Paris' (William Archer, 'Eleanora Duse – "The Second Mrs Tanqueray"', in *The Theatrical World for 1893* (London: Scott [1894]), pp. 125–37 (p. 128); 31 May 1893).

16 'there is reason to hope that before long the distinction between the theatre and the music-hall will be insisted upon by not a few who care for the actor's calling' ('Echoes from the Green Room', *Theatre* 24 (1894), 270–6 (p. 271)).

17 From Mrs Ormiston Chant, *Why We Attacked the Empire* (London: Marshall, [1895]), p. 21.

18 'Our Watch Tower. The County Council and the Music-Halls', *Theatre* 24 (1894), 277–81 (pp. 280–81).

19 William Archer, 'Eleanora Duse – A Society Butterfly – King Kodak', in *World for 1894*, pp. 143–51 (p. 147); 16 May 1894.

20 'A Society Butterfly', *Theatre* 23 (1894), 332–4 (p. 333).

21 H. D. Traill, 'The Literary Drama', *New Review* 5 (1891), 502–14 (p. 504).

22 William Archer, 'The Stage and Literature', *Fortnightly Review* n. s. 51 (1892), 219–32 (p. 232).

23 Henry Arthur Jones, 'The Literary Drama: a Reply', *New Review* 6 (1892), 89–96 (p. 95).

24 See Henry James, 'On the Occasion of "*Hedda Gabler*"', *New Review* 4 (1891), 519–30 (p. 521), where James writes of Ibsen's having 'mastered an exceedingly difficult form'.

25 The authors were: Thomas Hardy, W. E. Norris (31 August 1892); J. Henry Shorthouse, Lucas Malet (1 September); Frederick Anstey, A. T. Quiller Couch, Margaret L. Woods (2 September); Justin McCarthy, Mary Braddon, 'A Novelist' (5 September); George Moore (7 September);

Mrs Campbell Praed (8 September); Frank Harris (9 September); George Gissing (10 September); Harold Frederic (12 September); John Oliver Hobbes (13 September); Ouida (20 September). Despite this evidence, however, it is worth noting that at least three of these authors, Thomas Hardy, George Moore and John Oliver Hobbes, i.e. Pearl Craigie, later wrote plays.

26 Moore, 'Why I Don't Write Plays', p. 3. Moore did acknowledge, however, that the new drama criticism of Archer in particular was beginning to attract educated audiences away from farce and melodrama, and also went on to write a play, *The Strike at Arlingford*, which was produced by the Independent Theatre in 1893.

27 William Archer, 'The Free Stage and the New Drama', *Fortnightly Review* 50 (1891), 663–72 (p. 664).

28 Archer writes elsewhere of *The Second Mrs Tanqueray* that, 'It is the highest praise, then, that I can find for *Mrs Tanqueray* to say that its four scenes are like the crucial, the culminating, chapters of a singularly powerful and original novel' (*World for 1893*, p. 132).

29 Hamilton Aïdé, 'A New Stage Doctrine', *Nineteenth Century* 34 (1893), 425–57 (p. 452).

30 Henrik Ibsen, *A Doll's House, and Two Other Plays*, trans. by R. Farquharson Sharp and Eleanor Marx-Aveling (London: Dent, 1910), p. 67.

31 Frederic Wedmore, 'Ibsen in London', *Academy* (1889); quoted in Michael Egan (ed.), *Ibsen: The Critical Heritage* (London: Routledge and Kegan Paul, 1972), p. 107.

32 Clement Scott, '*A Doll's House*', *Theatre* (1889); quoted in Egan, *Critical Heritage*, p. 114.

33 William Archer, '"A Doll's House" – "A Scrap of Paper"', in *World for 1893*, pp. 155–62 (p. 157); 14 June 1893.

34 Critics sceptical about Nora's transformation include Clement Scott in the *Daily Telegraph*, the *Daily News* reviewer, and the *Spectator*'s reviewer. They are all quoted in Egan, *Critical Heritage*, pp. 102, 104, 110.

35 'Our Play-Box: "Her Own Witness"', *Theatre* n. s. 14 (1889), 301–2 (p. 302).

36 Clement Scott, '*Hedda Gabler*', *Daily Telegraph*, 21 April 1891, p. 3.

37 Review of *Hedda Gabler*, *Observer* (1891); quoted in Egan, *Critical Heritage*, pp. 230–1 (p. 231).

38 Clement Scott, review of *Hedda Gabler*, *Illustrated London News* (1891); quoted in *Critical Heritage*, pp. 225–8 (p. 227).

39 Bernard Shaw, '*Little Eyolf*', in *Our Theatre*, vol. II, pp. 256–64 (p. 261); 28 November 1896.

40 Mrs Patrick Campbell recalled in 1922:

Most successful actors and actresses are entirely dependent upon personality for their effect, aided, as the case may be, by the charm of their diction or their natural grace of gesture or personal beauty. Mediocre artists have risen to a considerable position on their quality of 'personality' [...] Plays are written around it, and many plays have been sacrificed to it. In an Ibsen play it is a very great misfortune, imprisoning the artist in his own narrow circle of individualism. (Mrs Patrick Campbell, *My Life and Some Letters* [London: Hutchinson, 1922], p. 66).

41 From Elizabeth Robins's unpublished autobiography 'Whither and How'; quoted in Thomas Postlewait, *Prophet of the New Drama: William Archer and the Ibsen Campaign* (Westport, CT and London: Greenwood Press, 1986), p. 72.

42 Review of *Hedda Gabler*, *The Times* (1891); quoted in Egan, *Critical Heritage*, pp. 218–19 (p. 219).

43 'An Ibsen Success – *Hedda Gabler* at the Vaudeville', *Pall Mall Gazette* (1891); quoted in Egan, *Critical Heritage*, pp. 220–1 (p. 221).

44 Review of *Hedda Gabler*, *Sunday Times* (1891); quoted in Egan, *Critical Heritage*, pp. 229–30 (p. 229).

45 William Archer, 'The Theatre: *Hedda Gabler*', *The World*, 29 April 1891, p. 24.

46 Laura Marholm Hansson, *Modern Women*, trans. by Hermione Ramsden (London: Lane, Bodley Head, 1894), p. 107.

47 Elizabeth Robins, *Ibsen and the Actress*, Hogarth Essays, second series, number 15 (London: Hogarth Press, 1928), p. 55.

48 Maurice Maeterlinck, 'The Modern Drama', *Cornhill* n. s. 7 (1899), 166–73 (p. 166).

49 With the brief exception of Beerbohm Tree the actor-managers were notoriously unsympathetic to Ibsen. Elizabeth Robins took the newly written *Master Builder* to Tree. Having already been told at a number of theatres that the play 'was wild! it was irritatingly obscure. It was dull, it was mad, it would lose money' (*Ibsen and the Actress*, p. 39), she turned to the man who had offered her the chance to stay on in the English theatre when she had feared she might have to return to America:

amongst other things that I owed to that versatile, generous, and lovable man, I owed to Beerbohm Tree the chance of being in the Ibsen saga at all. That much to explain why, though Mr Tree loathed Ibsen and had been one of the most vehement and picturesque fulminators against him, I finally took *The Master Builder* to the Haymarket.

Beerbohm Tree turned out to be the one manager in London who could see anything in the play. To my delight, what he could see was himself. Yes, he could produce it – on condition. The condition was that we should lift the play out of its sordid provincialism. We would do this by dint of making the people English; more particularly by making the Master Builder a sculptor. Many people in those days would have backed that view. (pp. 39–40)

When Ibsen did create, in his final play *When We Dead Awaken*, a sculptor-hero, Tree did not take up the role.

50 Interview with Marion Lea, *Illustrated London News* (1891); quoted in Postlewait, *Prophet of the New Drama*, p. 71.

51 Mrs Bell, also a friend of Henry James, was already an established writer, and had had plays produced by Coquelin (*L'Indécis*, 1887) and Charles Hawtrey (*Time is Money*, 1888).

52 J. T. Grein, 'Editor's Preface' to *Alan's Wife: A Dramatic Study in 3 Scenes* (London: Henry, 1893), pp. v–viii (p. viii).

53 Elizabeth Robins, *Theatre and Friendship: Some Henry James Letters* (London: Cape, 1932), pp. 146, 147.

54 It should, however, be noted that this instance of female collaboration was far from a utopian episode. Ameen resented the way in which her play was being used, and the fact that she was not fully consulted in the process of its translation to the English stage. For further details, see Angela V. John, *Elizabeth Robins: Staging A Life* (London and New York: Routledge, 1995), p. 90.

55 Eve Adam, ed., *Mrs J. Comyns Carr's Reminiscences* (London: Hutchinson, [c. 1926]), pp. 216, 237. Mrs Comyns Carr is herself an interesting figure in the issue of female collaboration, as she was very largely responsible in the later stages of Terry's career for her costumes. Of Terry's most famous dress as Lady Macbeth, subsequently best known, of course, through Sargent's painting, she writes, 'I was anxious to make this particular dress look as much like soft chain armour as I could, and yet have something that would give the appearance of the scales of a serpent' (p. 211). In her reference to the serpent, Comyns Carr is surely invoking Bernhardt.

56 Susan Bennett, *Theatre Audiences: A Theory of Production and Reception* (London and New York: Routledge, 1990), p. 149.

57 Quoted in Kate Flint, *The Woman Reader, 1837–1914* (Oxford: Clarendon Press, 1993), p. 315.

58 See *Theatre and Friendship*, p. 194.

59 Edith Lees, 'Olive Schreiner and her Relation to the Woman Movement' (1915), in Cherry Clayton (ed.), *Olive Schreiner* (Johannesburg: McGraw-Hill, 1983), pp. 46–51 (p. 46).

60 William Archer, '*The Wild Duck*: A Study in Illusions', in *World for 1894*, pp. 136–43 (p. 139); 13 June 1894.

61 Bernard Shaw, 'Two Plays', in *Our Theatre*, vol. I, pp. 140–8 (p. 147); 8 June 1895.

62 Bernard Shaw, 'Duse and Bernhardt', in *Our Theatre*, vol. I, pp. 148–54 (p. 149); 15 June 1895.

63 William Archer, 'Eleanora Duse – Ibsen Performances – The Independent Theatre – Five English Plays', in *World for 1893*, pp. 144–55 (p. 147); 7 June 1893.

64 Bernard Shaw, 'The New Magda and the New Cyprienne', in *Our Theatre*, vol. II, pp. 145–51 (p. 145); 6 June 1896.

65 William Archer, '*Heimat*', in *The Theatrical World for 1895* (London: Scott, 1896), pp. 193–202 (p. 201); 19 June 1895.

66 William Archer, 'The Rival Queens', in *World for 1895*, pp. 202–9 (p. 208); 20 June 1895.

67 Mrs Campbell is criticised precisely because she 'cannot enlarge or transform herself'. Rather she is trapped within what Archer describes as her 'irreproachable' gowns ('Fedora', in *World for 1895*, pp. 172–9 (pp. 175, 174); 29 May 1895).

68 William Ferrero, 'Woman's Sphere in Art', *New Review* 9 (1893), 554–60 (p. 557).

69 George Moore, *Modern Painting* (London: Scott, 1893), p. 220.

70 'Medusa's Head', in James Strachey (ed.), *The Standard Edition of the Complete Psychoanalytic Works of Sigmund Freud*, 24 vols. (London: Hogarth Press, 1955–74), vol. XVIII, pp. 273–4 (p. 274).

71 Henry James, 'After the Play', *New Review* 1 (1889), 30–46 (p. 41).

72 Henry James, *The Tragic Muse*, 3 vols. (London: Macmillan, 1890), vol. III, p. 150.

73 Bram Stoker, *Personal Reminiscences of Henry Irving*, 2 vols. (London: Heinemann, 1906), vol. II, p. 206.

74 An incident during Terry's performance of Viola at the Lyceum in 1884 links her to Lucy. During the production Terry had been troubled with a bad thumb, the pain of which almost prevented her appearing. Finally, it became so unbearable that Stoker took action, calling in his brother, a doctor, to lance Terry's thumb between acts. The following day it transpired that Terry had been suffering from blood-poisoning. This, combined with Stoker's tantalising 'hundredth night' present to Terry of a 'jewelled pin' during the run of *Hamlet* in 1879, involve the pair in the matrix of penetrative acts which permeates *Dracula*.

75 Bram Stoker, *Dracula* (Harmondsworth: Penguin, 1992), p. 213.

76 Elaine Showalter and Kathleen L. Spencer note that Lucy's predilection for marrying all her suitors might seem to counter the evidence for her virtue (See *Sexual Anarchy*, p. 180; and Kathleen L. Spencer, 'Purity and Danger: *Dracula*, the Urban Gothic, and the Late Victorian Degeneracy Crisis', *ELH* 59 (1992), 197–225 (pp. 209–10)). However, it may simply link her more effectively to the actress who was in some measure available to all her audiences.

77 George du Maurier, *Trilby* (London: Osgood, McIlvaine, 1895), p. 171. The novel was first published in 1894. References are made here to the first illustrated edition of the novel, issued in 1895.

78 As Nina Auerbach suggests in *Woman and the Demon: The Life of a Victorian Myth* (Cambridge, MA, and London: Harvard University Press, 1982), p. 18.

79 The principal aspects shared by this Athena and Trilby are, however, common to most statues of the goddess, as the *Lexicon Iconographicum Mythologicum Classicum* shows.

80 See 'Portraits. Mr Tree as Svengali; Miss Baird as Trilby', *Theatre* 26 (1895), 316. Dorothea Baird's later career further linked her with Terry when she married one of Irving's sons, and came to take the parts played by Terry opposite him.

81 Frederick Wedmore, 'The Stage. "Trilby"', *Academy* 48 (1895), 392–3.

82 'In the Provinces', *Theatre* 26 (1895), 232–5 (p. 233).

83 Bernard Shaw, 'Trilby and "L'ami des femmes"', in *Our Theatre*, vol. I, pp. 238–44 (p. 240); 9 November 1895.

84 'Caesar and Cleopatra has been driven clean out of my head by a play I want to write for them in which he [Johnston Forbes-Robertson] shall be a west end gentleman and she [Mrs Patrick Campbell] an east end donna in an apron and three orange and red ostrich feathers' (8 September 1897,

Christopher St John (ed.), *Ellen Terry and Bernard Shaw: A Correspondence* (London: Reinhardt and Evans, 1931), p. 234). It has also been suggested by Leonée Ormond that Leighton's relationship with Dorothy Dene may have been part of Shaw's inspiration.

85 This fact is ruefully recorded by Max Beerbohm who, having seen Paul Potter's adaptation of *Trilby* in New York, assured his half-brother that it was 'utter nonsense' and would fail in London. Luckily Tree decided to see for himself. This is recorded in Max Beerbohm, 'From a Brother's Standpoint', in *Herbert Beerbohm Tree: Some Memories of Him and of His Art*, collected by Max Beerbohm (London: Hutchinson, 1920), pp. 187–202.

86 William Archer, '"King Arthur" and "Guy Domville"', in *World for 1895*, 20–35 (pp. 31–2); 16 January 1895.

87 Bernard Shaw, 'Mr Grundy's Improvements on Dumas', in *Our Theatre*, vol. III, pp. 189–96 (p. 193); 17 July 1897.

88 Stanley Weintraub (ed.), *Bernard Shaw: The Diaries, 1885–1897*, 2 vols. (University Park and London: Pennsylvania State University Press, 1986), vol. II, p. 902. See also Postlewait, *Prophet of the New Drama*, p. 107.

89 Dan H. Laurence (ed.), *Bernard Shaw: Collected Letters, 1874–1897* (London: Reinhardt, 1965), p. 380.

90 Sequel to *Pygmalion*, in *The Complete Plays of Bernard Shaw* (London: Hamlyn, 1965), pp. 716–57 (p. 752).

CONCLUSION. WRITING ACTRESSES

1 'Introduction: Pier Desiderio and the Doll', in *For Maurice: Five Unlikely Stories* (London: Lane, Bodley Head, 1927), pp. xliv–li (pp. xlv, l).

2 Sarah Grand, 'Marriage Questions in Fiction: the Standpoint of a Typical Modern Woman', *Fortnightly Review* n. s. 63 (1898), 378–89 (p. 378).

3 Hubert Crackanthorpe, 'Reticence in Literature', *Yellow Book* 2 (1894), 259–69 (p. 266).

4 Janet E. Hogarth, 'Literary Degenerates', *Fortnightly Review* n. s. 57 (1895), 586–92 (p. 589).

5 Arthur Waugh, 'Reticence in Literature', *Yellow Book* 1 (1894), 201–19 (p. 219).

6 Bernard Shaw, 'Toujours Daly', in *Our Theatre*, vol. I, pp. 177–84 (p. 183); 13 July 1895.

7 William Archer, 'Eleanora Duse', *Fortnightly Review* 58 (1895), 299–307 (p. 301).

8 Helen Zimmern, 'Eleanora Duse', *Fortnightly Review* 67 (1900), 980–93 (p. 993).

9 Arthur Symons, 'Eleanora Duse', *Contemporary Review* 78 (1900), 196–202 (p. 201).

10 An alternative derivation for Duse's art, and one which also explicitly counters the parameters of Galatea's capacity, is suggested by Vernon Blackburn, who suggests that, 'If you subtract the imaginative creativeness

from each character which she impersonates, you are left with a quality of pure intellect, in each instance. This is the explanation of her everlasting variety and of the singleness of her simplicity' (Vernon Blackburn, 'Eleanora Duse', *New Review* 13 (1895), 39–44 (p. 41)).

11 Sidonie Smith, *A Poetics of Women's Autobiography: Marginality and the Fictions of Self-Representation* (Bloomington: Indiana University Press, 1987), p. 50.

12 T. L. Broughton, 'Women's Autobiography: the Self at Stake?', *Prose Studies* 14 (1991), 76–94 (p. 79).

13 Helena Faucit, Lady Martin, *On Some of Shakespeare's Female Characters* (Edinburgh and London: Blackwood, 1885), p. 90.

14 Elizabeth Robins, *Raymond and I* (London: Hogarth, 1956), p. 47.

15 Henrik Ibsen, *When We Dead Wake*, in *Ghosts, and Other Plays*, trans. by Peter Watts (Harmondsworth: Penguin, 1964), p. 242.

16 See Inga-Stina Ewbank, 'The Last Plays', in James McFarlane (ed.), *The Cambridge Companion to Ibsen* (Cambridge University Press, 1994), pp. 126–54.

17 This letter is dated Wednesday 14 June, and was received at the Lyceum a few days later in 1899. It interestingly replicates an undated latter sent by Robins to Irving when she was making efforts to stay in England rather than return to the States. In the earlier letter she writes of Portia to Irving, but this times offers to understudy, rather than to replace Terry. Both letters are in the Stoker archive, Brotherton Library, University of Leeds.

18 Letter of 6 September 1906; quoted in Auerbach, *Ellen Terry*, p. 283.

19 We should note, however, that Terry, 'clothed in her white samite draperies', nonetheless did successfully suggest to her audience 'the Niobe of the Louvre [...] a memory of the sorrow and dignity written by sculptors in marble, of those long lines of statues stolen by Europe from Greece, which stand now in our museums in the coldness of death, yet freshness of immortality' (St John, *Ellen Terry*, p. 83).

20 Ellen Terry, 'Stray Memories', *New Review* 4 (1891), 332–41; 444–9; 499–507. Also in the same volume of the *New Review* was Olive Schreiner's story 'The Woman's Rose' (pp. 540–3), which captures a moment of female understanding and appreciation beyond the resources of its male characters.

21 Nina Auerbach offers a different reading of Terry's autobiography, suggesting that by her 'suggestive presence' Christopher St John 'created the woman who wrote the Memoir [...] as consummately as Watts created Ophelia, or Henry Irving his womanly actress' (p. 415). This reading is only possible, however, if we disregard the evidence of Terry's earliest writings, which appeared before St John became known to Terry.

22 Ellen Terry's acting copy of *Nance Oldfield*, p. 6. The edition is kept at the Ellen Terry Memorial Museum, Smallhythe Place, Kent.

23 This copy of *The Story of My Life* is kept at the Ellen Terry Museum.

24 Edward Gordon Craig, 'Annex: A Plea for G. B. S.', in *Ellen Terry and Her Secret Self* (London: Sampson Low, 1932), pp. 26–7.

25 Virginia Woolf, 'Ellen Terry', in *Collected Essays*, 4 vols. (London: Hogarth Press, 1967), vol. IV, pp. 67–72 (p. 68).

Select bibliography

PRIMARY WORKS

Allott, Kenneth (ed.), *The Poems of Matthew Arnold*, 2nd edition ed. by Miriam Allott, London and New York: Longman, 1979.

Aristophanes, *The Frogs*, trans. by Benjamin Bickley Rogers, London: Heinemann; Cambridge, MA: Harvard University Press, 1968.

Beddoes, Thomas Lowell, *The Works of Thomas Lovell Beddoes*, London: Oxford University Press, 1935.

Bennett, W. C., *Queen Eleanor's Vengeance, and Other Poems*, London: Chapman and Hall, 1857.

Brontë, Charlotte, *Villette*, Harmondsworth: Penguin, 1979 [1853].

Brough, William, *Pygmalion; or, The Statue Fair*, Lacy's Acting Edition, London: Lacy, 1867.

The Poetical Works of Robert Buchanan, 3 vols., London: King, 1874.

Coleridge, Ernest Hartley, *Poems*, London and New York: Lane, Bodley Head, 1898.

Dickens, Charles, *Bleak House*, Harmondsworth: Penguin, 1996 [1853].

Dowson, Ernest, *Verses*, London: Smithers, 1896.

Du Maurier, George, *Trilby*, London: Osgood, McIlvaine, 1895.

Eliot, George, *The Works of George Eliot*, Cabinet edition, 20 vols., Edinburgh and London: Blackwood [n.d.].

Gilbert, W. S., *Pygmalion and Galatea: An Original Mythological Comedy*, in *Original Plays*, London: Chatto and Windus, 1876.

Goethe, Johann Wolfgang von, *Italian Journey*, trans. by W. H. Auden and Elizabeth Mayer, Harmondsworth: Penguin, 1962.

Elective Affinities, trans. by Judith Ryan, Princeton University Press, 1995 [1809].

Hallam, Arthur, *The Writings of Arthur Hallam*, New York: MLA; London: Oxford University Press, 1943.

Hardy, Thomas, *The Well-Beloved: A Sketch of a Temperament*, London: Macmillan, 1986 [1897].

Outside the Gates of the World: Selected Short Stories, London: Dent, 1996.

Hawthorne, Nathaniel, *Passages from the French and Italian Note-books of Nathaniel Hawthorne*, 2 vols., London: Strahan, 1871.

Hazlitt, William, *Liber Amoris, or The New Pygmalion*, Oxford and New York: Woodstock, 1992 [1823].

Heine, Heinrich, *The Prose Writings of Heinrich Heine*, ed. Havelock Ellis, London: Scott, 1887.

Ibsen, Henrik, *A Doll's House, and Two Other Plays*, trans. by R. Farquharson Sharp and Eleanor Marx-Aveling, London: Dent, 1910.

    When We Dead Wake, in *Ghosts, and Other Plays*, trans. by Peter Watts, Harmondsworth: Penguin, 1964.

James, Henry, *The Portrait of a Lady*, 3 vols., London: Macmillan, 1881.

    The Portrait of a Lady, New York edition, 2 vols., London: Macmillan, 1908.

    The Tragic Muse, 3 vols., London: Macmillan, 1890.

    The Complete Tales of Henry James, ed. Leon Edel, 12 vols., London: Hart-Davis, 1962–4.

    The Complete Notebooks of Henry James, ed. Leon Edel and Lyall H. Powers, New York and Oxford: Oxford University Press, 1987.

Jay, Harriett, *Through the Stage Door*, 3 vols., London: White, 1883.

Joyce, James, *A Portrait of the Artist as a Young Man*, London: Cape, 1964 [1916].

Lancaster, George Eric, *Pygmalion in Cyprus and Other Poems*, London: Clowes, 1880.

Lee, Vernon, *Miss Brown*, 3 vols., Edinburgh and London: Blackwood, 1884.

    For Maurice: Five Unlikely Stories, London: Lane, Bodley Head, 1927.

Works of Lucian, trans. by M. D. McLeod, 8 vols., London: Heinemann; Cambridge, MA: Harvard University Press, 1967.

Marryat, Florence, *My Sister the Actress*, 3 vols, London: White, 1881.

    Peeress and Player, 3 vols., London: White, 1883.

Meredith, George, *The Egoist*, 3 vols., Harmondsworth: Penguin, 1968 [1879].

Moore, George, *A Mummer's Wife*, London: Vizetelly, 1885.

Moore, T. Sturge, *The Poems of T. Sturge Moore*, London: Macmillan, 1931.

Morris, William, *The Earthly Paradise*, London: Ellis, 1868.

Ovid, *Metamorphoses*, trans. by A. D. Melville, Oxford University Press, 1986.

Pater, Walter, *The Renaissance: Studies in Art and Poetry*, Oxford University Press, 1986 [1873].

Pinero, Arthur W., *The Second Mrs Tanqueray*, London: Heinemann, 1895.

Pleon, Harry, *A Vision of Venus*, London: Dicks, [1893].

Racine, Jean, *Andromaque*, in *Œuvres de Racine*, Paris: Compagnie des libraires, 1713.

    Andromaque and other Plays, trans. by John Cairncross, Harmondsworth: Penguin, 1967.

Robins, Elizabeth and Florence Bell, *Alan's Wife: A Dramatic Study in 3 Scenes*, London: Henry, 1893.

Rossetti, Christina, *Poems of Christina Rossetti*, William M. Rossetti, ed. London: Macmillan, 1904.

Rousseau, J. J., 'Pygmalion. Scène lyrique', in *Œuvres Complètes de J. J. Rousseau*, 13 vols., Paris: Hachette, 1873.

Shaw, George Bernard, *The Irrational Knot*, London: Constable, 1905.

The Complete Plays of Bernard Shaw, London: Hamlyn, 1965.
Staël Holstein, Mme de, *Corinne, ou l'Italie*, 3 vols., London: Peltier, 1809.
Corinne, or Italy, trans. by Avriel H. Goldberger, London and New Brunswick: Rutgers University Press, 1987.
Stoker, Bram, *Dracula*, Harmondsworth: Penguin, 1992 [1897].
Tennyson, Frederick, *Daphne, and Other Poems*, London: Macmillan, 1891.
Trollope, Anthony, *He Knew He Was Right*, Harmondsworth: Penguin, 1994 [1869].
Ward, Mrs Humphry, *Miss Bretherton*, London: Macmillan, 1884.
Woolf, Virginia, *Freshwater: A Comedy*, London: Hogarth Press, 1976.
Woolner, Thomas, *Pygmalion*, London: Macmillan, 1881.
Zola, Emile, *Nana*, Harmondsworth: Penguin, 1972 [1880].

SECONDARY WORKS

Art history

Barrington, Mrs Russell, *George Frederick Watts: Reminiscences*, London: Allen, 1905.
Carr, Cornelia (ed.), *Harriet Hosmer: Letters and Memories*, London: Lane, Bodley Head, 1913.
Chapman, Ronald, *The Laurel and the Thorn: A Study of George Frederick Watts*, London: Faber and Faber, 1945.
Eastlake, Lady (ed.), *Life of John Gibson, R. A., Sculptor*, London: Longmans, Green, 1870.
Fraser, Flora, *Beloved Emma: The Life of Emma Lady Hamilton*, London: Weidenfeld and Nicolson, 1986.
Gombrich, Erich, *Art and Illusion: A Study in the Psychology of Pictorial Representation*, London: Phaidon, 1960.
Harbron, Dudley, *The Conscious Stone: The Life of Edward William Godwin*, London: Latimer House, 1949.
Haskell, Francis and Nicholas Penny, *Taste and the Antique: The Lure of Classical Sculpture, 1500–1900*, New Haven and London: Yale University Press, 1981.
Jameson, Mrs, *A Handbook to the Courts of Modern Sculpture*, Crystal Palace Library, London: Bradbury & Evans, 1854.
Jenkins, Ian, *Archaeologists and Aesthetes in the Sculpture Galleries of the British Museum, 1800–1939*, London: British Museum Press, 1992.
Jenkins, Ian and Kim Sloan, *Vases and Volcanoes: Sir William Hamilton and His Collection*, London: British Museum Press, 1996.
Jenkyns, Richard, *Dignity and Decadence: Victorian Art and the Classical Inheritance*, London: HarperCollins, 1991.
Jones, Stephen, Christopher Newall, et al., *Frederic Leighton*, London: Royal Academy of Arts and Abrams, 1996.
Jopling, Louise, *Twenty Years of My Life, 1867–1887*, London: Lane, 1925.
Loshak, David, 'G. F. Watts and Ellen Terry', *Burlington Magazine* 105 (1963), 476–85.

Macmillan, Hugh, *The Life-Work of George Frederick Watts, RA*, London: Dent, 1903.

Marsh, Jan, *The Legend of Elizabeth Siddal*, London: Quartet, 1989.

Moore, George, *Modern Painting*, London: Scott, 1893.

Moore, Lisa, 'Sexual Agency in Manet's *Olympia*', *Textual Practice* 3 (1989), 222–33.

Ormond, Leonée and Richard Ormond, *Lord Leighton*, New Haven and London: Yale University Press, 1975.

Read, Benedict, *Victorian Sculpture*, New Haven and London: Yale University Press, 1982.

Reid, Jane Davidson (ed.), *The Oxford Guide to Classical Mythology in the Arts, 1300–1990s*, 2 vols., Oxford University Press, 1993.

Robertson, W. Graham, *Time Was*, London: Hamish Hamilton, 1931.

Ruskin, John, *The Diaries of John Ruskin*, ed. Joan Evans and John Howard Whitehouse 3 vols., Oxford: Clarendon, 1957–9.

The Works of John Ruskin, E. T. Cook, and Alexander Wedderburn eds. 39 vols., London: Allen, 1903–12.

Sketchley, R. E. D., *Watts*, London: Methuen, 1904.

Swinburne, Algernon Charles, *Essays and Studies*, London: Chatto and Windus, 1875.

Tours, Hugh, *The Life and Letters of Emma Hamilton*, London: Gollancz, 1963.

Watts, M. S., *G. F. Watts*, 3 vols., London: Macmillan, 1912.

Wood, Christopher, *Olympian Dreamers: Victorian Classical Painters, 1860–1914*, London: Constable, 1983.

Literary criticism, and works on nineteenth-century writers

Adelman, Janet, *Suffocating Mothers: Fantasies of Maternal Origin in Shakespeare's Plays, 'Hamlet' to 'The Tempest'*, New York and London: Routledge, 1992.

Ashton, Rosemary, *G. H. Lewes: A Life*, Oxford: Clarendon Press, 1991.

Auerbach, Nina, *Woman and the Demon: The Life of a Victorian Myth*, Cambridge, MA, and London: Harvard University Press, 1982.

Romantic Imprisonment: Women and Other Glorified Outcasts, New York: Columbia University Press, 1985.

Barkan, Leonard, ' "Living Sculptures": Ovid, Michelangelo, and *The Winter's Tale*', *ELH* 48 (1981), 639–67.

Beer, Gillian, *Darwin's Plots*, London: Ark, 1983.

'The Reader's Wager: Lots, Sorts and Futures', *Essays in Criticism* 40 (1990), 99–123.

Blum, Abbé, ' "Strike All that Look upon Her with Mar[b]le": Monumentalizing women in Shakespeare's Plays', in *The Renaissance Englishwoman in Print: Counterbalancing the Canon*, Amherst: University of Massachusetts Press, 1990, pp. 99–118.

Bodenheimer, Rosemarie, 'Ambition and its Audiences: George Eliot's Performing Figures', *Victorian Studies* 34 (1990), 7–33.

Broughton, T. L., 'Women's Autobiography: the Self at Stake?', *Prose Studies* 14 (1991), 76–94.

Browning, Elizabeth Barrett, *The Letters of Elizabeth Barrett Browning*, 2 vols., London: Smith, Elder, 1897.

Carroll, David (ed.), *George Eliot: The Critical Heritage*, London: Routledge & Kegan Paul, 1971.

Crackanthorpe, Hubert, 'Reticence in Literature', *Yellow Book* 2 (1894), 259–69.

David, Deirdre, *Intellectual Women and Victorian Patriarchy: Harriet Martineau, Elizabeth Barrett Browning, George Eliot*, London: Macmillan, 1987.

Davis, Jill, '"This be different" – the Lesbian Drama of Mrs Havelock Ellis', *Women: A Cultural Review*, 2 (1991), 134–48.

Egan, Michael (ed.), *Ibsen: The Critical Heritage*, London: Routledge and Kegan Paul, 1972.

Eliot, George, *George Eliot's Life, as Related in Her Letters and Journals*, J .W. Cross, ed. Cabinet edition, 3 vols., Edinburgh and London: Blackwood, [n. d.].

   The George Eliot Letters, Gordon S. Haight ed. 9 vols., New Haven and London: Yale University Press, 1954–78.

   Essays of George Eliot, Thomas Pinney, ed. London: Routledge and Kegan Paul, 1963.

Ewbank, Inga-Stina, 'The Last Plays', in James McFarlane (ed.), *The Cambridge Companion to Ibsen*, Cambridge University Press, 1994, pp. 126–54.

Flint, Kate, *The Woman Reader, 1837–1914*, Oxford: Clarendon Press, 1993.

Friedman, Susan Stanford, 'Women's Autobiographical Selves: Theory and Practice', in Shari Benstock (ed.), *The Private Self: Theory and Practice of Women's Autobiographical Writings*, London: Routledge, 1985, pp. 34–62.

Gagnier, Regenia, *Idylls of the Marketplace: Oscar Wilde and the Victorian Public*, Stanford University Press, 1986.

Gray, Beryl, *George Eliot and Music*, Basingstoke: Macmillan, 1989.

Hogarth, Janet E., 'Literary Degenerates', *Fortnightly Review*, n.s. 57 (1895), 586–92.

James, Henry, *Henry James Letters*, Leon Edel, ed. 4 vols., London: Macmillan, 1974–84.

Jameson, Mrs, *Characteristics of Women, Moral, Poetical, and Historical*, 2 vols., London: Saunders and Otley, 1832.

Law, Helen H., 'The Name Galatea in the Pygmalion Myth', *The Classical Journal* 27 (1931–2), 337–42.

Leavis, F. R., *The Great Tradition*, London: Chatto & Windus, 1948.

Levenson, Shirley Frank, 'The Use of Music in *Daniel Deronda*', *Nineteenth-Century Fiction* 24 (1969–70), 317–34.

Litvak, Joseph, *Caught in the Act: Theatricality in the Nineteenth-Century English Novel*, Berkeley: University of California Press, 1992.

Lynn Linton, Mrs, *My Literary Life: Reminiscences of Dickens, Thackeray, George Eliot, etc.*, London: Hodder and Stoughton, 1899.

Maitland, Thomas [Robert Buchanan], 'The Fleshly School of Poetry: Mr D. G. Rossetti', *Contemporary Review* 18 (1871), 334–50.

Marsh, Jan, *Christina Rossetti: A Literary Biography*, London: Cape, 1994.

Miller, J. Hillis, *Versions of Pygmalion*, Cambridge, MA, and London: Harvard University Press, 1990.

Miller, Jane M., 'Some Versions of Pygmalion', in Charles Martindale (ed.), *Ovid Renewed: Ovidian Influences on Literature and Art from the Middle Ages to the Twentieth Century*, Cambridge University Press, 1988.

Noble, James Ashcroft, 'The Fiction of Sexuality', *Contemporary Review* 67 (1895), 490–8.

Poole, Adrian, '"Hidden Affinities" in *Daniel Deronda*', *Essays in Criticism* 33 (1983), 294–311.

Showalter, Elaine, *Sexual Anarchy: Gender and Culture at the* Fin de Siècle, London: Bloomsbury, 1991.

Smith, Sidonie, *A Poetics of Women's Autobiography: Marginality and the Fictions of Self-Representation*, Bloomington: Indiana University Press, 1987.

Spencer, Kathleen L., 'Purity and Danger: *Dracula*, the Urban Gothic, and the Late Victorian Degeneracy Crisis', *ELH* 59 (1992), 197–225.

Stigand, William, 'The Works of Elizabeth Barrett Browning', *Edinburgh Review* 114 (1861), 513–34.

Stutfield, Hugh E. M., 'Tommyrotics', *Blackwood's* 157 (1895), 833–45.

Sullivan, William J., 'Allusion to Jenny Lind in *Daniel Deronda*', *Nineteenth-Century Fiction* 29 (1974), 211–14.

Sutherland, John, *Mrs Humphry Ward: Eminent Victorian, Pre-eminent Edwardian*, Oxford University Press, 1990.

Swann, Brian, 'George Eliot and the Play: Symbol and Metaphor of the Drama in *Daniel Deronda*', *Dalhousie Review* 52 (1972–3), 191–202.

Symons, Arthur, *The Memoirs of Arthur Symons: Life and Art in the 1890s*, Karl Beckson ed. University Park and London: Pennsylvania State University Press, 1977.

Taylor, Ina, *George Eliot: Woman of Contradictions*, London: Weidenfeld and Nicolson, 1989.

Traub, Valerie, *Desire and Anxiety: Circulations of Sexuality in Shakespearean Drama*, London and New York: Routledge, 1992.

Vizetelly, Ernest Alfred, *Emile Zola, Novelist and Reformer: An Account of His Life and Work*, London: Lane, Bodley Head, 1904.

Waugh, Arthur, 'Reticence in Literature', *Yellow Book* 1 (1894), 201–19.

Wiesenfarth, Joseph, '*Middlemarch*: the Language of Art', *PMLA*, 97 (1982), 363–77.

Wilde, Oscar, *The Letters of Oscar Wilde*, Rupert Hart-Davis ed., London: Hart-Davis, 1962.

Witemeyer, Hugh, *George Eliot and the Visual Arts*, New Haven and London: Yale University Press, 1979.

Wolfe, Thomas P., 'The Inward Vocation: an Essay on George Eliot's *Daniel Deronda*', *Literary Monographs* 8 (1976), 1–46.

Theatre criticism, history, and biographies (excluding reviews of individual plays)

Aïdé, Hamilton, 'The Actor's Calling', *Nineteenth Century* 17 (1885), 521–6.
'A New Stage Doctrine', *Nineteenth Century* 34 (1893), 425–57.
Altick, Richard D., *The Shows of London*, Cambridge, MA, and London: Harvard University Press, 1978.
Anderson, Mary (Mme de Navarro), *A Few Memories*, London: Osgood, McIlvaine, 1896.
A Few More Memories, London: Hutchinson, 1936.
Archer, William, 'The Myths of Romeo and Juliet', *National Review* 4 (1884–5), 441–50.
'A Well-Graced Actress', *National Review* 7 (1886), 770–80.
'The Anatomy of Acting', *Longman's Magazine* 11 (1888), 266–81.
Masks or Faces? A Study in the Psychology of Acting, London: Longmans, Green, 1888.
'The Free Stage and the New Drama', *Fortnightly Review* 50 (1891), 663–72.
'The Stage and Literature', *Fortnightly Review* 51 (1892), 219–32.
'A New Stage Doctrine', *Nineteenth Century* 34 (1893), 425–57.
'Eleanora Duse', *Fortnightly Review* 58 (1895), 299–307.
The Theatrical World for 1893–9, London: Scott, 1894–7.
Arnold, Matthew, 'The French Play in London', *Nineteenth Century* 6 (1879), 228–43.
Aston, Elaine, *Sarah Bernhardt: A French Actress on the English Stage*, Oxford: Berg, 1989.
Auerbach, Nina, *Ellen Terry: Player in Her Time*, London: Dent, 1987.
Austin, Alfred, 'The Present State of the English Stage', *Temple Bar* 33 (1871), 456–68.
Baker, H. B., 'The Theatres', *Temple Bar* 39 (1873), 547–52.
Bartholomeusz, Dennis, *The Winter's Tale in Performance in England and America, 1611–1976*, Cambridge University Press, 1982.
Bennett, Susan, *Theatre Audiences: A Theory of Production and Reception*, London and New York: Routledge, 1990.
Beauties of the Modern Dramatists, London: Mann, 1829.
Bernhardt, Sarah, *My Double Life: Memoirs of Sarah Bernhardt*, London: Heinemann, 1907.
Blackburn, Vernon, 'Eleanora Duse', *New Review* 13 (1895), 39–44.
Booth, Michael R., *Theatre in the Victorian Age*, Cambridge University Press, 1991.
Victorian Spectacular Theatre, 1850–1910, London: Routledge & Kegan Paul, 1981.
Brownstein, Rachel M., *Tragic Muse: Rachel of the* Comédie Française, New York: Knopf, 1993.
Calonne, Vicomte de, 'The Stage in France', *Macmillan's Magazine* 34 (1876), 176–81.
Campbell, Mrs Patrick, *My Life and Some Letters*, London: Hutchinson, 1922.

Adam, Eve (ed.), *Mrs J. Comyns Carr's Reminiscences*, London: Hutchinson [c. 1926].

Cheshire, David F., *Portrait of Ellen Terry*, Charlbury: Amber Lane, 1989.

Chothia, Jean, *André Antoine*, Cambridge University Press, 1991.

Coleman, John, 'The Social Status of the Actor', *National Review* 5 (1885), 20–8.

Players and Playwrights I Have Known, 2 vols., London: Chatto and Windus, 1888.

The Elements of Dramatic Criticism. Containing an Analysis of the Stage under the following Heads, Tragedy, Tragi-Comedy, Comedy, Pantomime, and Farce. With a sketch of the Education of the Greek and Roman Actors; Concluding with Some General Instructions for Succeeding in the Art of Acting by William Cooke, Esq. of the Middle Temple, London: Kearsly, Robinson, 1775.

Craig, Edward Gordon, *Ellen Terry and Her Secret Self*, London: Sampson Low, 1932.

Craik, D. M., 'Merely Players', *Nineteenth Century* 20 (1886), 416–22.

Dark, Sidney and Rowland Grey, *W. S. Gilbert: His Life and Letters*, London: Methuen, 1923.

Davis, Tracy C., *Actresses as Working Women: Their Social Identity in Victorian Culture*, London and New York: Routledge, 1991.

Diderot, Denis, *The Paradox of Acting*, trans. by Walter Herries Pollock, London: Chatto & Windus, 1883.

'Echoes from the Green Room', *Theatre* 24 (1894), 270–6.

Forster, John, and George Henry Lewes, *Dramatic Essays*, ed. by William Archer and Robert W. Lowe, London: Scott, 1896.

Gold, Arthur and Robert Fizdale, *The Divine Sarah: A Life of Sarah Bernhardt*, London: HarperCollins, 1992.

Grant, George, *An Essay on the Science of Acting*, London: Cowie and Strange, 1828.

Hankey, Julie, 'Victorian Portias: Shakespeare's Borderline Heroine', *Shakespeare Quarterly* 45 (1994), 426–48.

Holledge, Julie, *Innocent Flowers: Women in the Edwardian Theatre*, London: Virago, 1981.

Holmström, Kirsten Gram, *Monodrama, Attitudes, Tableaux Vivants: Studies in Some Trends of Theatrical Fashion, 1770–1815*, Stockholm: Almqvist & Wiksell, 1967.

Irving, Henry, 'Shakespearean notes', *Nineteenth Century* 1 (1877), 327–30; 1 (1877), 524–30; 5 (1879), 260–3.

'Some Misconceptions About the Stage', *Nineteenth Century* 32 (1892), 670–6.

Irving, Laurence, *Henry Irving: The Actor and His World*, London: Faber and Faber, 1951.

James, Henry, 'The London Theaters', *Scribner's Monthly* 21 (1880–1), 354–69.

'London Pictures and London Plays', *Atlantic Monthly* 50 (1882), 253–63.

'After the Play', *New Review*, 1 (1889), 30–46.

'On the Occasion of "Hedda Gabler"', *New Review* 4 (1891), 519–30.

Wade, Allan (ed.), *The Scenic Art*, London: Hart-Davis, 1949.

John, Angela V., *Elizabeth Robins: Staging a Life*, London and New York: Routledge, 1995.

Jones, Henry Arthur, 'The Literary Drama: A Reply', *New Review* 6 (1892), 89–96.

Kendal, Madge, *The Drama*, London: Bogue, 1884.

Dame Madge Kendal, by Herself, London: Murray, 1933.

Kennard, Nina, *Rachel*, London: Allen, 1885.

Lewes, George Henry, *On Actors and the Art of Acting*, London: Smith, Elder, 1875.

Lilly, W. S., 'The New Naturalism', *Fortnightly Review* 38 (1885), 240–56.

'The Living Pictures', *New Review*, 11 (1894), 461–70.

Lynn Linton, E., 'The Stage as a Profession for Women', *National Review* 5 (1885), 8–19.

Macmillan, Dougald, 'Some Burlesques With a Purpose, 1830–1870', *Philological Quarterly* 8 (1929), 255–663.

'Planché's Early Classical Burlesques', *Studies in Philology* 25 (1928), 340–5.

Maeterlinck, Maurice, 'The Modern Drama', *Cornhill* n. s. 7 (1899), 166–73.

Martin, Helena Faucit, 'On Some of Shakespeare's Female Characters, by One Who has Personated Them', *Blackwood's*, 'Ophelia', 129 (1881), 66–77; 'Portia', 198–210, 'Desdemona', 324–45; 'Juliet', 131 (1882), 31–43, 'Juliet, Part 2', 141–69; 'Imogen, Princess of Britain', 133 (1883), 1–41; 'Rosalind', 136 (1884), 399–437; 'Beatrice', 137 (1885), 203–31; and 'Hermione', 149 (1891), 1–37.

On Some of Shakespeare's Female Characters, Edinburgh and London: Blackwood, 1885.

Martin, Theodore, 'Rachel', *Blackwood's* 132 (1882), 271–95.

'The English Stage', *Quarterly Review* 155 (1883), 354–88.

Helena Faucit (Lady Martin), Edinburgh and London: Blackwood, 1900.

Mayhew, Edward, *Stage Effect: or, the Principles which Command Dramatic Success in the Theatre*, London: Mitchell, 1840.

Meisel, Martin, *Realizations: Narrative, Pictorial and Theatrical Arts in Nineteenth-century England*, Princeton University Press, 1983.

Melville, Joy, *Ellen and Edy: A Biography of Ellen Terry and her Daughter Edith Craig, 1847–1947*, London: Pandora, 1987.

Modjeska, Helena, *Memories and Impressions of Helena Modjeska*, New York and London: Blom, 1969.

Mullin, Donald (ed.), *Actors and Actresses in Review: A Dictionary of Contemporary Views of Representative British and American Actors and Actresses, 1837–1901*, Westport, CT, and London: Greenwood Press, 1983.

'Our Watch Tower. The County Council and the Music Halls', *Theatre* 24 (1894), 277–81.

Pearson, Hesketh, *Gilbert: His Life and Strife*, London: Methuen, 1957.

Pollock, Juliet, 'The French Stage', *Macmillan's Magazine* 21 (1869–70), 400–4.

'The *Comédie Française*', *Contemporary Review* 18 (1871), 43–55.

'Art in its Dramatic Aspects', *Contemporary Review* 23 (1873–4), 363–79.

'The "*Théâtre Français*"', *Quarterly Review* 139 (1875), 138–69.

Postlewait, Thomas, *Prophet of the New Drama: William Archer and the Ibsen Campaign*, Westport, CT and London: Greenwood Press, 1986.

Robins, Elizabeth, *Ibsen and the Actress*, Hogarth Essays, second series, number 15, London: Hogarth Press, 1928.

Theatre and Friendship: Some Henry James Letters, London: Cape, 1932.

Raymond and I, London: Hogarth Press, 1956.

Rowell, George, *The Victorian Theatre, 1792–1914: A Survey*, second edition, Cambridge University Press, 1978.

'Mercutio as Romeo: William Terriss in *Romeo and Juliet*', in Richard Foulkes (ed.), *Shakespeare and the Victorian Stage*, Cambridge University Press, 1986, pp. 87–96.

Scott, Clement, *From 'The Bells' to 'King Arthur'*, London: Macqueen, 1896.

Shaw, George Bernard, 'Preface' to William Archer, *The Theatrical 'World' of 1894*, London: Scott, 1895, pp. xi–xxx.

Our Theatre in the Nineties, 3 vols., London: Constable, 1932.

Laurence, Dan H. (ed.), *Bernard Shaw: Collected Letters, 1874–1897*, London: Reinhardt, 1965.

Weintraub, Stanley (ed.), *Bernard Shaw: The Diaries, 1885–1897*, 2 vols., University Park and London: Pennsylvania State University Press, 1986.

Siddons, Henry, *Practical Illustrations of Rhetorical Gesture and Action*, London: Sherwood, Neely, and Jones, 1822.

St John, Christopher, *Ellen Terry*, London: Lane, 1907.

Stoker, Bram, *Personal Reminiscences of Henry Irving*, 2 vols., London: Heinemann, 1906.

Stokes, John, *Resistible Theatres: Enterprise and Experience in the Late-Nineteenth Century*, London: Elek, 1972.

'Rachel's "Terrible Beauty": an Actress Among the Novelists', *ELH* 51 (1984), 771–93.

Styles, DD, John, *The Stage: Its Character and Influence*, London: Ward, 1838.

Symons, Arthur, 'Eleanora Duse', *Contemporary Review* 78 (1900), 196–202.

Talma, *On the Actor's Art*, London: Bickers, 1884.

Terry, Ellen, 'Stray Memories', *New Review* 4 (1891), 332–41; 444–9; 499–507.

The Story of My Life, London: Hutchinson, 1908.

Ellen Terry's Memoirs, with Preface, Notes and Additional Biographical Chapters by Edith Craig and Christopher St. John, London: Gollancz, 1933.

St John, Christopher (ed.), *Ellen Terry and Bernard Shaw: A Correspondence*, London: Reinhardt and Evans, 1931.

Traill, H. D., 'The Literary Drama', *New Review* 5 (1891), 502–14.

'About that Skeleton', *Nineteenth Century* 36 (1894), 864–7.

Herbert Beerbohm Tree: Some Memories of Him and of His Art, collected by Max Beerbohm, London: Hutchinson, 1920.

Wedmore, Frederick, 'The Theatrical Revival', *Nineteenth Century* 13 (1883), 217–28.

Woodfield, James, *English Theatre in Transition, 1881–1914*, London and Sydney: Croom Helm, 1984.

Woolf, Virginia, 'Ellen Terry', in *Collected Essays*, 4 vols., London: Hogarth Press, 1967, vol. IV, pp. 67–72.

Zimmern, Helen, 'Eleanora Duse', *Fortnightly Review* 67 (1900), 980–93.

Works on social history, women, and sexuality

Acton, William, *Prostitution, Considered in its Moral, Social, and Sanitary Aspects*, second edition, London: Cass, 1972.

Austin, Alfred, 'Woman's Proper Place in Society', *Temple Bar* 33 (1871), 168–78.

Aveling, Eleanor Marx and Edward Aveling, 'The Woman Question: from a Socialist Point of View', *Westminster Review* n.s. 69 (1886), 207–22.

Bevington, Merle, *The Saturday Review, 1855–1868*, New York: Columbia University Press, 1941.

Blackwell, Dr Elizabeth, *The Human Element in Sex: Being a Medical Enquiry into the Relation of Sexual Physiology to Christian Morality*, London: Churchill, 1884.

Braddon, M. E., 'Whose Fault Is It?', *Belgravia* 9 (1869), 214–16.

Brandon, Ruth, *The New Women and the Old Men: Love, Sex and the Woman Question*, London: Secker & Warburg, 1990.

Chant, Mrs Ormiston, *Why We Attacked the Empire*, London: Marshall, [1895].

Chapman, Mrs, 'Women's Suffrage', *Nineteenth Century* 19 (1886), 561–9.

Cunnington, C. Willett, *English Women's Clothing in the Nineteenth Century*, London: Faber and Faber, 1937.

Dyhouse, Carol, *Feminism and the Family in England 1880–1939*, Oxford: Blackwell, 1989.

Ellis, Havelock, *Studies in the Psychology of Sex*, New York: Random House, 1936.

Escott, T. H. S., *Society in London*, London: Chatto & Windus, 1885.

'Female Poaching on Male Preserves', *Westminster Review* 129 (1888), 290–7.

Ferrero, William, 'Woman's Sphere in Art', *New Review* 9 (1893), 554–60.

Fischel, Dr Oskar and Max von Boehn, *Modes and Manners of the Nineteenth Century*, trans. by M. Edwardes, intro. by Grace Rhys, 4 vols., London: Dent; New York: Dutton, 1927.

Grand, Sarah, 'The New Aspect of the Woman Question', *North American Review* 158 (1894), 270–6.

'Marriage Questions in Fiction: the Standpoint of a Typical Modern Woman', *Fortnightly Review* n. s. 63 (1898), 378–89.

Halperin, David M., *One Hundred Years of Homosexuality, and Other Essays on Greek Love*, New York and London: Routledge, 1990.

Hansson, Laura Marholm, *Modern Women*, trans. by Hermione Ramsden, London: Lane, Bodley Head, 1894.

Helsinger, Elizabeth K., et al., (eds.), *The Woman Question: Society and Literature in Britain and America, 1837–1883*, 3 vols., Chicago and London: University of Chicago Press, 1983.

James, Henry, 'Modern Women', *Nation* 7 (1868), 332–4.

Jenkyns, Richard, *The Victorians and Ancient Greece*, Oxford: Blackwell, 1980.

Lee, Vernon, 'Deterioration of the Soul', *Fortnightly Review* n. s. 59 (1896), 928–43.

Lees, Edith, 'Olive Schreiner and her Relation to the Woman Movement' (1915), in Cherry Clayton (ed.), *Olive Schreiner*, Johannesburg: McGraw-Hill, 1983, pp. 46–51.

Loeb, Lori Anne, *Consuming Angels: Advertising and Victorian Women*, Oxford University Press, 1994.

Lonsdale, Margaret, 'Platform Women', *Nineteenth Century* 15 (1884), 409–15.

Lynn Linton, Eliza, 'The Girl of the Period', *Saturday Review* 25 (1868), 339–40.

The Girl of the Period, and Other Social Essays, 2 vols., London: Bentley, 1883.

'The Wild Women as Politicians', *Nineteenth Century* 30 (1891), 79–88.

'The Wild Women as Social Insurgents', *Nineteenth Century* 30 (1891), 596–605.

'The Partisans of the Wild Women', *Nineteenth Century* 31 (1892), 455–65.

Mayor, J. B., 'The Cry of the Women', *Contemporary Review* 11 (1869), 196–215.

'Modern Views about Women', *Tinsleys' Magazine* 5 (1869–70), 660–4.

'Modern Women', *Atlantic Monthly* 22 (1868), 639–40.

Mill, John Stuart, 'The Subjection of Women', in Stefan Collini (ed.), *On Liberty, and Other Writings*, Cambridge University Press, 1989.

Oliphant, Mrs, *Dress*, London: Macmillan, 1878.

Planché, J. R., *History of British Costume*, third edition, London: Bell, 1893.

Richardson, Benjamin Ward, 'Woman's Work in Creation', *Longman's Magazine* 8 (1886), 604–19.

Romanes, George J., 'Mental Differences Between Men and Women', *Nineteenth Century* 21 (1887), 654–72.

Stokes, John, *In the Nineties*, University of Chicago Press, 1989.

Tarnowsky, Benjamin, *The Sexual Instinct and its Morbid Manifestations, from the Double Standpoint of Jurisprudence and Psychiatry*, trans. by W. C. Costello and Alfred Allinson, Paris: Carrington, 1898.

Warner, Marina, *Monuments and Maidens: The Allegory of the Female Form*, London: Picador, 1987.

Weeks, Jeffrey, *Sex, Politics and Society: The Regulation of Sexuality since 1800*, London: Longman, 1981.

White, T. Pilkington, 'Woman in Politics', *Blackwood's Edinburgh Magazine* 161 (1897), 342–58.

Index

CAMBRIDGE STUDIES IN NINETEENTH-CENTURY
LITERATURE AND CULTURE

General editors
Gillian Beer, *University of Cambridge*
Catherine Gallagher, *University of California, Berkeley*

Titles published